An Orientation to Musical Pedagogy

An Orientation To Musical Pedagogy

Becoming a Musician-Educator

Birch Browning

OXFORD
UNIVERSITY PRESS

OXFORD
UNIVERSITY PRESS

Oxford University Press is a department of the University of Oxford. It furthers
the University's objective of excellence in research, scholarship, and education
by publishing worldwide. Oxford is a registered trade mark of Oxford University
Press in the UK and certain other countries.

Published in the United States of America by Oxford University Press
198 Madison Avenue, New York, NY 10016, United States of America.

Library of Congress Cataloging-in-Publication Data
Names: Browning, Birch.
Title: An orientation to musical pedagogy : becoming a musician-educator /
Birch Browning.
Description: New York, NY : Oxford University Press, [2017] | Includes
bibliographical references and index.
Identifiers: LCCN 2016039594 (print) | LCCN 2016040013 (ebook) |
ISBN 9780199928200 (cloth : alk. paper) | ISBN 9780199928224 (pbk. : alk. paper) |
ISBN 9780199928217 (updf) | ISBN 9780190668686 (epub)
Subjects: LCSH: Music teachers—Training of. | Music—Instruction and study.
Classification: LCC MT1 .B8 2017 (print) | LCC MT1 (ebook) | DDC 780.71—dc23
LC record available at https://lccn.loc.gov/2016039594

9 8 7 6 5 4 3 2 1

Paperback printed by WebCom, Inc., Canada
Hardback printed by Bridgeport National Bindery, Inc., United States of America

CONTENTS

ACKNOWLEDGMENTS

I come from a modern family. If you count all four of my parents, they included two librarians, a rocket scientist, and a reading tutor. From the outside, you might assume that reading lots of books, having an insatiable curiosity, and eventually writing a book would be expected. As an uncertain writer, I'm somewhat surprised that I've actually managed to finish this book, considering my nearly constant self-doubt.

But, while necessity might be the mother of invention, curiosity is the mother of books. My father was a reliability engineer at the Kennedy Space Center for over fifty years. That means he spent that time imagining: If this item fails, then what? So he was deeply enmeshed in thinking about and thinking in systems—how all of these variables interact. I must have inherited his fondness for thinking in systems, but I approach it from a slightly different perspective: If this newly discovered concept (new to me, anyway) is true, how does that affect everything else I've ever known?

During graduate school I had one of my "If this is true, this changes everything" moments while reading an article by Cornelia Yarborough. In this article she stated that perhaps the single most important task in teaching was to help students develop a level of understanding that enabled them to observe themselves and provide their own feedback. At that time, it shattered my idea that teachers (like me!) were experts and should provide correction and feedback so that students could pursue excellence. At this point in my career, I'm disappointed it took me so long to figure that out. What happened to me back then was what used to be called a paradigm shift— acquiring a completely new perspective on what was already known.

More recently, I've had two similar experiences. My friend Dr. William Bauer introduced me to two new books: *The Science and Psychology of Music Performance: Creative Strategies for Teaching and Learning*, edited by Richard Parncutt and Gary E. McPherson (Parncutt & McPherson, 2002) and *Preparing Teachers for a Changing World: What Teachers Should Know and Be Able to Do*, edited by Linda Darling-Hammond and John Bransford (Darling-Hammond & Bransford, 2005). These two books piqued my curiosity and led directly to this book, and subsequently led me in new directions of interest.

At some point I stopped counting the number of years I worked on this book and started counting in elephant gestation periods—it just seemed less painful. So, there are quite few people I need to thank for putting up with my blathering about the book and providing feedback and inspiration: Dr. Rita Klinger, my beloved first colleague at Cleveland State University (CSU), and my current colleagues Dr. Heather Russell, Dr. Barry Hartz, and Bill Zurkey. I'd also be remiss if I didn't thank my teachers—those who both encouraged me and humored me: Dr. John West, one of my high school band directors, for always selecting great repertoire for us to perform, and Drs. Jim Croft, Bentley Shellhammer, Clifford Madsen, Patrick Dunnigan, and George Riordan, all of Florida State University, for inspiring me and coaching me for so many years. There are many others, of course.

Finally, I need to thank my wife, Stephanie, our two children, and the rest of my extended family for putting up with me disappearing to write, which so often just looked like staring off into space.

My only advice to those of you who either choose to or are required to read this text is this: Follow your curiosity. Tug on each loose thread of information until you weave a complex and seemingly complete fabric of understanding. When you think you have it, go find a new thread to tug on.

CHAPTER 1

Introduction

There is a saying that I've heard: Be the teacher you wish you'd had. This is the book I wish I'd read when I first was considering becoming a professional musician or a teacher. I couldn't decide. (I still haven't decided.) Is it the last word on becoming a music teacher? Certainly not. It's also not the last word on becoming a musician.

I hope, in fact, that it can provide some first words—some first ideas—toward becoming a musician *and* a teacher. The process of becoming an artist or becoming a teacher takes a lifetime or more. There is no end to the process, only a continuous path. Pablo Casals, one of the greatest musicians of all time, was asked why he was still practicing even though he was ninety years old. His response? He said he still practiced because he was still making progress. Georg Solti, after all, recorded the Beethoven symphonies six times. In his eighties, Solti said he was just beginning to understand them.

Jerome Bruner, noted American psychologist and significant contributor to the understanding of human cognition, taught us that advanced knowledge in any field is the result of particulars being derived from a small set of accepted theorems or principles. For this reason, the book contains many fundamental concepts, ideas, frameworks, constructs, models, and lists as the basis of understanding musical pedagogy. Throughout the text, you will be encouraged to digest these concepts, summarize them, debate them, personalize them, and imagine their implications for the music teaching and learning processes. According to Bruner, "The curriculum of a subject should be determined by the most fundamental understanding that can be achieved of the underlying principles that give structure to that subject" (1977, p. 31).

Initially, you may find this emphasis on numbered lists a bit frustrating. Those who used preliminary versions of the text indicated that they didn't enjoy memorizing the lists. What they found later on, though, was that the lists of interrelated concepts, the frameworks of understanding, helped them think through various teaching and learning challenges. When prompted to recall the frameworks, they were surprised to discover how much they knew about the topic and that they could recognize the relationships between complex ideas.

The frameworks included in this text are not intended to frame or constrain the conversation but to start some dialog and even disagreement. As you start your career as a prospective music educator, you have many preconceived ideas about music teaching and learning. As you study the "fundamental understandings" about music teaching and learning, they may challenge your ideas. That's all right. Unless these preexisting beliefs and values are challenged, they will become the framework into which you will incorporate new knowledge and learning. Allowing this to happen will only codify existing practice without developing an intellectual basis for practice or change in practice. Therefore, prospective music education majors need to have the problem of becoming a music educator re-framed for them. I hope that reading and studying, along with writing and arguing about these fundamental understandings, will allow you to develop a secure foundation for the rest of your education in music pedagogy.

STRATEGY AND TERMS

Throughout the book, several different terms are used to describe teachers during various points in their careers. College students who are pursuing a music teaching license are referred to as *pre-service music teachers*. The term *student teacher* is used to describe students who are near the end of their college careers and are currently teaching in a school context under the supervision of a licensed professional music educator. The term *in-service* is used to indicate any person licensed and employed as a music educator. *Novice teachers* are in-service teachers who have attained an initial teaching license and are employed to teach music in a particular context but are in the early stage of their career—generally the first three to five years. (Preliminary teaching licenses are typically valid for two years. The body of research on teacher development suggests that teachers become competent after about five years of classroom teaching time.) *Expert teachers* are those who have been identified as master teachers, and they generally have many years of in-service experience.

FOR STUDENTS

Through reading this book, you will learn about the characteristics of excellent teachers. As you read, it may occur to you that excellent students share many of these characteristics. Many of the same behaviors and habits of mind that mediate excellent instruction are those that will enable you to be an excellent student—which you must be in order to become an excellent teacher. What exactly are these common characteristics?

First, and perhaps most important, excellent students and excellent teachers attribute successes or failures to their own efforts alone. They do not, for example, think that any of their abilities are based on gifts or talents; they do not think any success was just luck. Since everything is learned, they must have had experiences along their life course that allowed them to develop these abilities. Likewise, any failures are not based on bad luck.

Second, excellent students have a *mastery orientation* and a *growth orientation*. They set very high standards for themselves in terms of the musical or other academic work they produce and for the way they interact with and treat others. As an extension, they also realize that they can grow and improve to achieve any standard that they set for themselves. You can clearly see how these two orientations are directly related to attributing successes or failures to their efforts. Similarly, excellent students set high goals for themselves (as opposed to waiting for another person to motivate them), and are aware of not only their current abilities but also their progress toward those goals. They self-monitor or self-regulate their efforts and their use of time. Basically, they work hard until the task is done and then aggressively enjoy their free time.

Let's be clear: you are going to stumble and make mistakes along the way in your academic and musical career. This is inevitable. More important is the way you choose to respond to these stumbles. For example, you may receive some very negative feedback on a project that you thought met or exceeded the criteria. While such feedback can be distressing, you should look at it as an opportunity to excel . . . at a future date. Own the mistake; learn from it; and be even better next time.

Finally, excellent students are conscious of and tend to their relationships with peers, instructors, and professionals. They understand that productive working relationships are built on mutual respect and the need to avoid any disruptions to those relationships.

Let's consider each of the three characteristics or dispositions of excellent students—maintaining professional relationships, having an orientation toward mastery and growth, and attribution of results to themselves—as sets of interlocking behaviors in reverse order.

If your goal is to become a professional in your discipline and to attain a level of respect in the field, it is important for you to start practicing professional behaviors and dispositions as soon as possible. Think of a disposition as a learned behavior or perspective that has become so ingrained that it is not just a habit but feels instinctual. For example, because you are mindful of your professional relationships with your various instructors, you want to be respectful of their time. So, as a matter of habit, you should respond to all of their emails almost immediately, but within reason. You would not, for example, answer one instructor's email using your phone during another instructor's class because that would be disrespectful of that professional relationship. But you should generally consider twenty-four hours to be the outside parameter for responding to a professor's email; you'll want to respond more quickly if the subject is urgent, of course. Responding to email, as in this example, is more than simply a professional courtesy, however. It is in your enlightened best interest to show the professor that you are reliable. When you prove that you are trustworthy, the professor will entrust you with advanced opportunities.

How else can you learn to embody a professional disposition? To extend the email example, in addition to responding in a timely manner, you should be conscious of your use of language. You will want to address the instructor (or in-service professional) with his or her correct title, and you will want to use proper English grammar such as that taught in a composition course, not the casual language you use with your peers. This means using capitals at the beginnings of sentences, using proper spelling as opposed to spellings used in texting, and using no emojis. Keep in mind that it is difficult to properly convey tone in written communication, so be wary of accidentally offending or even angering an instructor owing to poor language choice. If you receive an email from a professor that includes some negative feedback, it is all too easy to respond in anger, in a way you might never respond in a face-to-face interaction. Never hit *Send* when you are angry; even if it makes you feel better in the moment, you will almost always regret it later. More important, it becomes a roadblock to your professional relationship with that instructor. Arriving on time and attending all class sessions and other scheduled meetings are just as important. Perhaps the most effective method of maintaining positive communication with your instructors is to proactively visit them during their office hours. (College and university instructors are usually required to have several hours set aside per week when students can have conferences without having to schedule one ahead of time.)

How else can you maintain a professional demeanor with your instructors, peers, and others? Primarily, by not giving them reasons to doubt you. This means always dressing appropriately for the circumstances. Never should you allow your personal appearance and personal hygiene to drop below a professional standard. You should take care, for example, to not wear casual attire such as beach clothes, jeans with holes in them, athletic wear, or other such items to class or to a professional obligation such as a field observation. On the other hand, it is possible to overdress; formal attire, such as you might wear for a concert, is not appropriate for some contexts. It is likely that your instructor will provide you with guidelines for any visits you might undertake at local schools. Likewise, you should maintain a professional appearance on any of your social media outlets. Even items shared "privately" via social media may not be as private as you think.

The second characteristic is having a *mastery orientation* and a *growth orientation*. How does this characteristic manifest itself in your daily life? With a growth orientation, you realize that it is all right and, in fact, desirable to know of skills you cannot execute yet or of some topic that you do not understand yet because you know that, if you work at it, you can develop that knowledge or skill. Simply realizing that you can learn whatever you want by working at learning it will eliminate a significant amount of frustration in your life.

At some point during your college career and your professional career, someone who has authority over you is going to tell you that something you did for them was unacceptable, that it did not meet the agreed-upon standard. How should you respond to negative feedback or criticism? If you know that you are capable of learning or improving your abilities, then you may accept this criticism as an opportunity to excel. You may decide to exceed the standards set by your instructor or supervisor and then set about developing a plan. Those who excel do so because they know they can. It's a positive feedback loop.

As you can see, those who take ownership of their professional relationships and ownership of their successes and failures attribute those outcomes to their effort, not to luck (good or bad) or to someone else. You will read about attribution theory in chapter 7 and learn how important those concepts are for student motivation and independence. For now, feel good about your accomplishments and own your mistakes. Those around you will respect you for it.

FOR INSTRUCTORS

The pedagogical design of this book is based in part on ideas from *How People Learn: Brain, Mind, Experience, and School* by John Bransford (2000). The main ideas from that text that are incorporated here are the following:

1. Naive ideas held by students must be challenged before more sophisticated understandings can take root. Throughout the text (and the course), students are challenged to examine their own experiences as

students, to examine the naive ideas about music, teaching, and learning that they assimilated during their K–12 experiences, and their own
identities as musicians and as educators.
2. New knowledge has to be integrated into a framework in order for it to
be useful. As Bruner stated, "To learn structure, in short, is to learn how
things are related" (Bruner 1977, p. 7).

Another book that informed the content of this text is *Preparing Teachers for
a Changing World* (Darling-Hammond & Bransford 2005). The main ideas
from that text incorporated here are as follows:

1. Pre-service teachers' ideas about teaching and learning are driven primarily by their own experiences as students.
2. Effective teachers have four kinds of specialized knowledge that mediate
their effectiveness.
3. One of the most important outcomes of a teacher education program is
that the candidate develop a clear understanding of what a [music] curriculum could be.
4. One of the major challenges for novice teachers is *enactment*—
purposefully incorporating the theories and methods learned during
the pre-service experience into their pedagogical approaches.

Other key concepts from various other sources include the following:

1. There is no such thing as talent; progress is the result of deliberate effort
(deliberate practice).
2. Deliberate practice—making a plan for an emphasis on fundamentals,
implementing it and obtaining specific feedback, and reflecting on what
went well and what can be done better the next time—acts as a model
for what teachers do for their students.
3. Synaptogenesis can be a model for learning and act as the bridge between
the biological and psychological experiences of living.
4. Musical understanding is the synthesis of musical knowledge and
musical skill.
5. Identity, role, and self are important factors in understanding the lived experience of a music educator. For example, you don't have to choose between
being a musician and being a pedagogue. But it is necessary to understand
that these are two interrelated disciplines. Expertise in one does not confer
expertise in the other. They both have to be mastered individually.

Other important ideas are sprinkled throughout the text. In many cases,
the original sources are cited so that faculty and students can extend the

conversation. The challenge, as always, is in helping the students see how these distinct concepts, ideas, and frameworks relate to one another and deepen our cumulative understanding. It's a gestalt thing: you have to see an overview of the entire system, break it down into tiny components, and then integrate them back together—like the score study process.

These other topics include structural and emotional communication as the key to musicality, the characteristics of professionals, and the role of personal disposition in developing expertise. In order for prospective teachers to become responsible for the learning experiences of hordes of students, they must first become responsible for their own learning.

In short, the book aims to help students develop adaptive expertise—the balance point between the efficiency of routines and improvement as a result of innovation—along with the disposition and skills to practice adaptive expertise as it relates to the learning and teaching of music. One outcome not only of this book but of any music teacher education program should be that the novice teachers be able to effect positive change within their new instructional context: the school where they obtain employment. The purpose of this text is to provide basic frameworks of understandings that set the young teachers up for success. Ultimately, it will be their professional responsibility to choose to use their knowledge and skills in an efficient and effective manner.

Assignments. Each chapter contain sterms, questions, and sometimes projects for the students to complete. When I have used this text to teach the orientation to music education course, a two-hour course for college freshmen, I have had them complete an outline for the chapter. Each section is usually condensed into one paragraph, so a full chapter may become four pages. I tell them that their goal is to take notes in such a way that they never need to read the chapter again but, rather, capture enough detail to study for an exam or to use the text as a resource. I have at various times asked them to define the terms, use each term in a cogent sentence, and write a paragraph or so using the terms. So far, the last has worked best in that they have to grasp the relationships between the terms and perhaps use them in an order other than the one in which they are listed.

As for the questions, sometimes the students have to submit written responses, sometimes I allow brief periods for small groups to develop responses, and at other times I've simply used them to guide classroom discussion. The goal during the discussion is always to help them understand the relationships between the concepts and their implications for the teaching-learning process. Some of the projects are well suited for individual work, while others can be used for group projects.

The key factor in all of this is the amount of time you can reasonably expect your students to commit to the course. When the section carried only one credit, it was enough to expect an outline for each chapter and reasonable answers during classroom discussion and on brief written exams. As the course expanded to two credits and students' field observation requirements increased, their responses became far more sophisticated. Within our faculty group, we also attempt to incorporate the same concepts and terms into subsequent coursework.

CHAPTER 2

Transitioning from Student to Teacher

For a moment, think back to the best educational experiences you had as a primary or secondary student. Then, take a moment and think about the worst educational experiences you had as a student. First-year music education majors rarely have difficulty with this task, and their responses are surprisingly consistent.

Their positive responses usually fall into one of the following categories:

1. A moving performance experience in their high school band, choir, or orchestra in which the performance just seemed to flow. Everyone in the ensemble knew exactly what they were supposed to do, and the performance seemed effortless.
2. An instance when a teacher, usually a music teacher but not always, was especially inspiring, demonstrated great personal character, or expressed particular admiration or concern for his or her students.
3. An opportunity they had to teach or lead another group of students that was particularly memorable.

Their negative responses are also similar and included these examples:

1. An instance when they were personally embarrassed by a performance by their high school band, choir, or orchestra, which led them to believe that there must be a better way to run an ensemble or music program.
2. An instance when a teacher, usually a music teacher but not always, demonstrated a surprising lack of professionalism or teaching ability, which is usually accompanied by publicly blaming or embarrassing the student.

Why is it important for you to consider these experiences? First, prospective music teachers often cite these kinds of experiences as their motivation for wanting to be a teacher. Consider the implications: they were so inspired or angered by a previous teacher that they decided to make it their life's work to either become like that teacher or to become anything other than that teacher. While these may be noble aspirations, they also become the defining concepts for the student of what it means to assume the role of a teacher.

Second, if we consider the task of becoming a teacher, the way you frame the task defines the way you approach learning to become a teacher. If, for example, you were inspired by a performance while you were a student, then you may want to instill that same love of music in your students. If you were particularly inspired by the behavior of one of your teachers, good or bad, then you may believe that teaching is about character. As you can see, the way you initially frame a problem such as determining what it means to be a teacher influences the strategies you choose to solve the problem (Bransford & Stein, 1993).

It is important, therefore, right as you start your teaching career, to reframe the questions for yourself in a way that will make your inquiries more productive. In this chapter we examine four topics that will help you reflect on why and how one becomes a music teacher. These include the purposes of schooling in the United States, a sophisticated understanding of what it means to be an effective teacher in light of these purposes, what you already know about being a teacher and why, and a framework that helps clarify what good teachers know and are able to do, along with the defining characteristics of competent teachers.

THE PURPOSES OF PUBLIC EDUCATION IN THE UNITED STATES

Music teachers do not work in an instructional vacuum. Not only do they often have fellow music teachers at their school but, unless they are the only music teacher in a district, they have colleagues who teach the students when they are younger or older.

It is important for you to develop a clear understanding of the purposes of public education in the United States because all instructional decisions must be grounded in these purposes. Teachers have their own personal reasons for entering the education realm, but professional educators understand that the function of education in the lives of their students is far greater than any personal agenda. Cadres of teachers working in harmony can achieve far greater results than those working at cross-purposes.

Fundamentally, the purpose of education is to prepare students to be functioning and contributing members of our democratic society. Naturally, a definition as broad as this provides little actual guidance and leaves much room for debate as to its meaning. There are four generally accepted realms for defining the outcomes of an education (Goodlad, 1984, as cited in Darling-Hammond, Banks, et al., 2005):

1. The **academic realm** deals with the knowledge (information) and skills (abilities) that enable the remaining three outcomes.
2. The **vocational realm** governs the ability to obtain and retain employment, which provides for personal financial responsibility and security.
3. The **social and civic realm** deals with the ability to function in complex social settings and contribute to them; and
4. The **personal realm** is concerned with self-knowledge, self-monitoring, and responsibility, along with the development of personal autonomy, purpose, talent, and expression.

Those of us who participate in music making realize that learning about music and making music with others can contribute to each of these outcomes. We'll explore the reasons for having music in schools and each of these outcomes in subsequent chapters. For now, it's important to keep in mind that all decisions about what is to be taught, how it is to be taught, and how teachers can be sure that students have mastered the subject are driven by the desire to obtain these four outcomes.

APPRENTICESHIP OF OBSERVATION

Most students know a lot about education and, therefore, they assume that they know a lot about teaching and what it means to be a teacher. Think for a moment, however, about the context wherein you gathered your knowledge about what it means to be a teacher. First-year college students usually have had at least twelve years of classroom experience, but as a student, not as a teacher. During these years they have watched teachers deliver countless lessons of exceptional variety and a wide range of quality, observed or been subjected to disciplinary interventions, and endured many quizzes and exams. However detailed their observations may be, their perspective is based on only on the parts of the instructional process that are available to students.

Consider the common activities of a typical mathematics teacher. He or she shows students how to solve certain kinds of mathematical problems using a formula or set of procedures, assigns sets of similar problems for students to practice solving, and then gives a series of quizzes or exams to motivate students to complete their homework. On the basis of these kinds of experiences, students develop a rather complete list of what their teachers do in a classroom and likely could imitate them to some extent. But the students are not able to observe the decision making that led the teacher to present a particular lesson or the choices that the teacher makes in the classroom during instruction and, therefore, do not have a complete view of the teacher's experience of being a teacher. Therefore, they lack the empathy to imagine the teacher's lived experience.

Lortie (1975, p. 65) coined the term *apprenticeship of observation* to describe the process whereby students learn about teaching by being taught in a classroom context. Although the students are able to observe the actions of the teachers in various classroom, they are not privy to the intentions of the teacher; they do not gain any insight into teaching that would allow them to do something different in a similar circumstance if they were the teacher. One thing is certain: students have many opinions about teachers and often would prefer that they do something different. Without additional knowledge and skills, young teachers would simply teach as they were taught and not be able to improve the overall educational process.

In any discipline, fundamental misunderstandings can impede future learning. As a consequence of an incomplete apprenticeship of observation, students often develop certain misconceptions about what it means to teach and to be a teacher.

1. Students think that teaching is easy and that teachers just follow a set of algorithms—simple rules and procedures—to determine classroom activities.
2. Students think that teaching is about telling, about transferring information from teacher to student. This, however, is only efficient in transferring simple, low-level information; telling is not an effective method for mediating complex understandings or skills. Think about all of the things your parents told you when you were growing up that you obviously didn't learn because they felt obliged to keep saying the same thing over and over again. Telling is not teaching.
3. Because students have experienced many kinds of learning activities, such as rehearsals, they think that they already know about them. Because they have had little or no experience designing learning activities, they have no ability to decide whether the activities were effective and how to modify them if they were not.
4. Young teachers tend to focus on the emotional and social aspects of teaching. This is especially true for music teachers owing to the uniquely

social nature of music making. Such important aspects of teaching as selecting and designing learning activities, delivering instruction effectively, and evaluating student learning are often neglected.

Consider again the positive educational experience that you were asked to recall above. What did the teacher do to make that experience unique? Could you design such an experience for your students? Is it possible that you might develop a great plan and yet your students do not have the same kind of experience you had? Could they have a unique learning experience in your class that happened serendipitously, by their discovering something wonderful by accident? Perhaps these considerations provide some insight into the nature of teaching and learning.

WHAT DOES IT MEAN TO BE A GOOD TEACHER?

No teacher can force a student to learn. Or, said another way, you can lead a student to knowledge but you can't make him or her think. Not only does the student have to be ready to learn, but often the student must make some kind of investment—time, effort, or both—in order for learning to occur. Thus, a teacher's primary task is to create an environment in which students can learn.

So, in reality, there is no such thing as teaching that is under the complete control of the teacher. Teachers can not dictate learning by decree. They are really facilitators of learning. The question is, What do expert teachers know about or know how to do that distinguishes them from their less-effective colleagues? Or, more simply, What enables a teacher to be effective? Below I discuss four key areas of teacher knowledge.

First, expert teachers *know a lot about their subject*, but not in a trivial kind of way. This means that their knowledge is not a collection of memorized yet isolated facts, the kind of knowledge that would help one be successful on *Jeopardy!* or in playing Trivial Pursuit. An expert's knowledge is organized in large conceptual frameworks of related ideas and concepts. This kind of interconnected understanding allows experts to quickly survey their intellectual landscape and apply the most appropriate knowledge or skills to novel problems.

The core ideas in any intellectual field are analogous to the steel framework of a well-constructed building. Once that framework is securely in place, complex systems can be added and supported. The same is true for learning any discipline. Once the framework of core ideas is secure, new information or skills can be integrated into the knowledge structure. Thus, when experts (or prospective experts like yourself) learn new information or skills, the new abilities are incorporated into existing knowledge and are available for solving problems.

Yet significant subject matter knowledge alone does not automatically enable one to be an effective teacher. For example, expert music critics have a specialized kind of knowledge about music and music performance, but that does not mean they are necessarily expert or even proficient performers. Similarly, performers have a specialized kind of knowledge about music, but it may not necessarily be helpful in conveying knowledge or skills to music students. What kind of knowledge makes it possible for someone to be an effective teacher—an effective designer and deliverer of learning experiences?

Effective educators have an additional kind of knowledge of their subject matter: They understand how knowledge in a particular intellectual domain develops over time and how that development is based on the structure of the subject. In other words, they know which facets of the subject matter are fundamental, which have to be learned first, and how that knowledge enables subsequent learning. Likewise, they understand how musical skills develop over time and what processes or knowledge can support skill development.

Why is this important? One of the key considerations in designing learning experiences involves student readiness; the teacher has to know whether these particular students are prepared to learn this particular bit of knowledge, this new skill, or this new perspective. One of the most common teaching errors is a failure to consider the prerequisites for learning. If the students do not have the necessary prior knowledge, skills or dispositions, then the learning experience will be frustrating to them and to the teacher. Expert teachers, because they understand the developmental process, realize the importance of student readiness and know how to select the right learning activity for a given group of students at their current level of ability.

Teachers also have an understanding of how students learn in general and how the individual characteristics, backgrounds, and experiences of particular students can positively or negatively influence their ability to learn. Ideas about student diversity are examined in a subsequent chapter, but you should know that, in addition to prior knowledge, factors such as age, race, cultural and national heritage, family experiences and expectations (both positive and negative), financial resources, social support, and personal identity can all impact a student's intellectual and emotional readiness to learn and must be taken into account when preparing and delivering instruction.

This is the second kind of specialized knowledge of effective teachers: *knowledge of students*, which includes an understanding of what motivates students as a demographic, as a group, and as individuals. For example, teachers who work with middle school students understand the unique psychology of students beginning to transition physically and emotionally from children to adults, they know about the backgrounds of the particular groups of students in their classes, and they have specialized knowledge about individual students. And they use those three types of knowledge of students to design and deliver their lessons.

Students are motivated when they find a challenge that is personally meaningful to them. More specifically, students are motivated by work that helps them accomplish a goal that they have set for themselves or helps them understand who they are and the world they live in. Effective teachers work to relate educational activities to their students' prior life experiences and their own aspirations—to make the lessons meaningful.

Next, think back to your experiences in various classes you have taken, especially secondary music ensembles. Your ensemble conductor probably had established certain routines with which to begin the rehearsal, commonly referred to as warm-ups. Likely, you can also recall circumstances that might have arisen, perhaps when working on a specific style of music or a particular performance fundamental, when you might have been able to predict what your teacher would have you do next. These activities are emblematic of the third kind of specialized knowledge that effective teachers have, which is a *repertoire of routines*, learning activities and instructional strategies that have been shown to promote specific learning outcomes. In other words, experts have a "bag of tricks" from which they can draw to help students learn. The academic term for the kind of knowledge that teachers use to plan and improvise instruction is *pedagogy*.

This low-level pedagogy is the kind of information that is most commonly covered in teacher methods courses. These routines promote instructional efficiency, and classroom management is sometimes dependent on routinizing certain activities. Such routines also make the instructional process easier for the teacher. The instructional challenge is knowing which routines to use when, and knowing when and how to break out of routines that might have outlived their usefulness.

Before moving on to the fourth type of specialized teacher knowledge, as you reflect on the first three kinds (knowledge of subject matter, of students, and of pedagogy), you may begin to realize that they interact with and support one another. These three understandings interact to form *pedagogical content knowledge* (PCK). Teachers use their PCK to design lessons (and rehearsals) and instructional units and to make moment-to-moment decisions based on the particular topic, the individual and collective characteristics of the students, and the chosen instructional method. Increased knowledge or improved understanding in one area has instructional implications for the teacher's knowledge in the other two areas. The ability to integrate subject matter knowledge, knowledge of students, and pedagogical knowledge is developed by planning instruction, interacting with students during the lesson, and reflecting on the effectiveness of the teaching afterward.

Think back again to your school experiences, and reflect on the different teachers and courses that you had. You probably recognized that each classroom seemed to have its own routines and its own rules about how the teacher interacted with the students and the students with one another. One class might be completely quiet, with the teacher providing directions, while another class, with essentially the same students, might be a hive of activity. Some of these differences can be attributed to the teacher, but experienced teachers know that groups of students have their own "personalities."

Learning is an inherently social activity. This is especially true in music. Each group of students, in combination with a particular teacher, develops its own little culture. Each school, as a collection of classroom-sized social contexts, develops its own characteristic culture. This schoolwide culture is also influenced by the demographics of the school, the academic expectations of the students, teachers, parents, and administrators, and the characteristics of the surrounding community. This realization helps clarify the fourth kind of specialized knowledge that experienced teachers develop: *knowledge of context.* Teachers are keenly aware that the *influences of the culture and setting* where the instruction occurs—the classroom setting, the school environment, and the community—all play a role in establishing expectations and in the success or failure of the students to meet the learning goals.

A FRAMEWORK FOR UNDERSTANDING TEACHING

To summarize, in order to begin to contemplate how effective teachers differ from less-capable instructors, you need to understand that effective teachers have four kinds of specialized knowledge:

1. They have a deep understanding of their subject, along with an understanding of the sequence in which to present material so that students can also acquire deep understanding.
2. They have an understanding of the way students learn, as well as the way the diverse backgrounds of students affect how individual students learn.
3. They have an understanding of the various instructional methods that are available to help students learn particular concepts and skills.

4. Finally, teachers have an understanding of the context in which teaching and learning occur, including both the social ecology of a group of students in a particular setting and the culture of that school in that community.

Throughout the remaining chapters of this text, I often refer to this framework as a way to understand excellent teachers and effective instruction. The next question to be addressed is, How does one go about becoming an expert teacher? In Chapter 3 we'll examine how expertise develops in general and consider the implications of expertise development on teacher development.

PROJECT

1. Explain the following terms:
   - Apprenticeship of observation
   - Pedagogy
   - Pedagogical content knowledge
2. What or who was your motivation to become a music educator?
3. For each of the four intended outcomes of public education, write a short paragraph explaining the relationship between music education and that particular purpose. Subsequently, write an organizing (first) paragraph and a concluding paragraph. Make sure to use the information contained in the rest of the chapter to support your thoughts.
4. As you look at the intended outcomes of public education, it's clear that the outcomes we generally associate with musical instruction fall into the first category—academic knowledge. But music teachers must also attend to the other three categories of outcomes—vocational, social-civic, and personal. What should the focus of a musical education be? What percentage of the intended outcomes should be musical and what percentage should be extramusical? How do these four categories of outcomes interact? Be aware that there is no one correct answer, and your answer is likely to change over the course of the semester and that of your career. Again, use the information in the chapter to support your thoughts.
5. Since you've been accepted as a teacher candidate in a music education licensure program, you obviously have exceptional abilities compared to the general population. Have you ever been told that you are talented or have "a gift"? Have you had special opportunities that others have not had? Or have you worked hard and stayed focused on your musical goals? Answer this question: To what to you attribute your success?

6. What is it about yourself—who you are—that will help you become a great teacher? How do you project those positive characteristics to others? People will have certain expectations of you as a teacher. Do you have the ability to meet their expectations, to not disappoint them, without impinging on who you are? How will you decide whether an expectation is reasonable or not?

7. Write a short narrative about a time when one of your previous teachers used his or her specialized knowledge about you—your personal background and experiences, or your personal goals—to communicate with you and was especially motivating or effective.

CHAPTER 3

What Is Talent?

Think for a moment about the people you know whom you would describe as talented. Likely, they are unusually good at something that brings them some kind of recognition. Maybe they excel at some kind of music making or at a sport such as tennis or snowboarding. While you might admire their ability and perhaps secretly would like to be able to do what they do, there's something about their ability that drives you a bit crazy. It just seems to come so easily for them, so effortlessly. If only you'd been given the same gift. If only you could find your talent. The issue may be how we generally understand the concept of talent. In our culture, we have a fairly common understanding of talent. It is a natural ability to do something better than most people can do it. That something is fairly specific—play golf, sell things, compose music, lead an organization. It can be spotted early, before the ability is fully expressed, and it is innate; you're born with it, and if you're not born with it, you can't acquire it (Colvin, 2008, pp. 20–21).

Over the centuries, the conceptualization of ability has oscillated. Some have considered ability to be a gift, either from God or from Nature, whereas others have thought that experience is the key to exceptional ability. This disagreement has resulted in political and philosophical debate: Descartes and his Enlightenment colleagues believed that we are all born exactly equal—an idea that led to the development of democracy as a form of government. Others, as the result of Darwin's ideas about evolution, believed in genetically endowed gifts. In fact, it was Darwin's cousin, Thomas Galton, who coined the phrase that so clearly defines this debate as "nature versus nurture."

The belief that special abilities are the result of a gift or talent is more widely held about music than any other field or endeavor. Approximately 75 percent of adults believe that musical talent is exactly that, something that you either have or you don't, and is often identifiable early in life. Several music performance researchers set out to determine whether this belief is justified. While investigating 257 music students at various levels of ability, they attempted to identify the early signs of talent in children who had later demonstrated greater musical ability than others had. They found that those who later exhibited some greater aptitude for music performance had, indeed, begun to sing at an earlier age than had the others (Howe, Davidson, Moore, & Sloboda, 1995). More specifically, they found that those who later showed superior musical skills were able to echo a tune at the age of eighteen months as compared to twenty-four months for the other students. At first glance, it seemed as if they had proved the existence of a talent for music and had identified a method for identifying children with the gift. But other differences in experience emerged from their research. Specifically, they found that those who could sing a tune earlier had parents and caregivers who sang to them more often. So, the comparatively early onset of their singing abilities was the result of environmental stimulus. No other study has been able to reliably document the precocious display of musical talent as a precursor to exceptional musical ability. Unless other evidence arises from future research, we can reasonably stop crediting special abilities with the magical idea of talent.

If it's not talent, perhaps the key to understanding exceptional ability is intelligence. Certainly, those with an above-average intelligence quotient (IQ) must at least be able to learn faster than others. As it turns out, this also is not true. Extensive examination of the effect of IQ on excellence has shown that those with higher IQs are able to assimilate new information a bit faster than others can, but that is to be expected—IQ exams are designed to measure that specific ability. Rather, other studies have shown that those who exhibit exceptional talents in some fields, such as sports or chess, do *not* generally exhibit higher average IQs than do their less accomplished colleagues.

If exceptional performance is not a consequence of talent or some other generalized ability such as IQ, then it must be the result of experience. After all, those who demonstrate mastery in any field have been working at it for a long time. But, as it turns out, this does not explain great accomplishment, either. We can all think of people who have been playing an instrument, singing, playing tennis, bowling, or participating in some other activity for a long time and yet they still don't show any exceptional ability, much less world-class performance. There is even evidence to show that experienced therapists, financial advisers, and some medical diagnosticians are often no better at achieving satisfactory results than are novices in those fields.

So, what factors lead to exceptional performance ability? In a follow-up study of the same 257 music students, Sloboda, et al. (1996) studied the amount of time the students engaged in formal practice and in informal playing such as improvisation, playing previously learned pieces, or other 'messing around.' As might be expected, they found a very high correlation between formal practice time and technical achievement but a weak correlation between informal practice and technical achievement. Most significant, however, they found no instances of high achievers' practicing less than any of the low achievers. Wait—read that again. Some of the low achievers were practicing as much as some of the high achievers did and yet were not being very successful; some of the high achievers practiced as little as some of the low-achievers did and still made exceptional progress. So, you have to practice in order to obtain exceptional performance abilities, but practice alone doesn't do it. What were are the high achievers doing that the low achievers were not? Could one practice differently, rather than simply practice more, to get better results?

First the bad news and then the good news. In a study at a conservatory in Berlin, Ericsson, Krampe, and Tesch-Römer (1993) examined the practice habits and practice histories of violinists who had been categorized as high achievers, likely to win an audition for a prestigious orchestra position, medium achievers, likely to play professionally but in a regional orchestra, and low achievers, who were focused on becoming music teachers rather than performers. On many measures, the groups were remarkably similar, including the fact that they had all been playing their instruments for about ten years. Any differences in starting age were insignificant. What they did find was fascinating.

They discovered that the members of the top two groups, the high and medium achievers, practiced alone for about 3.5 hours per day, for a total of about 24 hours per week. The low achievers practiced about 1.3 hours per day for a total of about 9.3 hours per week. The results, then, are, perhaps, predictable: more practice enabled greater skills. But what about the differences between the top two groups? How is it that they all practiced about the same amount yet some made more progress?

Their second big finding was that, on average, the high-achieving students had started their practice regime earlier than had the medium-achieving students. That is, they started to practice more hours per week at an earlier age than had the medium achievers. The differences could readily be predicted, on average, by their accumulated practice hours. By the age of eighteen the high achievers had accumulated, on average, more than 7,400 hours of practice; the second group averaged about 5,300 hours, and the future teachers averaged about 3,400 hours. Notice that these hours were accumulated by the age of eighteen. The researchers estimated that by the end of their conservatory career, the high-achieving violinists would have spent an average of 10,000 hours in practice.

So, here's the bad news: If you find yourself in that third category of performers, you might think: I can catch up with them if I only practice 2 hours more per day every day for the next four years. Unfortunately, the high achievers will still be putting in 3.5 hours per day, so they will be maintaining their lead. The researchers found that although it is mathematically possible to catch up, the realities of life, especially after the relatively distraction-free years at the conservatory, make it essentially impossible for the members of the third group to catch up with the top group in terms of practice hours.

Notice that all of these hour totals were averages. Some of the high achievers had practiced considerably less than 7,400 hours, and some of the medium achievers had practiced as much as the high achievers had. Therefore, there must have been yet another difference between them.This is the good news: While the amount of practice is a major determinant of achievement, the manner of practice is just as important. And these researchers figured out what the high-achieving students were doing differently. To describe it, they coined the phrase *deliberate practice.*

Their research confirmed the findings of many other studies: It takes approximately 10,000 hours of practice to achieve premiere status in an area of achievement, be it sports, the arts, business, or any other endeavor. But this practice must be of a particular type—deliberate practice.

COMPONENTS OF DELIBERATE PRACTICE

Deliberate practice isn't work and it isn't play, but is something entirely unto itself (Colvin, 2008, p. 66). It has five essential components.

1. It's designed to improve performance;
2. It can be repeated a lot;
3. Feedback on results is continuously available;
4. It's highly demanding mentally; and,
5. While it can be satisfying, it isn't much fun.

Let's take a short look at each of these factors.

It's Designed to Improve Performance

The key word here is *designed.* It has been shown (and you'll likely recognize this fact) that when people set out to work on getting better at something, they end up spending a considerable amount of time actually doing something they already know how to do rather than focusing on improving their abilities. Examples of this include the man who goes to the golf course to rather mindlessly hit a bucket of golf balls or the person who "works" on a musical piece by playing through it.

As it turns out, the old adage that practice makes perfect is not true. In reality, practice makes permanent. The purpose of deliberate training or practice is to move beyond one's current abilities. In order to do this, one has to know three things:

1. One's *current* level of ability. This requires subdividing the overall task, such as playing golf, into isolated tasks and then assessing one's ability at each of those tasks.
2. Then, it is essential to know *what* needs to be improved and what can be accomplished. We can think of tasks as being divided into three categories: the *comfort zone* (those we can already do), the *learning zone* (those we could do with some assistance or work), and the *panic zone* (those we're not ready for yet). Obviously, for effective learning one has to be working in the second category.
3. The third essential step in designing practice is to know *how* to work on the new task.

It Can Be Repeated a Lot

This component of deliberate practice functions as a check of the designed learning activity. One of the biggest problems in practice is a lack of focus on the fundamental performance problem. Let's go back to the golf example. Suppose our imaginary golfer has a terrible slice. (A slice is what happens when the ball fades to the right for a right-handed golfer.) Obviously, simply playing a round of golf is not going to improve the slice. This golfer needs the golf pro (a professional golf coach) to diagnose the cause of the slice and design a practice circumstance to eliminate the habit. Then the golfer needs to spend considerable time eliminating the habit by going to the driving range and not slicing. The golfer will have to transfer the new, improved drive to a round of golf, but that comes later.

What is the analogous circumstance for learning music performance? Suppose one is working on a true performance fundamental such as tone production. It's not enough simply to play or sing long tones in an effort to sound better. It is essential to know *why* the tone production is substandard. Only then can a teacher design or prescribe repeatable exercises to improve the tone production.

But what about when one is working on a specific piece? How does deliberate practice work? Again, practice can be designed to improve performance, but only after assessing which fundamental ability is the limiting factor. Suppose that the performer is challenged by a particular passage that requires a difficult fingering. The performance deficiency is not that passage but, rather, the fingering pattern. Practice sessions should include isolated practice of each segment of the difficult passage at a slower tempo. Then each component can be connected with the next and the tempo gradually increased to the target performance tempo. The assessment of success in this case is the successful transfer of the new skill into a run-through of the piece. This may only take a few minutes, or it may take dedicated work over a series of days or weeks.

In order for this procedure to be most effective, the tasks should be selected and the practice procedures designed *prior to* the beginning of the practice session. And that is also when goals have to be set. Otherwise, how would you know if or when you've been successful or even made any improvement? That's where the next factor comes into play.

Feedback on Results Is Continuously Available

At first, getting continuous feedback might seem complicated. You may have the impression that you need your teacher with you all the time so that you can get constant feedback, but that is not really the case. The secret is that you need to learn how to get your own feedback without the teacher. In fact, some research suggests that the key factor in improvement is learning to provide or obtain feedback on your own.

First, let's reconsider our imaginary golfer. Watching the flight of the ball and the extent of any slice certainly provides some feedback. But what if the golfer thinks he's doing it correctly and yet the ball continues to slice? A deliberate golfer will find a way to get feedback, either by asking another golfer or someone else he trusts to watch his drive to see if he is doing it right, or by videorecording his swing and seeing for himself. Obviously, in order to provide his own feedback, the golfer needs to be able to identify the differences between a proper swing and his own.

How does this transfer to music performance? The same idea is true: The key is to obtain quality feedback without the teacher's being present. The trick is to use a metronome, mirror, audio recorder or video recorder to gain new information about or a new perspective on the performance. Assuming that the practice task is well designed, recording one's attempts at correct performance and viewing or listening to them almost immediately helps one learn how to assess ones' efforts *during* performance—to make immediate changes in the approach to the playing or singing. This only works if one already has an accurate mental model of what one's performance should sound like.

It's Highly Demanding Mentally

This deliberate approach to practice requires one to be completely engaged in the process. These practice tasks have to be repeated intentionally, not mindlessly. The key is to constantly seek out areas that require improvement and work to make them better. That's what makes it *deliberate* practice instead of play. But that's also what makes it mentally challenging.

Ericsson et al. (1993) determined that both the high and the medium achievers they followed practiced about 3.5 hours per day, mostly because that was their upper limit. Some other studies have shown that 5 hours per day is the maximum. All of these studies, however, have shown some important similarities in the way high achievers schedule and approach their practice.

First, high achievers tend to practice in segments of approximately eighty minutes. If you think about the differences in the daily averages between the high and medium achievers (3.5 hours) and the low achievers (1.3 hours), it becomes fairly obvious that the top two groups practiced about three eighty-minute segments per day and the bottom group only one.

The high and medium achievers tended to practice in the middle of the day, between 10 a.m. and 2 p.m., when they were mentally and physically fresh. The future music teachers in this study tended to wait until mid-afternoon, the traditional siesta time, for their practice. Is it any wonder they weren't motivated to practice any more?

Finally, there was one more set of reliable differences, and this is potentially good news. The top two groups tended to sleep more, averaging 60 hours per week as compared to 54.6 hours for the lower-achieving group, and they napped a bit more, 2.8 hours per week as opposed to 0.9 hours per week on average. This does not mean that napping by itself will make you a better player, but rather it shows the importance of being mentally and physically fresh in order to take on the hard work of practicing.

It's Hard Work

The key challenge is motivation. Doing what we already feel confident about is reinforcing; it makes us feel competent. Deliberately seeking out that which we're not good at and doing it can make us feel incompetent, and therefore it is not very reinforcing. What is it that motivates exceptional performers to spend time working on activities that are challenging?

In *Drive* (Pink, 2009), Dan Pink explains that new research reveals three factors associated with high motivation:

1. **Autonomy**: There is a natural human desire to control one's own life. Engaging in deliberate practice helps one take control of one's own

learning and achievement, instead of being dependent on a parent, teacher, or coach.

2. **Mastery**: There is a natural human desire to want to do something better and better all the time. Engaging in deliberate practice satisfies that drive more effectively than does mindless practice, and leads one to seek out successively more challenging tasks.

3. **Purpose**: Humans are motivated by the desire to accomplish something or work toward a goal that is larger than themselves. Those who have participated in or listened to magical performances need no explanation about how music fits into this category.

As Ericsson et al. (1993) stated, deliberate practice is "not inherently enjoyable."

> If the activities that lead to greatness were easy and fun, then everyone would do them and they would not distinguish the best from the rest. The reality that deliberate practice is hard can even be seen as good news. It means that most people won't do it. So your willingness to do it will distinguish you all the more. (p. 72)

The key to overcoming the inherent challenges of deliberate practice seems to be developing a *growth mindset*. Once you realize that you are not reliant on your talent but, rather, that you are in control of your own progress (autonomy), then you are ready to practice deliberately. And, if you keep data from your self-generated feedback, then you will document your growth toward mastery. This is true whether your purpose is in music or any other challenge.

We will explore the fundamentals of motivation as they relate to teaching in subsequent chapters.

GETTING STARTED

Imagine that you now want to begin engaging in deliberate practice. What do you need to know in order to design a deliberate practice exercise? First, you have to have a clear understanding of the fundamental tasks you need to work on, how those tasks relate to one another, and how they contribute to exceptional performance. Second, you have to know what your current abilities are and what the next learning task is. Third, you have to know how to design a practice activity, implement it in the practice room, and assess your success or failure. If it didn't work, you have to draw on the first two kinds of knowledge to figure out why it didn't work and how you can try again differently during your next practice session.

Finally, you have to have control of your own learning environment, meaning the ability to choose your practice time and place and limit distractions. In other words, you have to create a learning context that works for you.

People who engage in deliberate practice (for ten years or more for twenty-four hours per week) become *exceptional performers*. People who design deliberate practice routines for others are called coaches or *teachers*. You are about to become both.

ACTION RESEARCH PROJECT

Your personal action research project is to incorporate deliberate practice into your standard practice routine. In order to do this, you will complete the Deliberate Practice Pre-Planning Form, figure 3.1. To start this process, let's first think about each of the five components of deliberate practice and how you will proceed.

1. *It's designed to improve performance.* Suppose that you have been assigned a particular piece to perform for your upcoming jury or the next student recital. Ideally, you should not be able to play it already—that would not allow you to learn anything new—and it should not be such a technical struggle that you are unable to invest in creating a musical performance. If that is the case, what should you work on? In order to figure this out, you need to know what you can already do and what needs to be improved. Then, you work on the *fundamental* skills that needs improvement, perhaps performing with great tone, correct musical style, longer phrase lengths, or dynamic range. When you determine what is holding you back from a great performance, work on that skill.

2. *It can be repeated a lot.* The task is to make the new skills automatic; you should not need to work at executing the new skills during performance. The only way to achieve this level of performance is to work at the *fundamental* skills in isolation over and over again. You may have to create a specific practice etude to develop and then polish that skill. Your applied instructor may also be able to assist you with this step.

3. *Feedback on results is continuously available.* You cannot know if you are being successful unless you have some way of knowing if you are correctly executing the new task. Since you likely do not meet with your applied instructor on a daily basis, you need a way to know *today* if you are making progress, and you need to plan how to obtain feedback before you start practice. Do you need visual or aural feedback? You may need to video record or audio record yourself to compare your performance with an ideal model and to compare it to your previous work to check for progress. You might

NAME: _____ DATE: _____

Etude/Excerpt: List the etude or the measures of an excerpt that you will be playing.	Goal: What would a successful performance look or sound like compared to your current ability?	Fundamental: What lack of fundamental knowledge or skill prevents you from performing the excerpt correctly?	Practice strategy: How will you develop the fundamental understanding or skill that will enable a satisfying performance? How will you incorporate your new learning back into the musical selection? What practice strategies will you use?	Feedback: How will you obtain feedback during practice as you develop?	Reflection: Record the minutes spent on this activity,rate your progress: (1 = poor, 5 = excellent), and note the practice strategies used.
					Minutes:Rating:
					Minutes:Rating:
					Minutes:Rating:
					Minutes:Rating:
					Minutes:Rating:
					Minutes:Rating:

Figure 3.1: Deliberate Practice Pre-planning Form.

just need a metronome or a tuner to supply feedback on steady tempo or pitch. Regardless, you have to decide how to obtain feedback. Then, you'll be better prepared for your next lesson.

4. *It's highly demanding mentally.* In order to make adequate progress, you need to schedule your practice sessions, and they need to take priority over less productive activities. But that's only the first task. The second and perhaps more difficult part is to stay on-task even when you get bored or somewhat frustrated. Keep a daily log of your practice so that you can track your effort and correlate it with your progress.

5. *It's hard work.* Maintaining your motivation is difficult, and the responsibility for it rest with you alone, not someone else. Keep in mind that you are in control, over time you will make progress that will distinguish you from the crowd, and all this hard work will allow you to perform music as you imagine it should be.

As a final note before you get started, you should not hesitate to get help with this process. Your applied teacher, your classmates, and older members of your studio may have valuable insights into deliberate practice. The goal is to learn to practice deliberately.

CHAPTER 4

Subject Matter of Music

You can have exceptional subject matter knowledge and not be a good teacher, but in order to be a good teacher, you have to have excellent subject matter knowledge. It is also true, however, that music serves many different functions for different people. In order to be able to communicate the power of music in our lives and in society, we have to understand the depth and breadth of the many different views of music held by people in our society.

There are just as many rationales for teaching music in our schools as there are views of the functions of music. In this chapter you'll be discovering the nature of music and the role it plays in our society in order to begin developing your personal philosophy of music education.

What should the final outcomes of the study of music be? Here's one attempt to answer that question: At the cessation of formal study, students should be able to consume, consider, and create music in ways that are personally, socially, and culturally useful, relevant, and meaningful.

As study progresses, students should be able to perceive sounds, think in sounds, and create sounds with ever-increasing ability. This means being able to hear and listen to complex sounds and perceive how they change over time and how they may be grouped and patterned at the moment and across time. It means being able to mentally recall and create groupings and patterns of sound, and it means being about to produce sounds and create (compose) new groupings (textures) and patterns (forms) of sound. All of these activities should occur in a manner that is personally, socially, and culturally relevant.

USES OF MUSIC

Ultimately, one must determine for oneself the meaningful role that music plays in one's life. But here are several ways to consider how music functions for people.

Music as Art or Personal Experience

One view of music is that it is a collection of *works* of art, and the study of music, then, is the study of these works. Thus, music is an object worthy of study.

Think back to a musical performance that you found to be particularly moving or meaningful. It's likely that you can recall the exact time and place of the experience, as well as the performers and those who were with you, unless you were alone. You may have been performing, listening to a live performance, or alone listening to a recording. You may have found the piece to represent something so profoundly beautiful or so inherently repulsive that the experience was essentially indescribable. In fact, that is one of the defining features of an artistic or *aesthetic experience*: that a description of it is an insufficient substitute for the actual experience.

What are the characteristics of this experience? See if these descriptors ring true (Ables, Hoffer, & Klotman, 1995):

1. It serves no practical purpose. It didn't pay the rent or drive you to work.
2. It involved feelings. Sure, almost everything involves feelings, but these were particularly intense.
3. It involved the intellect. At some point, you became keenly aware of the art (or music) object itself. This may have invoked a memory of a previous experience, musical or not.
4. It required a focus of attention. The object or the experience grabbed your attention and continues to re-engage you.
5. It had to be experienced. A description of the experience by someone else does not contain the same information.
6. Having the experience made life better or more meaningful.

You might wonder if a spectacular view of mountains or a visit to an exotic beachfront meet the criterion to be considered an aesthetic experience. Perhaps, but would those experiences be considered art? The term *aesthetics* is generally held to mean the study of beauty or the study of the philosophy of art. And art is generally held to be a purposeful (deliberate) act intended to communicate a particular view of life or living. There may be some debate about the exact scope and meaning of the terms *art* and *aesthetics*, but it's fairly certain that music and the study of music are germane.

Music as Communication or Interactive Experience

An old adage states that music is a universal language. While some societies are not as cultural-centric as it used to be, so we understand that while music might be universal, understanding of the music of another culture (or age group) is not automatic or universal.

Music can serve several communicative functions. Music can be used to refer to an extramusical idea or story. Examples of this include programmatic music such as Hector Berlioz's *Symphonie Fantastique*, in which a story is implied; operas, oratorios, and some ballets, in which the story is explicit; and pieces that describe places or objects, such as Modest Mussorgsky's *Pictures at an Exhibition* or John Mackey's *Frozen Cathedral*.

Music as a Cultural Activity

Music also serves as a kind of cultural communication. Consider the music associated with various ceremonies such as wedding, funerals, and inaugurations. The selection of certain musical repertoire, or the use of certain live performers or ensembles, sends a message about the importance of the event and the behavior expected of the participants. For example, one would expect different types of music at wedding ceremonies and at wedding receptions that correlate with the typical comportment of the attendees.

David Elliott takes the idea of music as communication one step further and defines music as a fundamentally human activity. He states that this activity has three dimensions: the doer, who is *musicking*, the musical product, and the cultural context in which the musicking occurs. Along with opportunities for music students (musickers) for personal growth and accomplishment in music and the intellectual study of music, musicking provides the chance for musickers to "formulate musical expressions of emotions, musical representations of people, places and things, and musical expressions of cultural-ideological meanings" (Elliott, 2005, p. 10). This is his definition of being musical.

Another way to define music might be from a more pragmatic, "person-focused" perspective (Lehmann, Sloboda, & Woody, 2007). In this approach, music is defined by the use or purpose assigned to the activity by the person using it. According to this view, one might identify four roles in music, those of the creator, the teacher-student dyad, the listener, and the user. From this perspective, the creator could be a composer, arranger, producer, or performer—the person or group that produces the musical product. The teacher-student dyad encompasses the musical mentor-mentee interaction that may occur between two individuals or in a group setting. The listener is an individual who is actively focused on a musical performance (either live or recorded) for cultural, artistic, or personal ends. The (casual) user is a passive listener who includes background music as a part of the milieu of his or her life experiences.

Music as a Physical Phenomenon

You have heard the classic question, "If a tree falls in the woods and no one is there to hear it, does it make a sound?" Students commonly respond in one of two ways: "Of course! How could it not?!?" or "How would we know?" It all depends, of course, on your definition of *sound*.

Now what?

Fundamentally, music is made up from sounds and silence, and sound is the result of a physical phenomenon. (It may be helpful to imagine the sound from a handbell as you read this section.) Any object that produces sound vibrates in some fashion. As it vibrates and pushes and pulls against the air, it creates waves of high pressure and troughs of low pressure. Like the ripples on a pond caused by a dropped pebble, the waves and troughs travel out in concentric circles, either resonating through or reflecting off nearby objects. Again, just like ripples in a pond, the waves and troughs combine into chaotic patterns. It's this jumbled mess of interacting waves that reaches our eardrums, and we process it into perceived sound. Thus, sounds only exist in our minds as perceptions of physical phenomena.

We perceive the amplitude of the waves and troughs, their height and depth, as volume; the stronger or higher the amplitude, the louder we perceive the sound to be. We perceive the frequency of the waves, the time from one peak to the next, as pitch; the faster the frequency of the waves expressed in cycles per second, the higher the perceived pitch. Humans with undamaged hearing mechanisms generally can perceive frequencies between 20 Hertz (Hz, cycles per second) and 20,000 Hz.

If we were to graph out a sound over time, to create a sound envelope, we would see that each sound envelope has four parts: attack, decay, sustain, and release (ADSR). See Figure 4.1.

1. The **attack** is the time it takes for sound to go from zero or nil to its maximum. In this example, it would be the time from the moment the clapper strikes the bell until the bell reaches its maximum vibration.
2. The **decay** is the time of the subsequent reduction from the energy of the initial attack down to a sustained vibration.
3. The **sustain** is the time during which the sound either maintains or gradually loses amplitude or volume.
4. The **release** is the cessation of vibration and sound production.

Some items, such as bells, tend to vibrate at and sustain a particular frequency, or pitch. Like a pendulum swinging at a particular rate owing to its

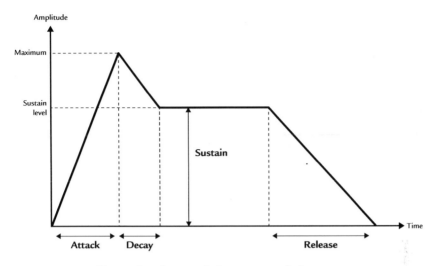

Figure 4.1: Parts of the sound envelope: attack, decay, sustain, and release

length, certain frequencies will sustain in some items owing to their mass, size, and construction. These items are said to resonate at that pitch. This is their *resonant pitch*. Other items, such as square sheets of metal, do not tend to vibrate efficiently at any particular frequency and therefore expend their energy fairly quickly. Finally, other items, such as bricks, either do not have a resonant frequency or resonate at a frequency above or below our threshold of perception.

Items often also vibrate at frequencies that are multiples of their resonant frequency or resonant pitch. For example, standard tuning pitch is A440. That means that the standard frequency of the A above middle C on a piano is to be tuned to 440 Hz, or cycles per second. If you listen to a pure tone (sine wave) of that pitch, as you can on Wikipedia, it has no color or character. It sounds cold and electronic.

If you strike that pitch on a piano, however, you do not obtain only that single frequency, or pitch. The piano string will also vibrate at multiples of the fundamental pitch: 880 Hz, 1320 Hz, 1760 Hz, and so on. Multiples of the fundamental are called overtones; 880 Hz is the first overtone, 1320 Hz the second overtone, and so on. These overtones provide the individual color or timbre of a sound. Timbre is what allows you to distinguish between a sine wave, a piano, and an oboe all playing the same pitch. The piano and the oboe have different colors because they have different ratios of overtones; some overtones are stronger on the piano than on the oboe and vice versa. When we say that an instrument or voice has a characteristic tone, we are saying that the overtones are in the correct proportion.

Summary

These four descriptions of the uses of music are simply lenses through which we can view and consider music. None is absolute or exclusive. You will need to decide for yourself which of these uses resonate or ring true for you, and the function of music may change depending on the context and your own subjective emotional or intellectual state. In many ways, the beauty of music is that, even as we decide for ourselves the value of music and the arts in our lives, a definitive explanation of music is still elusive.

COMPONENTS OF ORGANIZED SOUND

Whether you are thinking of music as a collection of sound envelopes or as the aural component of a cultural activity, composers and improvisers organize the components of musical sound into patterns to create musical structure (form) and to express emotion. It is generally accepted that music has five basic components. They are listed below in no particular order.

- **Rhythm**, the most basic component of music and the most easily accessible, is the mechanism by which time is measured, subdivided, and combined in music. The unit of measurement is the beat. The rhythmic elements may or may not have a definable pitch.
- **Timbre** is the tone color of the various notes expressed rhythmically or melodically. The timbre that is perceived is based on the ratio of the overtones to one another.
- A **melody** is a sequential grouping of two or more discrete musical notes, not necessarily with different pitches. The notes may be expressed in some rhythmic manner, in that they may be divided or combined. Each note in the sequence may or may not have the same timbre.
- **Harmony** is the simultaneous sounding of two or more pitches. They may or may not have the same rhythm or timbre.
- **Form** is the manner in which various musical elements are combined, either through repetition, contrast, or variation, to complete a musical design.

Text, though an integral part of many musical performances, is technically extramusical in that it does not directly utilize any of the fundamental components of music. That does not mean, however, that text cannot be *combined* and integrated with musical elements to make a more complete and expressive work of musical art.

Music as a Neurological Phenomenon

How is it that we perceive these vibrations as sounds? How is it that we turn physical vibrations in the environment into perceptions with meaning so powerful that we demand *live* music performances for special moments in our lives? First let's deal with the physiology of hearing. The hearing mechanism has three parts, the outer ear, the middle ear, and the inner ear. The outer ear consists of the pinna, the cartilage, and the auditory canal. The purpose of the outer ear is to assist in locating the direction from which the sound arrived and to deliver the sound to the middle ear. The middle ear consists of the eardrum and three small bones that convert the sound energy from the actual pressure waves into mechanical energy and transfer the mechanical energy to the inner ear.

The inner ear consists primarily of the cochlea, which looks not unlike a snail shell, and several other small components. The purpose of the cochlea is to convert the mechanical energy delivered to it from the middle ear into neurological electrical signals that are then transferred to the brain.

Neurological Perception

Consider for a moment the immense complexity of the sounds of almost any musical performance. These sounds arrive at your eardrum as an chaotic mess of sound frequencies and volumes. How is it possible for your brain to make any sense of that mess whatsoever? The neurophysiology of sound and music perception is far beyond the scope of this book, but the overall process is fascinating.

The primary auditory cortex functions as a traffic cop for the sounds that enter your brain, which have now been converted into electrical signals. The primary auditory cortex interprets the signal and separates out the individual streams of information—volume, timbre, and verbal language, say—and sends them off to different parts of the brain, the secondary auditory areas, for simultaneous processing. Now the sound information has gone from one undifferentiated mess to several information streams in various parts of your brain. How can it process all of that information and make sense of it instantly, as more music keeps pouring in?

One of the remarkable processes that your brain uses to defend itself from information overload is called grouping. You do this visually when you see a forest instead of many trees. Your brain does this, too, when processing music. Instead of hearing a collection of frequencies that happen to align in a series of overtones, you hear a trombone. When you hear two instruments playing the same line, your brain combines them into one sound object. Instead of hearing a saxophone and a trombone, you hear a completely new sound object: a saxobone or trombophone. Again, that is only if they are playing simultaneously. If they are playing different lines, or if they are not playing together, your brain will make two sound objects—a more complex sound.

Now consider the effort your brain undertakes to understand the sounds of a choir. Assuming undamaged hearing physiology and normal neurological function, the primary auditory cortex divides the signal information into various streams and directs it to other areas of the brain for processing. The pitch information is sent to nearby structures for determination of relationships between pitches. These relationships can be sequential (one to the next) as in a melody, or they can be simultaneous, as in harmonies. One signal is sent to the cerebellum, in the back of your brain, which processes it for beat and tempo. Another stream is sent to other areas of the brain to process any text or language. Then the various streams are recombined and compared to all previously known music to determine whether it has been heard before, and the emotional areas of the brain respond accordingly. All the while, the frontal cortex is trying to predict what might happen next in the music.

At this point, it is sufficient for you to know two things: (1) the process of perceiving and responding to music is highly complex and not yet fully understood, and (2) more areas of the brain are used for processing music than for any other human activity.

MUSICALITY AND MUSICAL PERCEPTION

If you have ever played around with any of the music software packages that play back your notation, you understand intuitively that what is produced sounds mechanical and unmusical. It is as lifeless as computer-generated speech. The problem with the unmusical playback is that it is too perfect. The software creates a literal production of the music notation—a nominal performance. There is no variability in the timing between notes, note length, volume, or tempo. In short, it's missing the imperfection that brings music to life.

On the other hand, listeners, even those without extensive musical training, almost always recognize exceptional performers and performances. The performances communicate in a way that seems magical. Somehow, while being completely absorbed in the moment, the listener has an intuitive awareness that the work had a beginning and is progressing to some reasonable conclusion.

How exactly does the magician or the musician manipulate physical or sound objects to fool our senses? Surprisingly, both use the psychology of expectation and timing to create their desired effect. The performances may *seem* to be magical, but the performers follow well-established guidelines and procedures to communicate with their audiences.

From one piece to the next, human performers are remarkably consistent; many musicians and ensembles can be identified in recordings because of their unique yet consistent sound or style. When compared to a nominal (mechanical) performance, however, musicians are remarkably inconsistent. They demonstrate neither perfect timing nor consistent volume and tone color from one note to the next. Some of this variation is random variation due to the limitations of human physiology and cognition. Other variations are made for purposes of musical expression. Whereas performers use a musical *nuance* to change the shape (ADSR) of a single note,

> [e]*xpression* refers to the small-scale variations in timing, loudness, and other parameters that performers insert at specific points in a performance. An expressive gesture can be completely contained within a sequence of a few notes [or a phrase]. *Interpretation* refers to the way in which many individual expressive acts are chosen and combined across an entire piece to produce a coherent and aesthetically satisfying experience. Expressive devices are thus the basic building blocks of an interpretation. (Lehmann, 2007, pp. 89, italics added)

Effective musicians use purposeful variations in timing, timbre, dynamics, and articulation to communicate emotion as well as musical form and structure to the listener. In order to achieve successful musical communication, the performer and the listener must agree on certain rules similar to vocabulary, grammar, and syntax in spoken language. Whence do these rules arise? They are formed by the temporal and embodied experiences of being alive (notice the term "gesture" in the quotation above) and the expressive qualities of spoken language.

Listening to music and perceiving musical intent, as opposed to merely hearing, is a complex process based on refined perception and musical expectation, both of which are formed from prior listening experiences. Sophisticated music listening requires the ability to group various sound experiences into a single sound object and then to create a hierarchy of sound objects. For example, a melodic sequence—a series of short note groups that are repeated at various pitch levels—might be thought of at two different levels: the sequence as sound object is made up of several smaller sound objects. This grouping process, as explained by *gestalt theory*, is integral to recognizing musical structure. The performer's task is to communicate the structure and emotion of a musical selection as clearly and deliberately as possible. Each of the tools that musicians use to communicate structure and emotion are examined individually, followed by an explanation of how they are synthesized into a musical whole.

Structural Communication

Structural communications is one of the two major expressive mechanisms used by performers to bring the music to life. Humans experience consciousness as an awareness of time; they can recall the past, experience the present, and predict future events and experiences. In music, an awareness of form and structure allows the listener to experience the passage of time within the musical work.

As outlined in the rest of this subsection, musical performers use subtle, sometimes almost imperceptible changes in tempo (timing) and dynamics to indicate small- and large-scale musical structure. These techniques might be used to dictate musical structures as small as a group of two notes—perhaps grammatically analogous to a noun phrase—or a structure as large as a movement from a symphony. When a listener becomes aware, even subconsciously, of a yet incomplete form, he or she is able to form predictions about the eventual outcome of the formal development based on prior experiences with similar musical forms. That these predictions can be either satisfied or thwarted at the conclusion of the work may be thrilling or frustrating to the listener.

Meter and Rhythm

The most accessible component of music is the beat, or tactus. This progression of beats, measured in beats per minute, corresponds with the way you would likely tap your foot when listening to music. Beats can be subdivided, usually into two, three, or four parts. Beats can be grouped into measures, usually of two, three, or four beats, and subsequently into groups of measures.

As an example of the effect of meter, consider the melody presented in Figure 4.2. Without thinking about it too much, try to sing the tune in solfège.

Compare the feel of the first tune with the one shown in figure 4.3.

A nominal, mechanical performance of each should sound exactly the same despite the differences in notation. Yet a human performance will

Figure 4.2: A tune

Figure 4.3: The same tune written differently

have a completely different feel. Some may even find it difficult or at least uncomfortable to sing the tune as presented in figure 4.2. Even without explicit training, musicians subconsciously place a slight emphasis on the first beat of each measure. In order to do this, performers will both accent the note—start at a slightly higher volume level and then return to the nominal level—and stretch the time value of the note. These performance practices appear to be derived both from dance, in which the dancers generally take a large or heavy step on beat one, and from language, in which certain syllables are naturally accented and lengthened to provide perceptive clarity and emphasis.

Melody, Note Groupings, and Phrases

In figure 4.3, the note groupings (eight-beat groupings) line up with the beginning of every other measure, but this is not always the case. Phrases are groups of measures that, when taken as a single whole, have some sort of acquired musical meaning. A common analogy to a musical phrase is a complete sentence in spoken or written language. Each is assembled into a meaningful whole from various subcomponents; written or spoken language has words and clauses whereas musical language has measures, note groupings and sub-phrases. In music, often the phrases and note groupings align to some extent with the meter and barlines, but not always. This alignment tends to reinforce the internal structure.

Within a phrase, notes can be grouped together into small melodic units. Such groupings can be obvious, as with melodic sequences, or more opaque. A complete examination of this topic is beyond the scope of this text but, in general, the way a phrase is segmented can have a significant impact on its musical meaning. As an analogy, consider the effect of two different phrase groupings on an excerpt from the early English play *Ralph Roister Doister* (as cited in Hovey, 1976, p. 58).

Do and say what you wish, you shall never please me;
But when you are merry, I will be all sad;
When you are sorry, I will be very glad;
When you seek your heart's ease, I will be unkind;
At no time in me shall you much gentleness find.

Do and say what you wish. You shall never please me
But when you are merry. I will be all sad
When you are sorry; I will be very glad
When you seek your heart's ease. I will be unkind
At no time. In me shall you much gentleness find.

Read each verse aloud and consider how you communicated the two different structures to potential listeners. If you read each verse in a nominal manner, you would have simply pronounced each word at a more or less even tempo; you may recall hearing young children read in this manner. More likely, you used timing and dynamics to indicate the groupings. Slight pauses indicate breaks between the various sentence clauses that are separated by commas; slightly longer pauses are used to break up the complex sentences that are separated by semicolons; longer pauses are used to indicate the ends of sentences. You also likely started each sentence rather quickly and slowed down just a bit toward the end, but not at the same rate for each. Depending on the desired effect and the intended note grouping, performers will either increase or decrease volume at the end of groupings. As you changed the groupings in the text, you likely decoded different meanings. You may even have subconsciously changed your tone and timing to reflect the altered emotional content. These same processes work in musical expression.

If you read the verses aloud using these techniques to indicate the structure, you are using the same techniques that effective musicians use to indicate musical structure. When performers create a complex representation of a phrase structure, they create a hierarchy of related groupings. Performers generally save their strongest effects for the more important structural elements, changing their timing and dynamics more at the ends of the most important structures. These tendencies are so ingrained that musicians do not notice subtle changes as variances from a steady tempo. They do, however, notice these slight pauses if they are inserted in the middle of a phrase or note grouping. The implication is that there are unspoken rules of performance practice that, because they are so commonly used, are not noticed unless they are violated.

If the verse above were set to music, each verse might be considered the top level of the hierarchy, with each complete sentence and then each clause occupying a lower level of the hierarchy.

Harmonic Tension and Release

Two or more musical tones that sound in sequence have a *melodic* relationship to one another. Two or more musical tones that sound simultaneously are said to have a *harmonic* relationship. Because children generally grow up surrounded by a culturally defined musical soundscape, they develop a tacit understanding of the local musical culture through a process called *acculturation*. For example, in Western music, certain intervals are considered consonant and others are considered dissonant. As a result of acculturation, listeners develop a level of expectation for the sequence of melodic and harmonic structures. In general, any deviation from these expected sequences results in a kind of musical tension. Similarly, a return to an expected norm after a period of tension causes a kind of musical release. Composers in all genres use these techniques to enhance emotional and structural communication.

In order to more fully understand the concepts of harmony, harmonic tension, and harmonic release, we have to examine the physical phenomenon of sound a bit more. Air pressure waves are created by a vibrating object such as the cone of a speaker or the reed in a clarinet. We experience those pressure waves as sound. The pitch that we perceive is determined by the frequency of the vibrations. The frequency for middle C on the piano is 261.6 Hz, or cycles per second. The frequency of the C one octave above middle C is about 523.2 Hz. Every time the frequency is doubled, we perceive the note to be one octave higher; if the frequency is half as fast, we perceive it as one octave lower.

For the sake of convenience, let's pretend that the frequency of the b-flat a little more than two octaves below middle C is 60 Hz. (It's actually 58.27 Hz, but using 60 will make the upcoming explanation a bit easier to understand.) Thus, one octave above our reference b-flat is also a b-flat, but with a frequency of 120 Hz. Another octave higher, at 240 Hz or four times our fundamental pitch, is yet another b-flat. Now it gets interesting. What about three times the fundamental? The resulting pitch is 180 Hz, which is perceived as an f one and a half octaves above the fundamental. If we transpose that f down one octave, its frequency is 90 Hz, it is still is perceived as an f, and it is considered to be a fifth above the fundamental because that f is the fifth degree of a b-flat scale. If we go down from the fundamental b-flat that same distance, five degrees on a diatonic scale, we arrive at a perceived e-flat at approximately 40 Hz. The fact that these two pitch intervals have a 3:2 frequency relation will be important below.

Returning to the original fundamental b-flat, the next interesting pitch is the one that occurs mathematically and perceptually halfway between the b-flat and the f above. This note has a 5:4 frequency relation to the fundamental (so, approximately 75 Hz in this case) and is perceived as a d. Together, these three pitches—b-flat, d, and f—create a harmonic sound that you would find familiar: a major chord. While this sound forms a basis of Western music, note that its genesis is in the mathematical relation between the perceived pitches. This particular chord is often referred to as a I chord, because it's built on the first degree of the scale.

If we, in turn, build the same harmonic relationship from the f (the fifth scale degree above the b-flat) we obtain three pitches—f, a, and c—and we call this a V chord because it's built on the fifth note of the scale, which is a fifth above the b-flat. If we perceive the b-flat I chord as the home (tonic) chord, moving away from it to the V chord causes a bit of harmonic tension. Returning to the I chord from the V sounds and feels like a release of that tension. In conceptual and perceptual terms, this is the basis of harmonic tension and release in Western music. This V–I harmonic movement has a name; it's called an authentic cadence.

If, instead of building the V chord on f, we build a major triad on the e-flat, we obtain a combination of pitches—e-flat, g, and b-flat—that build the IV chord. The IV–I harmonic movement (still the movement of a fifth) also has a name; it's called a plagal cadence. When you hear it, you will likely recognize it as the "Amen" cadence that is common at the end of Christian hymns.

Once you start to recognize these sounds and the relationships between them, you may begin to realize that the vast preponderance of Western music is based on a I–IV–V–I or a I–IV–I–V–I harmonic motion. In general, the V–I motion, also known as dominant-to-tonic motion, is the strongest harmonic movement. Several other points are important.

- Using accidentals, it is also possible to create chords with root, third, fifth, and seventh scale degrees (seven chords) and secondary dominant functions, such as II^7–V^7–I;
- The dominant-tonic movements are emphasized because of half-step motion in particular voices between the chords; and
- The farther away harmonically one goes from the home key, the stronger the release will be when returning to the home key.

If you are using this book as a text for an introductory music education course, it's likely that you are simultaneously taking some sort of music theory course, during which you will discuss these concepts in greater detail.

The key point of this section about structural communication is that listeners, because they have absorbed certain understandings about music through the acculturation process, will subconsciously perceive, recognize, and respond to musical structure. Effective musical artists use this process to their advantage to both satisfy and surprise their listeners.

Emotional Communication

The other facet of musicality to be explored is expression, or emotional communication. Although many consider it to be the most important facet of an effective performance, instruction in expressive performance is often neglected, perhaps because it seems somewhat magical or seems to exist primarily in the realm of expert performers. Recent research has begun to unlock the code to expressive performance and provide important pedagogical insights and tools.

There are two elements to expressive performance: intentionality and accuracy. Since all renderings of a piece—especially those of less-than-expert performers—are somewhat inconsistent and contain random changes, expressive performance requires that the musician intend to communicate a specific emotion. And, for performances to successfully communicate a specific emotion, the listeners must be able to accurately discern which emotion is intended. Researchers have tested intentionality and accuracy by asking musicians to perform with a specific emotion in mind and then questioning listeners as to what emotion they perceived in the work. With trained performers and listeners, the intentional communication of musical emotion was successful approximately 75 percent of the time. This rate of success generally matches the rates of successful facial or vocal expression and recognition.

In an effort to understand emotional communication in music, performances were recorded and analyzed to determine exactly how the performers were able to communicate specific emotions (Juslin & Persson, 2002). It was determined that the performers used *expressive cues* to convey the intended emotion. The four most effective expressive cues were found to be tempo (or timing), dynamics, timbre, and articulation (style). See figure 4.4.

Furthermore, each performance was subsequently analyzed to determine how each of the expressive cues was manipulated in order to communicate specific emotions. (See Table 4.1.)

Figure. 4.4: The communication of musical emotion (based on material in Juslin & Persson, 2002)

Table 4.1: MUSIC EXPRESSION CUES

Emotion	Cue Utilization
Happiness	fast tempo, small tempo variability, *staccato* articulation, large articulation variability, high sound level, bright timbre, fast tone attacks, small timing variations, increased durational contrasts between long and short notes
Sadness	very slow tempo, *legato* articulation, small articulation variability, low sound level, dull timbre, large timing variations, reduced durational contrasts between long and short notes, slow tone attacks
Anger	high sound level, sharp timbre, spectral noise, fast tempo, *staccato* articulation, abrupt tone attacks, increased durational contrasts between long and short notes, no *ritardando*, sudden accents, accents on tonally unstable notes, *crescendo*, phrase *accelerando*
Tenderness	slow tempo, slow tone attacks, low sound level, small sound-level variability, *legato* articulation, soft timbre, moderate timing variations, reduced durational contrasts between long and short notes, final *ritardando*, accents on stable notes
Fear	staccato articulation, very low sound level, large sound-level variability, fast tempo, large tempo variability, very large timing variations, bright spectrum, pauses between phrases, sudden syncopations

Source: Based on material found in Juslin & Persson, 2002).

If you have ever tried this on your own, you may have discovered some of the musical cues. Notice that there is some overlap; there is not a one-to-one mapping of performance technique with a corresponding emotion. It is the mixture of the various cues that seems to hint at the intended emotion in the listener. Just for fun, go back and reread the excerpt from *Ralph Roister Doister* and encode one or more of the various emotions using the musical emotional cues. (Note that the two verses have different explicit meanings based on the phrase groupings, so some emotions might be more appropriate for one version than for the other.)

When you read the verses, did you do so in exactly the same manner all the way through? Did you use the exact same inflection, volume, and timing? Of course not. Listeners would tune you out after a very short period of time. Throughout the verses, you likely emphasized some syllables more than others, changed your dynamic to indicate increasing anger or decreased it to indicate a quiet intensity, and rushed through some clauses while perhaps taking a dramatic pause before the climax. Each clause brings on its own subtle shift in the emotions expressed in the verse as the text adds more meaning. Music is (or should be) like this, too; the emotions of a single phrase can modulate from beginning to end, and surely each phrase or large section should have its own character. The philosopher Susanne Langer makes this relationship explicit when she states, "Music is the tonal analogue of emotive life" (Langer, 1953, p. 27).

If the shifting emotional content of music represents the internal, dynamic "emotive life," how do performers know how to encode those emotions in sounds, and how do listeners know how to decode those sounds back into core emotions? Your reading of the verses above should supply an essential clue to the answer: we learn to encode and decode musical emotions based on our similar experience encoding emotions into and decoding them from spoken (or yelled or whispered) language.

The ability to break the musical emotional code reflects the process through which meaningful spoken communication arises. A child's earliest experiences with spoken language are with her parents and other caregivers. They use a special kind of language, called *motherese*, when interacting with infants. In fact, it's often referred to as infant-directed speech (IDS). This speech style, characterized by high pitch, glissandi, soft articulation, and short, repeated syllables, is more successful than adult speech in keeping an infant's attention. Later, child-directed speech includes more variation, with short, accented syllables used to indicate disapproval. The fact that caregivers use IDS intuitively and infants understand it innately suggests that there are underlying genetically encoded brain mechanisms at work, but they remain unidentified.

Consider songs that are intended to communicate anger and the musical characteristics associated with anger as listed in table 4.1. Composers carefully use these expressive elements to convey anger. You recognized the music as angry because, at some point in your life, an angry person yelled at you using these exact same expressive elements. The process works in the same manner for the other four emotions listed in table 4.1.

How Musicians Make It Work

Those who are unaware of the knowledge gathered from research on musical expression may cling to the myth that musicality is an innate talent that is not teachable—either you have it or you don't. Great performers sometimes unknowingly contribute to the myth that expression is innate or unteachable precisely because they are unable to explain it adequately. This may be due in part to the tacit nature of expert knowledge; they no longer remember not knowing how to be expressive, and therefore think they've done it all along. Those who know better understand the relation between emotion, language, and musicality, and therefore work as teachers to establish a link between the subjective world of the performer (for example, imagery, metaphor, emotion) and the objective features of performance (for example, articulation).

Forging this link can be accomplished through several pedagogical techniques. The first, alluded to above, is by using metaphor, analogy, and imagery to activate appropriate emotional states within the performer during practice or prior to performance. This is similar to the techniques used by method actors. The challenge is that teachers cannot conjure up emotional states in their students that are dependent on prior experiences if the students lack experiences that previously evoked those emotions.

The second useful technique is modeling, either through live performance or recordings, which is when the teacher essentially shows the student how to play the excerpt. There are drawbacks and challenges to this method. For one thing, unless the teacher verbally describes and aurally differentiates the specific performance details he or she is attempting to pass along, the student may not discern the expressive gesture in enough detail to implement it himself or herself. For another, this instructional method may not help the student form an explicit link between the subjective emotion to be conveyed and the objective technique required to produce it.

Consider the vast size of the repertoire that professional musicians must know intimately in order to earn and maintain employment. How can they possibly remember all of that music, especially the details of various expressive gestures that make for effective performance? Quite simply, they don't. This is one of the reasons why expressive performance appears to be innate or intuitive; it's a result of the process that expert musicians use to create those performances.

As a way of understanding this process, consider professional accompanists. They are often required to sightread complicated works and produce musically convincing performances with limited practice or rehearsal time. How do they make that happen? Beyond the technical skills required to sightread (a process discussed elsewhere in this text), and because of their vast experience, expert accompanists have assimilated the rules of expressive performance and use those rules to generate musically satisfying performances on the fly. Not only are they able to discern and communicate the musical structure, but they are also able to recognize the musically expressive potential in the work of the composer—the various dynamic expressions of emotion built into the work—and select the appropriate musically expressive cue to use at that moment in the piece. As complex as this may seem, it is not unlike the expressive work in use when professional actors improvise scenes or give readings of plays. With some practice at it, you, too, might become quite good at generating expressive readings on the fly.

Experience plays a key role in this process, along with years of study. Like accompanists, expert musicians recognize when the current piece is like another piece they may have studied in detail and then apply the same musically expressive rules to the new piece. Consider how conductors might approach a monumental work such as a Brahms symphony. If they've never studied Brahms before, then the process might be somewhat intimidating. If, however, they have conducted the other three Brahms symphonies, learning the last new one may not be as troublesome.

Although your artistic goal might be to give performances that listeners perceive as magical, the artistic processes used to render such performances are not magical at all—they are based on solid research on music perception, cognition, and performance.

In Chapter 5 we'll look at the purposes and outcomes of public school music education, the subject matter content as defined by the National Standards for Music Education, and their implications for defining musical understanding and performance.

So, what should we want as outcomes from the teaching process? What is it that we want students to know and do? We teach singers and instrumentalists to control the sound envelope. We teach them to listen to and perceive sound. We teach them to appreciate music. We teach them to use music and to create music that is culturally relevant. We teach them to be musical—to think with and communicate in sounds.

PROJECT

1. Explain the following terms in your own words:
   - Aesthetic experience
   - Perception and cognition
   - Attack, decay, sustain, and release
   - Rhythm, timbre, melody, harmony, and form
   - Random variation, nuance, expression, and interpretation
2. Consider the four uses of music as described in this chapter. For each, share a short personal narrative about how music functioned in that way for you.
3. Think about a performance recording that you consider to be highly expressive. Search around on the Internet and find a MIDI or synthesized nominal performance of the same piece. Compare the two versions and describe in detail how the musical performer used structural and emotional musical cues.
4. Explain how the communication of musical emotion works. Be sure to explain the concept in general, its relation to language, and the specific way in which each emotion works.

5. Select a fairly simple, short melody. You may use a child's tune or a simple etude. Your task is to perform it five different ways, representing each musical emotion, for a friend. The friend should fill out the Musical Emotional Response Form shown in Figure 4.5. The goal is for the listener to recognize which of the five musical emotions—happiness, sadness, anger, tenderness, and fear—you intended to convey.

You are about to hear five renditions of the same simple melody. Each time it is performed it will represent one of five emotional states: happiness, sadness, anger, tenderness, or fear. All you have to do is to circle the emotion portrayed in each performance.

Performance	Emotion				
1	Happiness	Sadness	Anger	Tenderness	Fear
2	Happiness	Sadness	Anger	Tenderness	Fear
3	Happiness	Sadness	Anger	Tenderness	Fear
4	Happiness	Sadness	Anger	Tenderness	Fear
5	Happiness	Sadness	Anger	Tenderness	Fear

Figure 4.5: Musical Emotional Response Form

CHAPTER 5

Music as Subject Matter

One of the continuing challenges to music education is the perception by members of the general public and education administrators that music, and the arts in general, are "extras" rather than core subjects in the curriculum. Unfortunately, this perception is often shown to be correct in that music education in many cases is practiced as an extracurricular activity, even if it occurs during the regular school day.

Over the course of the past several decades, there have been considerable efforts to disseminate rationales that justify including music as a core subject. In the past, these efforts sometimes focused on such collateral benefits of music study as improved SAT scores, better reading scores for younger children, and the social benefit from group interaction in ensemble courses. Music education policy, if based on these premises, fails to support music as indispensable because these benefits can be obtained through other educational efforts. Many music teachers have been complicit in this failure to justify the existence of their programs.

Yet those who have participated in music education programs in the past have a tacit understanding of the educational benefits of music study. The recent challenge has been to make those implicit understandings explicit and to marry together research about music learning, music education philosophy, and music education policy in order to communicate the value of music study to the general public and to advocate with educational and governmental decision makers for continuing financial support of music study.

In this chapter, I investigate the idea that music can be a curricular subject along the lines of mathematics, language, or history and why it is important for students to study music. Second, you will read about the national standards for music education, including the history of the standards and how they seem to define music itself. Finally, we'll explore the relationships between the national standards for music education and a taxonomy of cognitive processes and knowledge domains.

REDEFINING SUBJECT MATTER

Although leaders in music education have been seeking to define music as a subject worthy of study in the schools for a number of years, they were not the first to seek a vocabulary for communicating the educational value of various disciplines. In 1948 a group led by education researcher Benjamin S. Bloom developed a system to classify learning outcomes based on evaluations of students' work products. They developed a taxonomy with three major domains, each divided into subdomains (Bloom, 1956, pp. 7–8). These are the three major domains.

> **Cognitive domain**: the recall or recognition of knowledge and the development of intellectual abilities and skills;
> **Psychomotor domain:** the manipulative or motor-skill area; and
> **Affective domain:** changes in interest, attitudes, and values, and the development of appreciations and adequate adjustment.

Cognitive Domain

Bloom's original organization of the cognitive domain involved six levels that were hierarchical in that each of the higher levels required preexisting lower-level knowledge. They are

1. **Knowledge**: remembering and recalling facts;
2. **Comprehension**: understanding the relations and interactions between facts, understanding rules and theorems, and understanding the relation between questions and answers;
3. **Application**: using knowledge, rules, and procedures to solve novel problems;
4. **Analysis**: dissecting a complex system (such as a musical work or social interaction, or any system with interacting variables) into component parts to gain an understanding of the system;
5. **Synthesis**: having completed an analysis, understanding the complex interactions between the various components of a complex system; and
6. **Evaluation**: assigning a value or making a judgment about a concept or product, or the process by which the concept or product was developed.

Let us use a musical example to obtain a clearer understanding of these three higher-level processes. Imagine that you are presented with the problem of selecting and preparing a new piece of music to play for your jury at the end of the semester. You might

1. *Analyze* the basic musical content of the piece—the technical elements such as the pitch range, rhythms, and articulations employed in the piece; analyze the interrelationships between the basic elements that you discover in order to determine the form and structure of the piece; analyze the skills required to perform the piece; and analyze your current skill level.
2. Next, you would need to *synthesize* what you learned from your analysis of the piece into a complex understanding of the work; synthesize your knowledge of how to practice and of the piece to create a practice plan; and use your prior knowledge of the piece and musicality to create an artistic representation for performance.
3. *Evaluate* the basic elements and construction of the piece to determine whether it is worth investing the time and effort to perform it and evaluate whether your current knowledge and skills are well matched with the procedural knowledge required to perform the piece successfully. And, afterward, you would have to evaluate your performance product and the process you used to prepare for the performance, with an eye toward preparing and performing better in the future.

If you think carefully about what students would do in order to demonstrate various levels of knowledge, you will realize that there is a conflict, however. Is an analysis something you create, or is it something you do? Is it a product or a process? (This is an example of the process-versus-product debate, which we will revisit later in the book.)

Psychomotor and Affective Domains

The two other domains, the psychomotor and the affective, dealing with the acquisition of skills and of values, respectively, are explained in detail in subsequent chapters. For now, you only need to understand two concepts. First, while the subdomains of the psychomotor domain describe the various skill levels one reaches as one progresses from simple imitation to high-level performance that appears to be natural or innate, the demonstration of skills is primarily a cognitive process, in that the mind controls the body. Second, just as in the other domains, the values represented by the various subdomain levels in the affective domain develop over time from simple awareness and recognition to internalized values that appear to be natural and to be part of one's personality. Just as in the psychomotor domain, values are driven by the cognitive domain—knowledge of the consequences of actions and the empathic knowledge of how one's decisions and actions affect other people's quality of life.

Benefits of This Taxonomy

This three-part taxonomy is itself an instance of conceptual knowledge in that it helps teachers organize their understanding of the cognitive processes their students should engage in and the types of knowledge that enable those cognitive processes. It establishes the clear link between knowledge and cognition—one is not possible without the other. Teachers can then apply their understanding of the taxonomy to generate instructional plans, implement the instruction, analyze their students' progress, critique the strengths and failures of the instruction, and then use that knowledge to improve the quality of the plan.

A firm understanding of the taxonomy provides the common terminology (a kind of factual knowledge) that enables communication with educators in other disciplines to explain the value of musical education. Specifically, it mediates the communication of the importance of procedural and strategic planning (a kind of metacognitive knowledge) in the creative process. Explaining that these processes are essentially cognitive rather than skill-based will go a long way toward helping other educators understand that a musical education is as valid as the knowledge gained by study of any other discipline.

Tables 5.1, 5.2, and 5.3 explain each of the domains in more detail and provide action verbs that correlate with each level.

THE NATIONAL STANDARDS IN THE ARTS AND MUSIC
The History of the 1994 National Standards for Music

In 1983, a report titled "A Nation at Risk: The Imperative for Educational Reform" was published by the National Commission on Excellence in Education, a presidential commission established by President Ronald Reagan. The report, which indicated that America's schools were failing to maintain superiority or even parity with many school systems in other parts of the world, was a watershed in the national educational reform movement. The report cited five areas in particular that needed to be addressed in order

Table 5.1: COGNITIVE DOMAIN

Level	Definition	Sample verbs
Knowledge	Recalls and remembers information.	defines, describes, identifies, knows, labels, lists, matches, names, outlines, recalls, recognizes, reproduces, selects, states, memorizes, tells, repeats
Comprehension	Understands the meaning, translation, interpolation, and interpretation of instructions and problems. States a problem in his or her own words. Establishes relationships between dates, principles, generalizations, or values.	comprehends, converts, defends, distinguishes, estimates, explains, extends, generalizes, gives examples, infers, interprets, paraphrases, predicts, rewrites, summarizes, translates, shows relationship of, characterizes, associates, differentiates, classifies, compares
Application	Uses a concept in a new situation or uses an abstraction unprompted. Applies what was learned in the classroom to novel situations in the workplace. Facilitates transfer of knowledge to new or unique situations.	applies, changes, computes, constructs, demonstrates, discovers, manipulates, modifies, operates, predicts, prepares, produces, relates, solves, uses, systematizes, experiments, practices, exercises, utilizes, organizes
Analysis	Separates material or concepts into component parts so that the organizational structure may be understood. Distinguishes between facts and inferences.	analyzes, breaks down, compares, contrasts, diagrams, deconstructs, differentiates, discriminates, distinguishes, identifies, illustrates, infers, outlines, relates, selects, separates, investigates, discovers, determines, observes, examines
Synthesis	Builds a structure or pattern from diverse elements. Puts parts together to form a whole, with emphasis on creating a new meaning or structure. Demonstrates originality and creativity.	categorizes, combines, compiles, composes, creates, devises, designs, explains, generates, modifies, organizes, plans, rearranges, reconstructs, relates, reorganizes, revises, rewrites, summarizes, tells, writes, synthesizes, imagines, conceives, concludes, invents, theorizes, constructs
Evaluation	Makes judgments about the value of ideas or materials.	appraises, compares, concludes, contrasts, criticizes, critiques, defends, describes, discriminates, evaluates, explains, interprets, justifies, relates, summarizes, supports, calculates, estimates, consults, judges, measures, decides, discusses, values, accepts/rejects

Source: Bloom's Taxonomy (n.d.).

Table 5.2: PSYCHOMOTOR DOMAIN

Level	Definition	Sample verbs
Imitation	Includes repeating an act that has been demonstrated or explained, and it includes trial and error until an appropriate response is achieved.	begin, assemble, attempt, carry out, copy, calibrate, construct, dissect, duplicate, follow, mimic, move, practice, proceed, repeat, reproduce, respond, organize, sketch, start
Manipulation	Includes repeating an act that has been demonstrated or explained, and it includes trial and error until an appropriate response is achieved.	(similar to imitation): acquire, assemble, complete, conduct, do, execute, improve, maintain, make, manipulate, operate, pace, perform, produce, progress, use
Precision	Response is complex and performed without hesitation.	achieve, accomplish, advance, exceed, excel, master, reach, refine, succeed, surpass, transcend
Articulation	Skills are so well developed that the individual can modify movement patterns or to fit special requirements or to meet a problem situation.	adapt, alter, change, excel, rearrange, reorganize, revise, surpass
Naturalization	Response is automatic. One acts "without thinking."	arrange, combine, compose, construct, create, design, refine, originate, transcend

Source: Bloom's Taxonomy (n.d.).

Table 5.3: AFFECTIVE DOMAIN

Level	Definition	Sample verbs
Receiving phenomena	Awareness, willingness to hear, selective attention.	asks, chooses, describes, follows, gives, holds, identifies, locates, names, points to, selects, erects, replies, uses
Responding to phenomena	Active participation on the part of the learners. Attention to and reaction to a particular phenomenon. Learning outcomes may emphasize compliance in responding, willingness to respond, or satisfaction in responding (motivation).	answers, assists, aids, complies, conforms, discusses, greets, helps, labels, performs, practices, presents, reads, recites, reports, selects, tells, writes
Valuing	The worth or value a person attaches to a particular object, phenomenon, or behavior. This ranges from simple acceptance to the more complex state of commitment.	completes, demonstrates, differentiates, explains, follows, forms, initiates, invites, joins, justifies, proposes, reads, reports, selects, shares, studies, works
Organization	Arranging of values into priorities by contrasting different values, resolving conflicts between them, and creating a unique value system. The emphasis is on comparing, relating, and synthesizing values.	adheres, alters, arranges, combines, compares, completes, defends, explains, formulates, generalizes, identifies, integrates, modifies, orders, organizes, prepares, relates, synthesizes
Internalizing values	Having a value system that controls behavior. The behavior is pervasive, consistent, predictable, and most important, characteristic of the learner.	acts, discriminates, displays, influences, listens, modifies, performs, practices, proposes, qualifies, questions, revises, serves, solves, verifies

Source: Bloom's Taxonomy (n.d.).

to maintain educational excellence: content, standards and expectations, time, teaching, and leadership and financial support. Regarding standards and expectations, the commission recommended that "schools, colleges, and universities adopt more rigorous and measurable standards, and higher expectations, for academic performance and student conduct" (National Commission on Excellence in Education, 1983).

Subsequently, the National Council on Education Standards and Testing called for a set of national standards in the core subjects: math, English, science, history, and geography. Leading arts and music education organizations, fearful that the study of the arts would eventually be defunded or excluded from schools, began a tremendous push to prevent that catastrophe.

In the policy arena, the Music Educator's National Conference (MENC, now known as the National Association for Music Education, NAfME) led a consortium of arts education organizations to obtain federal funding to develop national standards for education in the four unique arts disciplines—music, visual arts, theater, and dance—for grades K–12. According to MENC, "These voluntary standards describe the knowledge, skills, and understanding that all students should acquire in the arts, providing a basis for developing curricula" (Consortium of National Arts Education Associations, 1994). The arts education standards state that students should be able to (1) communicate at a basic level in the four arts disciplines, (2) communicate proficiently in at least one art form, (3) have an informed acquaintance with exemplary works of art from a variety of cultures and historical periods, and (4) relate various types of arts knowledge and skills within and across the arts disciplines.

The conference's efforts in the political arena were no less significant. After an intense lobbying campaign, the arts were designated a core subject under federal law in the Goals 2000: Educate America Act, along with English, mathematics, history, civics and government, geography, science, and foreign language. These two accomplishments—developing the national standards and validating arts study as a core curricular subject—have had lasting positive benefits for students.

As published in 1994 by MENC, the National Standards for Music Education contained the following nine content standards.

1. Singing, alone and with others, a varied repertoire of music
2. Performing on instruments, alone and with others, a varied repertoire of music
3. Improvising melodies, variations, and accompaniments

4. Composing and arranging music within specified guidelines
5. Reading and notating music
6. Listening to, analyzing, and describing music
7. Evaluating music and music performances
8. Understanding relationships between music, the other arts, and disciplines outside the arts
9. Understanding music in relation to history and culture

Each content standard contained between three and six achievement standards, which described what students must do to meet the content standards, grouped into grades K–4, 5–8, and 9–12. It might be useful to examine excerpts to gain a stronger understanding of their structure. Table 5.4 provides an overview of Content Standard 6, including one associated achievement standard with its assessment strategies and descriptions of student response, for each grade-level grouping as outlined in *Performance Standards for Music* (MENC, 1996).

Later, MENC developed supplemental standards and additional documentation explaining and expanding upon the national music standards. Examples of these many useful publications include *Opportunity-to-Learn Standards for Music Instruction*, which set benchmarks for music learning environments including standards for curriculum and scheduling, staffing, materials and equipment, and facilities, *Performance Standards for Music*, which is designed to help teachers assess student learning in music, and many volumes in the Strategies for Teaching series.

New National Standards for Music Education (2014)

In 2006, the National Executive Board of MENC empowered the Task Force on National Standards to review the relevance of the 1994 standards and to determine whether they should be revised to reflect the current state of music education in the United States. After careful consideration, the task force (Hoffer et al., n.d.) recommended that

1. The 1994 Achievement Standards be replaced by a set of recommended Achievement Standards developed by MENC for each grade level in the general music program through grade 8 and for each elective course offering in the secondary school.
2. The content standards be reviewed subsequent to the revision of the Achievement Standards (though it noted the validity of the 1994 Content Standards).

Table 5.4: CONTENT STANDARD 6

Grade Levels	Achievement Standard 6a	Assessment strategy	Description of response
K–4	Students identify simple music forms when presented aurally.	Three short recorded examples are played for the student, who is asked to identify the form of each example. Forms may include ABA, AABA, ABACA, other forms involving not more than three sections (not counting repetitions), or call and response. Each example is heard three times. Both instrumental and vocal examples are included.	*Basic Level*: By the end of the third hearing, the student can identify the form of one of the three examples. *Proficient Level*: By the end of the third hearing, the student can identify the form of two of the three examples. *Advanced Level*: By the end of the third hearing, the student can identify the form of all three examples.
5–8	Students describe specific music events in a given aural example, using appropriate terminology.	The student is asked to describe or explain what is happening musically in a given listening example. For example, what instruments are playing the melody? What instruments are playing the accompaniment? How is variety achieved? In what ways is the melody altered when it reappears? What is happening harmonically at this point? There are approximately two hearings for every three questions.	*Basic Level*: 1. The student can answer 50 percent of the questions, though the answers may be incomplete or inaccurate in certain details. 2. The student's responses use the technical vocabulary of music in some instances but not in others. *Proficient Level*: 1. The student can answer 75 percent of the questions accurately. 2. The student's responses use the technical vocabulary of music in almost all instances. *Advanced Level*: 1. The student can answer 90 percent of the questions accurately. 2. The student's responses reflect a high level of familiarity with the technical vocabulary of music.

| 9–12 | Students analyze aural examples of a varied repertoire of music, representing diverse genres and cultures, by describing the uses of elements of music and expressive devices. | The student is asked to analyze three representative works in various styles, at least one of which is from a non-Western culture. All are presented aurally. Each work is approximately three to five minutes in length. For each work, the student is asked to (1) identify the medium (e.g., name the instruments or ensemble; identify the voices); (2) describe the form, structure, or basis of organization of the music (e.g., theme and variation, call and response, strophic); (3) describe the melodic characteristics of the work (e.g., emphasis on extended ranges, much chromaticism, frequent use of embellishments, based on a non-Western scale); (4) describe the rhythmic characteristics of the work (e.g., use of a rhythmic motive, use of 3 against 2 simultaneously or sequentially, steady beat despite frequent meter changes); (5) describe the harmonic or textual characteristics of the work (e.g., gradual but extreme dynamic changes, wandering melodic line to symbolize confusion, deceptive cadence to symbolize surprise). Each work is played four times, with two minutes between hearings. | *Basic Level:* The student is able to make one relevant and accurate observation concerning three of the six characteristics listed (i.e., medium, form, melody, rhythm, harmony or texture, and expressive devices) for one of the works.

Proficient Level: The student is able to make one relevant and accurate observation concerning four of the six characteristics for two of the works.

Advanced Level: 1. The student is able to make one relevant and accurate observation concerning five of the six characteristics of all three works. 2. The student is able to describe in detail three significant or unusual events occurring in the examples (e.g., an added sixth, a modulation to a remote key, brief use of Dorian mode or an Indian raga). |

Source: National Standards for Music Education (1994).

3. The Opportunity-To-Learn Standards for Music Instruction be reviewed and updated

The remaining recommendations are available from the NAfME website.

In order to develop new national standards for music education, NAfME representatives joined with leaders from other national arts organizations to form the National Coalition for Core Arts Standards (NCCAS). Working together, the members of NCCAS developed the National Core Arts Standards: A Conceptual Framework for Arts Learning (http://www.nationalartsstandards.org/content/conceptual-framework). The purposes of the new arts standards were to unify the conceptual underpinnings for all arts instruction in the United States and to specify intended learning outcomes across all arts disciplines based on common standards. Unlike the old national standards, which specified artistic *products*, the new standards were designed to encourage the use of common artistic *processes*: creating, performing/presenting/producing, responding, and connecting. Within each of these four processes, anchor standards indicated the kinds of work students would do.

Creating
1. Generate and conceptualize artistic ideas and work
2. Organize and develop artistic ideas and work
3. Refine and complete artistic work

Performing/Presenting/Producing
4. Select, analyze, and interpret artistic work for presentation
5. Develop and refine artistic techniques and work for presentation
6. Convey meaning through the presentation of artistic work

Responding
7. Perceive and analyze artistic work
8. Interpret intent and meaning in artistic work
9. Apply criteria to evaluate artistic work

Connecting
10. Synthesize and relate knowledge and personal experiences to make art
11. Relate artistic ideas and works with societal, cultural, and historical context to deepen understanding

Within each of the arts disciplines included in the new standards (dance, media arts, music, theater, and visual arts), discipline-specific enduring understandings and essential questions were developed for each anchor standard, along with grade-level-specific learning outcomes, which are specified according to various artistic components.

The music standards are divided into five strands, each with grade-level-specific process outcomes (for more details see table 5.5):

1. Music (general), Pre-K to 8
2. Music: Harmonizing Instruments: Novice, Intermediate, HS Proficient, HS Accomplished, HS Advanced
3. Music: Composition and Theory, HS Proficient, HS Accomplished, HS Advanced
4. Music: Traditional and Emerging Ensembles, Harmonizing Instruments: Novice, Intermediate, HS Proficient, HS Accomplished, HS Advanced
5. Music: Technology, HS Proficient, HS Accomplished, HS Advanced

The National Standards as a Vision for Curriculum

By themselves, the new national standards for music education are highly unified across the various strands. The new National Core Arts Standards demonstrate the commonality of artistic processes across the various artistic domains. Across each of the five music discipline areas—music (general), harmonizing instruments, composition and theory, traditional and emerging ensembles, and technology—the process strands, anchor standards, enduring understandings, and essential questions are identical. Only as the artistic components are specified are the outcomes differentiated. Take a look at table 5.5. Under the Creating Strand, the four artistic components—imagine, plan and make, evaluate and refine, and present—are identical across all of the disciplines and grade levels. Only the grade-level performance standards (not listed in the table) differ from one discipline to another. The complete listing of all of the performance standards is extensive, but the organization and unity lend credence to the total package of standards.

You are encouraged to develop a more comprehensive understanding of the standards by reviewing the various discipline-specific documents at http://www.nationalartsstandards.org. In addition, the NAfME is developing Model Cornerstone Assessments for grade levels 2, 5, and 8 and for middle school and high school ensembles. All of the information on the new national music education standards can be viewed at http://www.nafme.org/my-classroom/standards/. Educators can create a custom standards handbook that would be specific to their instructional context via http://www.nationalartsstandards.org/customize-handbook.

Table 5.5: MUSIC STANDARDS

Artistic Components	Strand
Imagine	**CREATING STRAND** **Anchor Standard 1**: Generate and conceptualize artistic ideas and work. **Enduring Understanding:** The creative ideas, concepts, and feelings that influence musicians' work emerge from a variety of sources. **Essentials Question(s):** How do musicians generate creative ideas?
Plan and Make	**Anchor Standard 2:** Organize and develop artistic ideas and work. **Enduring Understanding:** Musicians' creative choices are influenced by their expertise, context, and expressive intent. **Essential Question(s):** How do musicians make creative decisions?
Evaluate and Refine	**Anchor Standard 3:** Refine and complete artistic work. **Enduring Understanding:** Musicians evaluate and refine their work through openness to new ideas, persistence, and the application of appropriate criteria. **Essential Question(s):** How do musicians improve the quality of their work?
Present	**Anchor Standard 3:** Refine and complete artistic work. **Enduring Understanding:** Musicians' presentation of creative work is the culmination of a process of creation and communication. **Essential Question(s):** When is creative work ready to share?
Select	**PERFORMING STRAND** **Anchor Standard 4:** Select, analyze, and interpret artistic work for presentation. **Enduring Understanding:** Performers' interest in and knowledge of musical works, understanding their own technical skill, and the context for a performance influence the selection of repertoire. **Essential Question(s):** How do performers select repertoire?
Analyze	**Anchor Standard 4:** Select, analyze, and interpret artistic work for presentation. **Enduring Understanding:** Analyzing creators' context and how they manipulate elements of music provides insight into their intent and informs performance. **Essential Question(s):** How does understanding the structure and context of musical works inform performance?
Interpret	**Anchor Standard 4:** Select, analyze, and interpret artistic work for presentation. **Enduring Understanding:** Performers make interpretive decisions based on their understanding of context and expressive intent. **Essential Question(s):** How do performers interpret musical works?

Artistic Components	Strand
Rehearse, Evaluate, and Refine	**Anchor Standard 5:** Develop and refine artistic techniques and work for presentation. **Enduring Understanding:** To express their musical ideas, musicians analyze, evaluate, and refine their performance over time through openness to new ideas, persistence, and the application of appropriate criteria. **Essential Question(s):** How do musicians improve the quality of their performance?
Present	**Anchor Standard 6:** Convey meaning through the presentation of artistic work. **Enduring Understanding:** Musicians judge performance based on criteria that vary across time, place, and cultures. **Essential Question(s):** When is a performance judged ready to present? How do context and the manner in which musical work is presented influence audience response?
	RESPONDING STRAND
Select	**Anchor Standard 7:** Perceive and analyze artistic work. **Enduring Understanding:** Individuals' selection of musical works is influenced by their interests, experiences, understandings, and purposes. **Essential Question(s):** How do individuals choose music to experience?
Analyze	**Anchor Standard 7:** Perceive and analyze artistic work. **Enduring Understanding:** Response to music is informed by analyzing context (social cultural, and historical) and how creators and performers manipulate the elements of music. **Essential Question(s):** How does understanding the structure and context of the music influence a response?
Interpret	**Anchor Standard 8:** Interpret intent and meaning in artistic work. **Enduring Understanding:** Through their use of elements and structures of music, creators and performers provide clues to their expressive intent. **Essential Question(s):** How do we discern the musical creators' and performers' expressive intent?
Evaluate	**Anchor Standard 9:** Apply criteria to evaluate artistic work. **Enduring Understanding:** The personal evaluation of musical work(s) and performance(s) is informed by analysis, interpretation, and established criteria. **Essential Question(s):** How do we judge the quality of musical work(s) and performance(s)?

(Continued)

Table 5.5: CONTINUED

Artistic Components	Strand
	CONNECTING STRAND
	Anchor Standard 10: Synthesize and relate knowledge and personal experiences to make art.
	Enduring Understanding: Musicians connect their personal interests, experiences, ideas, and knowledge to creating, performing, and responding.
	Essential Question(s): How do musicians make meaningful connections to creating, performing, and responding?
	Anchor Standard 11: Relate artistic ideas and works with societal, cultural, and historical context to deepen understanding.
	Enduring Understanding: Understanding connections to varied contexts and daily life enhances musicians' creating, performing, and responding.
	Essential Question(s): How do the other arts, other disciplines, contexts, and daily life inform creating, performing, and responding to music?

As you review the documentation of the National Standards for Music Education, pay close attention to the *processes* students use to meet the performance standards and create musical *products*. Your vision of what a musical curriculum could be is what you imagine your future students doing and how you will go about supporting them in their musical efforts. Do not let your past limit your students' future.

In the Chapter 4 you garnered some insights into the knowledge about music held by expert musicians, about how music functions, and about how that knowledge is obtained. In this chapter, you have learned about the kinds of cognitive processes that define and justify any subject matter as worthy of being studied and looked at the National Standards for Music as a way of organizing the processes and *outcomes* of musical instruction. In subsequent chapters you will read about how students learn, how musical understanding develops over time and, eventually, how to design and implement instruction.

PROJECT

1. Explain the following terms:
   - Cognitive domain
   - Psychomotor domain
   - Affective domain
2. How might a comprehensive understanding of the taxonomies for cognitive, psychomotor, and affective domains be useful to teachers?
3. Based on your reading of the history of the National Standards, what can you infer about the history of music education in the United States? About the current state of music education in the United States?
4. Examine the 2014 National Standards for Music Education at the NAfME website: http://nafme.org/my-classroom/standards. Create a custom standards handbook for a specific instructional content area of your choosing. Compare the curricular vision represented by your custom handbook to your K–12 music experience.
5. Examine the handbooks for Harmonizing Instruments, Composition and Theory, and Music Technology. How does the vision of music education curriculum of each fit with your philosophy? Do these topics belong in a public music education program? Are you prepared to teach in any of these areas? If not, what do you need to do to adequately prepare for your future students?
6. Go online and locate the music standards for your state. First, examine them sufficiently to determine how they are structured and organized. In what ways do they resemble and differ from the 1994 and 2014 national standards? More important, are your state music standards more similar to the product-orientaed national standards from 1994 or the process-oriented national standards from 2014? Since any standards reflect a certain view or philosophy of music education, how do the priorities of your state standards compare to the national standards? How might those various outcomes and priorities have an impact on music instruction in your state?

CHAPTER 6

How Students Learn

In order to be an effective teacher, one has to understand the nature of knowledge and how students learn. This chapter explores four main points that will be essential in your development.

1. Learning has both a neurological and a psychological expression.
2. Knowledge is only valuable to students if it is useful to them.
3. Incorrect prior knowledge can interfere with new learning.
4. Using knowledge is a habit that can be learned.

A lot is packed into these four statements, so let's take some time to dissect them.

NEUROLOGICAL BASIS FOR LEARNING

At birth, the human brain is endowed with certain large structures, each with functions essential for the survival of the infant. The neurons that make up the brain are largely, but not entirely, disorganized and disconnected from one another. During the first months of life, infants are generally unable to distinguish or make sense of the stimuli they receive from their environment. In fact, various stimuli activate large sections of the brain; sounds stimulate what will eventually become the visual cortex, and light may activate areas that eventually process sound.

Over time, infants gradually become able to distinguish between light, sounds, and other sensations and stimuli. Their brains, and quite literally their minds, are developed and shaped in response to the stimuli in their environment. Through a process called *synaptogenesis*, individual neurons grow connections with one another as the brain processes each stimulus. A repeated stimulus reinforces and adds to existing connections. As more neurons become connected, and as networks of connected neurons connect to one another, the experiences become richer and the infant's comprehension of the stimulus becomes more sophisticated. Each unique neural network represents a unique memory, which is experienced as a *representation* of the prior experience.

Think for a moment about a route you take on a regular basis. Imagine the starting point, important turns and reference points along the way, and the ending point. Imagine a map of the route showing these same details. The map is a symbolic representation of the territory. Your mental image of the territory is a mental representation of the territory. Your mental image of the route is a separate mental representation of the route. Your mental image of the map is a mental representation. Each of these individual representations is stored in your brain as a unique collection of connected neurons. Thus, there is a one-to-one correlation between the neural networks of your brain and the mental representations stored in your mind.

The map is a symbolic representation of the territory. In the end you have two mental representations in your mind: one of the actual territory and one of the map—which is in turn a representation of the territory. But most important, you have the useful knowledge of the correlations between the map, the actual territory, and your mental representation of each, which allows you to do something important and meaningful: to get from one place to another without getting lost.

It is necessary to consider the value of the map and, in turn, your representation of it. The map (representation) cannot be 100 percent accurate. In order to achieve perfect accuracy, it would have to be a literal reproduction of the territory. At that level of detail, it would require too many mental resources and would lose its usefulness as a stand-in for the territory. A symbolic representation, the map in this case, is optimally meaningful at the level of detail at which it is most efficient for obtaining some end—to enable one to think about and solve a problem. The information contained in a representation becomes meaningful when it is used to "image, problem solve, anticipate, teach, remember, learn, practice [or] create" (Lehmann, Sloboda, and Woody, 2007, p. 19). A single representation can itself have varied levels of detail and can be connected to other representations to form a mental map of the intellectual territory. To extend our map analogy, this is how you can improvise a novel route to a destination when your primary route is somehow blocked.

Recognition occurs when you note a stimulus in your environment as something to which you can attach a label, or an instance of something.

Cognition (thinking) occurs when you recognize something in the environment as something meaningful. How is it that a person or an object can have meaning to a person? It has to do with the number of associations between the representation of that person or object and other representations. The more representations one has accumulated, the more complex understandings can develop. According to Grühn (2005), "This means that one gains multiple opportunities to recognize something as something, one develops a broad range of interpretations of meaning" (p. 102). These vast, interconnected neural networks and associated representations of knowledge, skill, and dispositions define what we know, what we are able to do, and who we are.

MEANINGFUL, USEFUL KNOWLEDGE

Imagine that you wrote down everything you know by putting each bit of information or knowledge on its own index card. You could keep your index cards (your knowledge) in one big pile, but the pile might not be very helpful if you needed to find some particular fact or procedure. You'd probably want to keep the cards organized in some way. Consider for a moment how many different ways you could organize the cards. You might discover connections between previously unrelated cards. How, then, would you organize them? It might be possible to make copies of the cards that belong in multiple places, but then how would you change all of those cards if you realized that one contained a mistake? How would you know where to file new cards?

Imagine that you could arrange the cards in some kind of multidimensional patterns. Doing so would allow you to find specific bits of information, find related information, and add new information in the right spot so that you could find it later. There would be other huge advantages of organizing the cards this way: you could see patterns in the way the information was organized. Seeing patterns would help in identifying collections of information that might be useful in solving particular problems.

Fortunately, this is analogous to the way your brain works. Your life experiences are encoded in the physical structure of your brain. When you learn something new, physical connections among groups of neurons grow. When you recall any bit of information—an experience, fact, emotion, smell, or sound—or execute a previously learned skill, those same collections of neurons fire again. Every time these patterns are used, they are reinforced, and the connections become stronger.

PRIOR KNOWLEDGE AND NEW LEARNING

The human brain, and by extension the mind, are uniquely evolved to create patterns out of the chaos of your life experiences. Every new experience is compared to all of your previous ones to see if there's a match. If the patterns match exactly, the previous patterns are reinforced again. Any slight variations in the new experience from the previous are also encoded. This process is known as assimilation; the new information is incorporated, or assimilated, into the preexisting knowledge structures.

A few scenarios have to be considered.

1. What happens if there are no existing patterns of information to match the current experience? The answer in this case is fairly straightforward: new knowledge structures (new connections between neurons) are constructed. There is no guarantee, however, about the accuracy or usefulness of this new knowledge.
2. Consider that at some baseball game in the recent past, a group of fans decided to invert their hats during the bottom of the ninth inning and it just so happened that the team rallied for a win. In the fans' minds, there was a connection between their inverted caps and the rally. Thus, the idea of the rally cap was born. The mind seeks to make patterns out of the randomness of life, and sometimes it makes meaningful connections between two randomly occurring, unrelated events.
3. What happens if the new information conflicts with the prior knowledge structures? There are several possible responses:
   a. The new information is ignored or dismissed as irrelevant or wrong. Believe it or not, this happens fairly often. Many people have deeply ingrained opinions or biases that are highly resistant to change. This is especially true if these opinions have been the basis for many subsequent opinions or decisions or underpin one's identity.
   b. The new information is merged with the existing knowledge structures in a way that expands the conceptualization of the topic. In this way, the knowledge structure becomes more sophisticated and more useful.
   c. The old structures are discarded and replaced by the new ones. This is only likely to occur if the old structures are weakly encoded.
4. What happens if existing knowledge structures cause the mind to misinterpret the new experience? What if these existing patterns contain inaccurate representations of real-world knowledge? This is problematic. If new knowledge is misinterpreted, it can get misfiled. However accurate the new information, it can be useless if it is based on a false premise. It can also contribute to future misinterpretations of subsequent new

information. Over time, complex yet inaccurate knowledge structures can develop, become resistant to change, and create challenges to new learning.

A HABIT THAT CAN BE LEARNED

Let's examine one common misperception about knowledge and under-standing. All too often, students (and teachers) operate under the assumption that the purpose of schooling is the transmission of information from a more knowledgeable agent (teacher) to a less knowledgeable target (student). (Many who have never studied human development in an unbiased manner seem to harbor this misconception.) Consider what a learning environment based on this assumption would look like. It would involve the teacher's providing information to the students, either via lecture or by directing access to reading materials, and subsequently testing the students' ability to recall the discrete bits of information. (You already know that recall is the lowest form of knowledge in Bloom's Taxonomy of Cognitive Objectives, and this type of assessment also fails to address the other two domains: psychomotor and affective.)

But what if the teacher's task was to help the students prepare themselves to solve previously unencountered problems? One might still observe the transfer of information, but in addition the students would be actively engaging with a complex problem that required the application of the new information in order to create a solution. What do the students need in order to solve novel problems? The information itself is necessary, but not sufficient. The information has been organized into systems or frame-works that facilitate recall and also the ability to accommodate and then apply new information. The systematic knowledge enables the students to enact their understandings in order to solve problems. *Understandings* are systems of information that are prepared for action, and *enactment* is the process through which understandings are turned into action.

How do students enact their understandings, or turn their knowledge into action? Primarily, they are conscious of their own efforts and approach them in a deliberate fashion. In the first phase of their approach to a new problem, they analyze the problem itself by breaking it down into smaller, more manageable components, determine what fundamental concepts are involved in the problem, and imagine what conditions might be like when the problem is solved. As a result, they then consider what they already know that might be applicable to the problem, and what they might need to learn to attack the problem successfully. In the second phase, they use strategies that are appropriate to the specific problem to solve the various components of the problem, and then merge the potential solutions in an effort to solve the problem. Finally, they evaluate the solution and their efforts. They may discover that their solution is acceptable or inadequate, or they may discover that the process was flawed even if they created an acceptable solution. The end goal of the process is for the students to become more effective in solving similar problems in the future. This process of designing goals, using strategies to solve problems, and self-monitoring during the process is known as *metacognition*, or being aware of and guiding one's own thinking.

In summary:

1. Synaptogenesis is the neurological basis of learning. A representation is the psychological basis of learning.
2. Knowledge is only valuable if it enables action.
3. Students sometimes have inaccurate understandings that must be addressed in order for them to efficiently acquire new understandings; and
4. The enactment of knowledge (understanding) can be learned and habituated (metacognition).

EXPERTISE

As a way of understanding advanced abilities in music, we will first examine the characteristics of expertise (extraordinary ability) that apply across disciplines. By definition, only a relatively small percentage of people who undertake any particular endeavor become experts in that activity or achieve world-class status. There is nothing wrong with pursuing an activity simply for the pleasure of participating. However, understanding the characteristics of expertise and how it develops has implications for music performance and instruction. What are the characteristics of expertise, and exactly how do they allow for expert performance? What are the implications for teaching?

The characteristics of expertise and expert performance are now well-known, but researchers organize that information in a variety of ways. We're going to consider three global characteristics of expertise.

1. Experts are able to recall information because their knowledge is stored in meaningful "chunks." Their recall is cued by circumstances and context.
2. Experts have exceptional content knowledge in their domain. These understandings reflect a highly organized, rich network of interconnected patterns of useful or usable knowledge that is primed for enactment during problem solving.

3. Experts have well-defined routines for solving common problems; experts are able to consciously adapt to and innovate in new contexts and circumstances and when faced with novel problems.

There are two common misconceptions about expertise. The first is that experts are able to achieve at a high level because they have exceptional intelligence. This is not true. Barring a mental deficiency, almost anyone can achieve at a very high level. In fact, many who suffer from autism or savant syndrome attain world-class performance levels, even in music. (For more information and a list of exemplars, see http://en.wikipedia.org/wiki/savant_syndrome.) The second fallacy is that experts may have superior memories. It is true that they may develop tremendous memory skills in their domain, but there is no evidence that their mechanisms for memory are innately above average.

Recall

It is commonly believed that most people can normally hold seven items, plus or minus two items, in their short-term memory at any time, and research has supported this idea. (It is not a coincidence that phone numbers without the area code are seven digits long.) Researchers wanted to test whether short-term memory abilities could be expanded through practice (Ericsson & Chase, 1982). For this experiment, they recruited an undergraduate college student and confirmed that the student had essentially average intelligence and memory skills.

For one hour per day, three days per week, the subject was read a sequence of random numbers at a rate of one per second. If the student recalled the sequence correctly, the next sequence was lengthened by one digit; if the sequence was not recalled correctly, the next sequence was shortened by one digit. After twenty months of steady practice, or approximately 230 hours, the subject was able to reliably recall sequences of eighty digits! What is really interesting about this result is the strategy the subject used to increase his ability to recall. His brain didn't suddenly develop new memorization abilities; he trained himself to use techniques—mnemonic devices—to remember long number sequences.

When they first started the training process, the subject tried to remember the string of numbers by repeating them to himself, much as one might recite a telephone number repeatedly until able to write it down. After five sessions the subject was able to recall sequences of twelve digits, but it appeared that the strategy of repeating numbers had reached a practical limit. The subject, as it turns out, was a long-distance runner. In subsequent sessions he encoded various three- and four-digit strings as typical running times. For example, he encoded 3492 as "3 minutes and 49.2 seconds, near world-record mile time." Thus he was able to rapidly increase his recall of digit strings. To further expand this ability, the subject grouped the running times together, each group containing three or four running times. He "maxed out" at about seven supergroups, each containing three subgroups of three or four running times, as one might expect.

Three interesting points are applicable to general learning and to music performance. First, the subject was able to recall more by creating *chunks* of information. In essence, the chunks of four numbers became only one item that he had to recall instead of four. On top of that, he created another system to help him recall the groups. His limit of seven items was not expanded significantly, but he created a network or schema in which vast quantities of information could be stored and reliably recalled.

Second, the discrete numbers were grouped together in a manner that was personally meaningful to the subject. His existing knowledge about running allowed him to improvise a new memory system that worked for him. In fact, later in the experiment, the subject was given number sequences that did not lend themselves easily to being encoded as running times. Consequently, the subject developed an alternative schema to encode the information; for example 893 was encoded as "89 point 3, a very old man."

Third, the subject's prior knowledge enabled him to assimilate more new information. This particular encoding system would not work for someone without knowledge of running. The general rule is that we learn—we encode new information—on a basis of preexisting representations and neural networks.

Knowledge

Some of the earliest studies of expertise and expert thinking involved an examination of the thinking processes of chess players. De Groot (1965) Studied world-class chess players and the way their cognitive activities compared with those of lower-level players. In one experiment, de Groot placed the chess pieces in arrangements that might be observed in typical games. Subsequently, he removed the pieces and asked the subjects to re-create the arrangement. As one might expect, the more-expert players were able to do so with significantly more accuracy than were the less-experienced players. De Groot was concerned that perhaps the more expert players had better general memory skills that mediated their chess-playing skills. So, he arranged pieces randomly on the chessboard and asked both groups to re-create the arrangement. In this experiment, the less-expert players matched the abilities of the experts.

What de Groot determined was that, just as the subject who memorized strings of random numbers had done so by grouping them, the expert chess players had encoded the positions of the pieces in meaningful chunks. Instead of trying to recall fifteen or more unique positions, the experts only had to recall three or four meaningful groups or patterns of pieces. DeGroot wanted to know what made the groupings meaningful to the experts but not meaningful to the less-expert players.

In order to find out, de Groot again placed the pieces in typical game positions and then asked the subjects, both experts and less-experienced players, to think aloud about what their next moves would be. Now, there are several common misconceptions about how chess experts approach their decision making. The first is that they consider all of the possible moves available to them. The second is that they then consider all of the possible responses to each of those moves and then essentially play out all of these game scenarios to their logical conclusion. Only then do they decide which move gives them the best advantage. Consider the cognitive load of such an exercise would: If the player only considered ten possible moves with ten possible responses to each move, after only one turn there would be one hundred different possible arrangements of the pieces. Given what we know about short-term memory, the player can reasonably only be expected to recall about seven arrangements, so this strategy is unworkable.

De Groot determined that none of the players exhausted all of the possible moves, and yet the chess masters consistently picked better moves. De Groot determined that, owing to their many hours of experience and background knowledge, the chess masters organized the pieces into strategically meaningful groupings. Thus, their knowledge was not organized around memorizing positions on a grid or around the many possible moves of individual pieces. The experts' knowledge was organized around the fundamental "big ideas" of chess: providing the maximum number of ways to beat your foe while simultaneously limiting his or her offensive options.

Subsequent studies in a variety of fields such as electronics design, computer programming, and radiology have confirmed the primary findings of Ericsson and de Groot: First, information is stored in patterns. Across a variety of domains, competent individuals use meaningful patterns to store vast quantities of information. Data stored in this fashion are more readily accessible for use in problem solving.

Second, because knowledge is organized around fundamental big ideas that may be unique to the domain, the knowledge organization strategies of experts are more effective than those of less-capable individuals. Thus, experts can encode new information more quickly and accurately than can non-experts and can recall useful information because it is organized around the core concepts of the field.

These two ideas might lead one to believe that experts are able to solve problems more quickly than are non-experts. In one sense, that is true: When experts encounter problems similar to ones they have previously encountered and solved, they are able to recognize the relations between the problem and the core ideas of the field, while non-experts only look at the surface features. For example, when faced with certain types of problems, college physics students will categorize the problems according to the most apparent features of the problem, such as the use of an inclined plane or pulleys. The physics experts are more likely to categorize the problems by the core ideas that lead to solutions, such as Newton's Second Law of Motion.

Third, the organization of knowledge around the big ideas of the domain, and encoding information in rich, interconnected networks of chunks and patterns, allow experts to recognize the key issues in problems (those directly related to the big ideas) and more fluently retrieve information that might be applicable.

It's counterintuitive, but often experts take longer to decide on a problem-solving strategy than do non-experts. When faced with novel problems, non-experts often decide on a solution very quickly, whereas experts will employ various search-and-recall strategies prior to testing a solution. For example, when asked to write a short essay in response to questions, experts will take time to search their experiences for useful, pertinent information and then organize their entire response, whereas non-experts will seize on their first inkling of a response and immediately begin writing, organizing their thoughts as they write.

The process of improvising a solution to a problem for which one might be unprepared results in an extremely high cognitive load, not unlike trying to solve a complex calculation with an older, overloaded computer. Because of their extensive experience and knowledge base, experts are able to dispense with many problems in a routine manner that might stump one with less experience and knowledge. This allows them to maintain focus on larger issues that might escape others.

Adaptive Expertise and Metacognition

Expertise manifests itself in different ways in different contexts. Some types require the ability to reliably execute a task or series of tasks the exact same way each time. This type of expertise is called *routine*, not because it is common but because it requires the accurate execution of routines. Employees involved in construction or manufacturing, for example, are valued more highly if they can build their product exactly the same each time; an auto worker who "creatively" welded parts together would not be considered very expert.

Expertise is also manifested in ways that require adaptability to various contextual circumstances. In reality, most efforts require a bit of compromise between the efficient use of routines and changing routines to become more effective. Auto manufacturing serves as an example of adaptive change that led to increased efficiency. Henry Ford, a maniacal tinkerer, was the first to use an assembly line to build autos. Prior to his innovation, each worker assembled cars by himself. He had to know how to assemble an entire car on his own.

Teachers, like many other professionals, have to find an appropriate balance between the use of routines and innovation. Routines can allow one to be more efficient at a given task, but excessive use of routines can become predictable and boring. Innovation and adaptability allow one to increase one's effectiveness. On the other hand, attempts to adapt too quickly can result in feeling overwhelmed. Adaptive experts manage to find a balance between these two ideals along the optimal adaptability corridor (see figure 6.1). You will read about the relation between classroom routines and effective classroom management, and how instructional routines relate to instructional effectiveness.

Just as accommodating new information can sometimes be challenging, so can changing one's habitual approach to solving problems or completing tasks such as learning a new piece of music or practicing musical

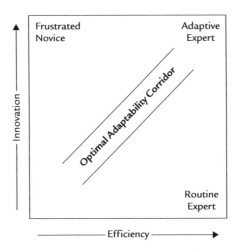

Figure 6.1: Adaptive expertise, adapted from Bransford, Derry, Berliner, and Hammerness (2005, p. 49)

fundamentals. This can be especially true if your old routines have afforded you a certain level of success or you are somehow emotionally attached to your processes. Making purposeful adjustments to one's approach to any task first requires an awareness of one's current knowledge and abilities, both their strengths and their limitations. Before selecting a strategy for solving the problem, you may need to do some research or hone your skills. Only then will you be prepared to solve the problem efficiently. Subsequently, you should evaluate the outcomes of your effort and make the appropriate adjustments for the future. This whole process requires metacognition, or awareness of your current knowledge, problem-solving strategies, and thought processes.

Implications for Teaching

Expertise does not develop overnight. As stated in Chapter 3, it is developed by enacting deliberate practice in a single discipline for about ten thousand hours. Expertise also develops in stages. In any domain, learners gradually move from novice to competent performer to expert. Novices know essentially nothing about the field. Competent performers are able to consistently apply certain well-established routines to solve common problems. Experts are able to apply their extensive knowledge and experience to problems and create innovative solutions, and do so in a way that appears to be nearly effortless.

What do learners need in order to move through this process? After all, expertise or competence is not likely to occur just because someone invests a certain number of hours working at at task.

First, they need opportunities to engage in authentic, competency-appropriate problems. Authentic problems are real-world ones as opposed to contrived ones. For example, in mathematics, working on an authentic problem might mean solving a series of word-based problems rather than working through a list of calculations. Authentic historical problems would involve discovering the past through research rather than memorizing dates and names. In music, students should prepare themselves for performances, compose, conduct, and improvise. Students should engage with problems that they can solve on their own or with minimal assistance.

Second, they need to develop true understanding of the core concepts of the domain—the big ideas—and strategies for applying them to real problems. Every discipline has a collection of domain-specific understandings that underpin it. From these, all other understandings can be derived and decisions can be supported; specific information does not contradict these core understandings but adds detail and nuance. In music, for example, students need to understand that excellent musical form involves a balance between variety and repetition. Only then can they understand the purpose of and value the effect of sonata allegro form.

Third, they need feedback, from others and through self-evaluation, about how successful their problem-solving efforts were. They also need opportunities to reengage with the problems until they develop deep understanding of the core concepts. When students engage in authentic problems that involve the big ideas in a discipline and they have specific feedback on both their problem-solving process and their product (answer or conclusion), then they learn how to enact their core understandings to solve new problems on their own.

So what do teachers actually do to help students develop "pre-expertise"? They create opportunities for their students to engage in the three kinds of activities listed above: They help students understand the big ideas by giving them strategies to solve appropriate problems, and help students learn to self-evaluate by providing feedback. There's a lot to unpack from that statement. For now, what you need to know is that teachers create environments in which students can learn. The goal is for learners to become independent and *self-regulated* by using appropriate learning strategies, accepting feedback and to self-evaluate, and being self-motivated.

PROJECT

1. Explain the following terms:
   - Synaptogenesis
   - Recall
   - Representation
   - Knowledge
   - Expertise
   - Understanding
   - Enactment
   - Metacognition
   - Chunk
   - Self-regulation
   - Routine expertise
   - Adaptive expertise
2. What is the difference between knowledge and recall?
3. How do students enact their understandings, or turn their knowledge into action?
4. Because of their extensive experience and knowledge base, experts dispense with many problems in a routine manner that might stump one

with less experience and knowledge. This allows them to maintain focus on the larger issues that might escape others. If this is true, what are the implications for becoming an expert teacher or expert musician?

5. Tell a story about a routine you have had to change recently. How did you go about it? Has your practice routine changed this semester? What metacognitive strategies did you use to change your routine?

6. Knowledge is organized around the fundamental big ideas of any discipline. What are the big ideas in the following domains?
   - Teachers and teaching
   - The purposes of education
   - Music
   - How students learn

7. More important, how are the big ideas in each of these domains related? Draw a map to represent the connections.

8. Deconstruct the following statement: Competent teachers help students understand the big ideas by giving them strategies to solve appropriate problems and help students learn to self-evaluate by providing feedback. Does this statement align with your current ideas about what it means to be a teacher? What are the implications of this statement for what you need to do over the next few years to become a competent teacher?

9. Name an area in which you consider yourself a competent novice. What would you have to do to become an expert?

CHAPTER 7

How Students Acquire Musical Understanding

In this chapter we expand our understanding of learning to discover how people learn music. Naive explanations of musical learning might include knowledge about music (for example, music history or music theory) and being able to perform on an instrument or sing a song, but these would be inconsistent with what is known about learning in a general sense. Musical learning is defined as the development of musical representations (sound images along with related factual and procedural knowledge) and corresponding neural connections in response to musical stimuli.

MUSICAL KNOWLEDGE AND DEVELOPMENT

Despite seeming helpless and practically inert, babies are born with an astonishing array of musical abilities. Newborns attend more to sounds that they have been exposed to repeatedly prior to birth. In fact, researchers have shown that newborns are able to "recall" sounds that they heard prior to birth. When given a choice between two dissimilar sounds, newborns will innately attend to sounds played for them in utero. Even five-month-olds are sensitive to subtle changes in familiar melodic patterns—ones that differ from what they expect to hear based on prior exposure.

The value of the role of the parents and caregivers in the development of musical skills should not be underestimated. Babies' earliest musical training comes in the form of a special speaking style employed by caregivers. This *motherese*, as it is called, is more song-like and rhythmic than normal speech, and its use appears to promote bonding. In general, motherese is higher pitched, slower, and more expressive than normal speech. Children are more attentive to words that are sung in this manner than to spoken words. Children also imitate the patterns of motherese when babbling. This preverbal interchange between infant and caregiver is essentially musical in nature. In infancy, communication is based primarily on tone, pitch, and volume rather than on words. Therefore, musical communication becomes a part of a child's mental development from the beginning.

Children are surrounded by the musical sounds of their native culture. Through a process called *acculturation*, children absorb not only the musical grammar and syntax of their surroundings but also the cultural and social functions of music. In this respect, family and community play an important role in a child's informal music learning. Factors such as a parent's musical listening selections at home or in the car, music at religious gatherings, attendance at music performances, and formal music involvement by parents or older siblings influence a child's understanding of the function of music in one's life. Early exposure to musical activity, especially singing by the parents and caregivers, is the most significant factor in early and long-term musical development (Davidson, Howe, Moore, & Sloboda, 1996).

Early Developmental Factors and Skill Development

One of the most important cognitive developments in infants and young children is the ability to group distinct auditory stimuli into meaningful chunks, for example, grouping a series of pitches into a melody or grouping note sequences into rhythmic patterns. Although there is some evidence that formal training can accelerate the acquisition of these skills, the constraints of the developmental process are the primary limiting factor. At this stage, those without early training catch up to those who have had prior musical experiences.

The process of learning musical language and skills parallels the development of spoken and written language skills. For each skill, the first step is for the child to actively attend to an aural stimulus in the environment. The sound stimulates the development of neural connections, which the child experiences as a mental representation of the modeled sound. When the child speaks, he or she is attempting to reproduce the sound based on this mental model.

The essential cognitive function in all of these efforts by the child is the oral-aural feedback loop. (See figure 7.1.) This feedback loop allows the child to aurally compare his or her oral production (speaking or singing) with the previously acquired mental model of the end product. Each time

Figure 7.1: The oral/aural feedback loop

the child speaks (or sings), he or she modifies the effort in order to more accurately reproduce the sound. The limiting factor is the accuracy of the child's aural model. The parents' role is not to model the physical production of the sound but, rather, to stimulate and clarify the child's mental model, which the child then reproduces.

The essential sequence is this: (1) presentation of an aural stimulus, (2) development of a mental model (representation) of the sound, which may not be entirely accurate, (3) attempts to orally reproduce the musical representation, and (4) a "polishing" process based on aural feedback, during which the child mentally compares the musical product to the representation. This step, along with repeated hearings of the model, improves the accuracy of the representation.

Musical development in children occurs slowly as they create representations based on musical models and through musical activities such as singing, listening, and moving. At first, their understanding is procedural; they only know how to participate in musical activities. Only gradually do they know *about* music and develop verbal and symbolic representations. Below you will see how this simple model explains much about how children and adults acquire musical understanding.

Development of Rhythmic Skills

It is generally thought that the perception of rhythm precedes the perception of melody. Infants, of course, have been exposed to the sound of their mother's more-or-less even heartbeat throughout gestation. Newborns, in fact, can distinguish between regular and irregular heartbeat sounds. Between the ages of three and four children can begin to distinguish between slow and fast tempi, and this seems to be their primary concern in music.

Children begin coordinating their movements to music by the time they reach their second birthday. Although they still generally cannot synchronize their movements with others', they often can imitate rhythms verbally that they cannot reproduce physically. This suggests that their perceptive skills are more advanced than their physical coordination might indicate.

Typically they can coordinate their rhythmic movements with others' by about the age of five.

Development of Singing Skills

Infants attend to the melodic and rhythmic contours of their caregiver's intuitive use of motherese. To the child, these sounds function as precursors to both language and music. Most commonly, the first intentional sounds produced by a child are descending glissando figures. These gradually come to include ascending glissandi, repeated ascending or descending glissandi, and various combinations of each.

Not until around a child's first birthday can she distinguish between proto-speaking from proto-singing. Children begin this process by using a single syllable on the glissandi. Gradually, these efforts evolve into short, repeated "phrases" consisting of stable syllables and melodic contour at a variety of pitch levels. Between about three and four years of age, children can repeat song fragments and combine these components into something resembling a melody yet completely distinct from speaking. Some researchers have observed children reproducing the lyrics, rhythms, and even the form of simple songs by the age of four. At this age, children sometimes loop through song fragments or sing simple songs with the phrases out of order.

By the age of six or seven, children have acquired a range of about an octave, and they have assimilated the diatonic system (if that is their cultural model). Absent additional musical training and practice, the development of new singing skills ceases at about the age of eight. In fact, according to Gembris, "[t]he singing abilities of untrained adults are not much different from those of 8- to 10-year-old children" (2002, p. 495).

Learning to Read Music Notation

The issue of when and how to introduce music notation to children is a complex problem that over the centuries has been addressed by many music educators, perhaps most notably by Johann Heinrich Pestalozzi, Shinichi Suzuki, and Zoltán Kodály. In conceptual terms, learning to use music notation for music performance is analogous to learning to use written language, the most significant point being that children typically have acquired a working vocabulary of nearly five thousand words prior to their initial efforts at reading. With such a sizable vocabulary, young children are capable of sophisticated communications without any ability to read or write. Likewise, children experience and use sounds prior to their use of symbolic notation for those sounds. To learn to read, children map the visual symbols—the written text—onto their existing sounds and meanings. Written text only becomes decipherable and meaningful to children when it is paired with sounds and meanings they already understand. This process is analogous to the importance of knowing how before knowing about.

During this process, children learn "knowledge about the uses of print, how print represents sounds, how words are formed, how sentences are put together, and how sentences become stories or reports" (Brunning, Schraw, & Ronning, 1999, p. 242). This allows students to learn how to extract new meaning from written text. The process of learning to understand notation is similar in that it "requires knowledge about the use of notation, how notes represent sounds, how phrases are formed, how melodies are put together, and how melodies become compositions" (McPherson & Gabrielsson, 2002, p. 104).

Look again at the oral-aural feedback loop presented in figure 7.1. The process of learning to decipher musical notation is essentially identical. Prior to reading musical notation, the child acquires a musical representation from a musical aural model such as a rhythmic or melodic pattern. When using notation, however, the existing musical model is cued by an appropriate symbolic representation—the music notation. This process is the same as that for written language, in which a symbol (the text) is paired with a child's existing vocabulary. With music notation, the symbols (the notes on the page) are paired with a child's existing repertoire of pitches, rhythms, and melodies. Compare the production-aural feedback loop shown in figure 7.2 with the oral-aural feedback loop shown in figure 7.1.

Early musical learning occurs primarily through acculturation and informal experiences. Children absorb music from their environment. Many school-age children continue their musical development by participating in musical activities at their schools or by studying privately during the later years of primary education.

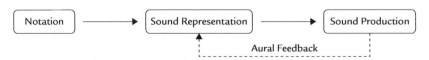

Figure 7.2: The production/aural feedback loop in music

Later Development
Formal Instruction in Music

As mentioned above, acculturation and informal learning can only foster a certain level of musical skill and understanding; without particular kinds of deliberate musical activities, musical development will stagnate at about age eight. This is not to suggest that informal activities are not also essential for later musical development. But children who actively participate in music every day develop skills and abilities faster than those whose main musical stimulus is passive consumption. According to Howe and colleagues, [o]ne of the few reliable early predictors of later musical achievement is the age at which a child first started to sing recognizable songs" (Howe, Davidson, Moore, & Sloboda, 1995, p. 41). Therefore, early musical activities are likely to be a major influence on later musical development.

Formal music instruction can be productive at any age provided that the activities are appropriate for the learner's age and motivation level. The informal music learning that children have experienced to this point in their lives has been a kind of play rather than work. Successful early instruction, including classroom instruction, builds on these informal play-like qualities rather than confounding them.

Research shows that children younger than four generally cannot focus on systematic instrumental instruction, and students younger than six cannot practice without direct supervision: "All early instruction requires high levels of skillful adult support and interaction to sustain a productive yet game-like environment" (Lehmann, Sloboda, & Woody, 2007, p. 35). Most professional musicians began formal instruction between the ages of six and eight, especially on instruments that require extreme dexterity and coordination, such as violin and piano. Other instruments, including most wind instruments, may be started at an older age when the students are physically capable of manipulating the instrument.

Outcomes of Formal Instruction

From a practical perspective, formal music instruction should foster the ability to perform intentional musical acts such as "listening, performing, imagining, moving or dancing, composing, improvising, or conducting" (Grühn, 2005, p. 106). On the surface, these activities appear to be quite different: performing written music, moving and dancing, conducting, and improvising seem to be physical skills, whereas listening, imagining, and composing might appear to be cognitive tasks. In fact, there are common understandings (representations) that mediate these activities. Musical representations support all aspects of musical thinking and development, from remembering sounds, to reproduction, to creating (composing and improvising). Findings by McPherson and Gabrielsson supports the idea that the common denominator of musicality is a person's ability to "encode and manipulate musically relevant information, in essence, to construct and manipulate mental representations" (Lehmann et al., 2007, p. 21).

These representations are not only auditory in nature. They may also include emotions, images, kinesthetics, or related concepts, such as linguistic labels, and symbols. Thus, the representations required for mechanical reproduction of sound, whether singing or manipulating an instrument, and for performing in any musically meaningful manner are necessarily complex. Therefore, if a main outcome of formal instruction is the development of musical representations, then the instruction must be designed to provide opportunities for these representations to develop. In the following section, we'll explore the nature of these representations and how they are developed.

PRACTICE

Most people think of practice as the work that is required to learn a particular piece of music. As a consequence, they make certain decisions about how to approach their practice and how to judge their success or failure. A better definition of practice suggests that it is any effortful activity that results in learning—an observable change in ability. However, knowledge and skills are intertwined; an increase in certain kinds of knowledge may result in improved performances. Therefore, many of the activities associated with musical learning—reading a book about music, mock performances and auditions, listening to recordings of self and others, for example—may not appear on the surface to be practicing, yet they contribute directly to ongoing changes in behavior and should therefore be considered a form of practice.

What kinds of musical representations enable effective practice? What kinds of knowledge and skills foster expertise and allow expert musicians to learn new repertoire quickly? First, they have the fundamental performing skills (playing or singing) that allow them to manipulate their voice or instrument with ease. This ability is developed slowly over time.

Second, they have fundamental musical knowledge that allows them to decipher a new piece quickly and develop complex understandings of the piece from various perspectives and at different levels of detail, ranging from the exact style, timbre, length, and volume of a particular note to the formal design of a longer work. That ability also is developed over time.

Therefore, the practical outcomes of practice should be twofold:

1. To obtain various generic knowledge and skill representations that will assist in learning additional repertoire quickly; and
2. To learn new music from a variety of perspectives, not just the skills required to execute the notes.

Skill Development

One might question the relation between skill development and mental representations. Isn't manipulating an instrument or your voice primarily a physical skill? In a word, no. It may appear so on a superficial level, but what is observed is an embodiment of the mental representations behind the skill. Remember, all learning can be defined as a mental representation, and representations are analogous to neurological connections. When learning a skill, one is creating and then reinforcing the neurological connections that facilitate that performance. By analogy, you might think of practicing and learning a skill as writing a mental program for that skill. Then, when you execute that skill, for example, riding a bicycle, you are mentally running the "ride a bicycle" program. If you've programmed yourself correctly, the program can run automatically.

Brain scans of expert musicians show neurological changes that directly coincide with the quality and intensity of practice. For example, the neurological areas associated with the left hand in string players have been found to be significantly larger than those associated with their right hands. Through the process of neuroplasticity, the areas of their brain that control the left hand have developed complex connections that expand and take over nearby neurological space. As areas expand, they may actually begin to overlap and interfere with one another.

Music practice can also result in finely tuned context-specific audio discrimination skills. For example, musicians develop fine discrimination of frequency (pitch) and loudness (volume), but these abilities are only employed when they are listening to music. This skill does not automatically transfer to increased discrimination of frequency and pitch when listening to speech. Melodic performers develop sensitivity to pitch height (intonation), and percussionists develop heightened awareness of duration. Conductors develop the ability to deliberately monitor exceptionally large auditory spaces. That is, they can selectively attend to specific facets of large ensemble performances, or choose to monitor the entire ensemble. All of these abilities are the result of learned representations and the associated neurological connections.

The connections associated with performance or listening discrimination are not limited to discrete areas of the brain but actually extend into related areas of the brain. Listening to known music activates not only the associated auditory areas of the brain but also the areas of the motor cortex associated with the performance of that piece. For example, brain scans of pianists taken while they listen to a piece they already know how to perform show that the areas of their brains associated with their hands are activated exactly as if they were performing that piece.

Performers pass through three sequential phases when developing skills, as seen in figure 7.3: a cognitive stage, an associative phase, and an autonomous stage (Barry & Hallum, 2002).

The cognitive stage requires the performer to engage higher mental processes to guide the acquisition of task and motor skills, as well as representations. In other words, this phrase requires the investment of significant effort to figure out the new skill. It is as if the part of your brain that knows about the skill is telling the motor areas of your brain what to do. During the associative stage, the performer practices the psychomotor task and develops an awareness of how it feels to perform the piece. This stage still requires significant mental effort to execute the skill without error. Any distraction may reduce the accuracy of the performance. In order to reach the autonomous stage, the performer must attain a level of learning at which the physical task requires minimal mental direction the performer is free to deal with matters other than the skill itself—the execution of the skill must seem to "flow." This automaticity requires an understanding of the piece that cannot be developed through mere repetitive practice. I now turn to this interaction between skill-related representations and musical representations, this integrated music understanding.

Figure 7.3: Stages of skill development

Musical Knowledge in Relation to Practice

The act of performing music is a reconstructive process. Sound objects that have been encoded as mental representations are reconstituted as new sound events. This process of mental recall and physical production is highly dependent on how the music is encoded in the representations. For this reason, one of the two main intentional outcomes of practice should be a detailed, comprehensive mental map (representation) of the repertoire at various levels of detail.

Think back to the experiment in expert recall in Chapter 6 in which the subject was encoding long sequences of numbers. His first strategy was to encode meaningful chunks that he could string together to recall the entire number sequence. After a short a time, he reached the limit of this type of recall of sequences of chunks. Musicians often learn and perhaps memorize music in this fashion. Through repeated playings, they develop a sequence of interconnected chunks. This method of learning is called *forward chaining*. The downside of learning music his way is that the only memory cue for each chunk is the previous chunk; failure to recall any given chunk results in failure to recall the remainder of the sequence, whether the recall task is a series of numbers or a series of notes.

You'll recall that the subject of the number memorization experiment was able to substantially increase his number sequence recall by the use of various deliberate strategies. When he reached the limit of forward chaining, he began to create super chunks that each contained smaller chunks. He created a hierarchical representation of the number sequence. Expert musicians use this same strategy to create hierarchical representations of the pieces they are learning for performance. The other key to number series recall was that the retrieval cues for the various chunks were personally meaningful. By the time of the performance, expert memorizers have multiple inter-related representations (formal, textual, tactile, and so on) that enables them to use another set of memory retrieval cues should one set fail.

Best Practices

If there is no such thing as talent (defined as a genetic gift), then the only way to achieve excellence is through practice. The relevant questions are, How much practice is necessary? and What kind of practice is most effective for certain tasks? Fortunately, the answers to these questions are readily available in the body of research on music learning.

Practicing and Time Use

There is a general consensus that approximately ten thousand hours of practice time is necessary to attain expertise in music performance (Ericsson et al., 1993). The amount of time per week spent in practicing, though it varies considerably, is useful in predicting musical success. Estimated practice time for those achieving expertise ranges from fifteen to twenty-five hours per week as an adolescent to twenty-five to fifty hours per week immediately prior to winning a professional position. It appears, however, that the most important factor in practice effectiveness is not only the number of hours but how those hours are organized. This is equally important to those who are not seeking a professional performance position and must have time available for other career development, such as learning how to be a teacher. Based on the research on effective practice, several generalities can be listed.

1. Practice that is spread over an extended period of time, as opposed to "cramming," is both more efficient for learning and performance is more likely to be retained.
2. Daily practice time should also be divided and coordinated with specific tasks and goals. Short practice sessions are best for simple tasks, but longer and more complex tasks require longer practice sessions.
3. Practice sessions of between one hour and one and one-half hours appear to be most effective, with breaks between sessions rather than during sessions. There is evidence that experts tend to schedule their longest and most difficult practice sessions during late morning and not later in the day, when they may already be mentally and physically fatigued. Practice sessions should be scheduled, and the schedule should be followed.
4. As musicians develop, they are able to practice for longer periods of time. Like athletes, musicians should practice up to the point at which they become mentally and physically fatigued but not beyond it. Part of the point of practicing is learning to do it more efficiently and for longer periods. In effect, one is not only practicing the music but also practicing practicing.
5. Formal practice generally includes exercises to develop generic skills (such as etudes, scales, along warm-up exercises) along with practicing specific repertoire. Informal practice (playing by ear, improvising, jam sessions, sightreading, and other enriching activities), which contributes to overall achievement by allowing musicians opportunities to consolidate and apply learning, should not be neglected.

Mental Practice

One of the main goals of practice is to develop mental representations that facilitate performance. It is convenient, therefore, that there are several purely cognitive practice techniques that can be used to reinforce existing representations. Recall that for musicians with rich connections between sound representations and skill execution, listening to recordings of known repertoire can activate motor programs in the brain used to play those pieces; there is a two-way connection between the sound representation and the physical skills required to perform the piece. Simply imagining the sound of a piece and imagining the efforts used to perform the piece can strengthen those representations. This process cannot be used to learn a new piece without already having some experience with it.

Oxendine (1984, as cited in Barry & Hallum, 2002, p. 153) describes three circumstances during which mental practice may be most productive:

1. Review that immediately precedes, follows, or coincides with performance;
2. Formal or informal rehearsal between periods of physical practice; and
3. Musical decision-making related to the strategy-making phases of the activity that occur during (or between) periods of physical practice or performance.

Learning New Music

Research on practicing musicians has provided a list of common activities employed in learning a new piece of music. These are the kinds of strategies musicians should use during the initial cognitive-verbal-motor stage of learning.

1. In the initial stages of practice, musicians attempt to develop an internal aural representation of the piece—to mentally hear the piece with only the score.
2. They analyze the piece and use the structure of the piece to determine how to divide the piece into practice units. The more challenging the task is, the smaller the units are.
3. As they become more proficient in the technical aspects of the piece, the practice units become longer, and the practice becomes more focused on musical aspects rather than technical. (Barry & Hallum, 2002, p. 156)

MOTIVATION, SELF-REGULATION, AND ACHIEVEMENT.

How is it that some musicians are able to maintain a high level of motivation, often across many years or decades? As it turns out, this, too, is fairly well understood as the result of years of research on professional musicians.

Motivational Factors

Motivation is often misunderstood. Many believe that it is a feeling that comes and goes. Students talk about not feeling motivated to practice or waiting until they feel motivated to work on an assignment. This is not a new idea. In Greek mythology, the Muses are responsible for the creative inspiration in the arts. Modern ideas of motivation list three factors involved in motivation: extrinsic motivation, intrinsic motivation, and personal attributes and effort. Although it may sometimes seem like it, none of them require divine intervention.

Extrinsic and Intrinsic Motivation

Generally, people are intrinsically attracted to music because making music and listening to music are rewarding activities. Infants are innately attracted to music without any outside motivating factors. For infants and young children, listening to and making music are associated with play. Many successful musicians and those who continue effortful music-making as adults report some sort of "peak musical experience" as a young child. Although this kind of experience may not predict future musical involvement, it appears to be enabling.

Extrinsic factors may be the first critical determinant of continued musical involvement. Particularly negative experiences with music for children, such as being told they are not musical or that they cannot sing, can negate music's intrinsic motivational factors. Such negative experiences seem to have the opposite effect of peak experiences because they tend to prevent future musical involvement.

Parents and caregivers are a child's first music teachers, providing informal musical instruction in singing and dancing. Recall that the best predictor of future music success is the age at which a child can sing a recognizable song, which is the consequence of early parental modeling and motherese. Parents continue to play an important role in facilitating formal instruction by providing funding and transportation. Parents without extensive musical training still play a critical role in a child's musical achievement by sitting in on lessons and by supervising practice efforts. Most successful musicians can recall being required by parents to practice. Only later, after they began to experience public and personal recognition of their progress, did they begin to motivate themselves to practice. This is when students reach a tipping point between extrinsic motivation and intrinsic motivation.

Initial music instruction should build on the playlike aspects of early music learning. High-achieving music students describe their first teacher as warm, friendly, encouraging, and fun to be with, and report that they looked forward to their lessons. Those who gave up lessons described their first teachers as critical, unfriendly, cold, and directive. Until age ten or eleven, disliking the music teacher often morphs into disliking music.

Subsequent teachers are sources of motivation because they help the young musician develop a productive belief system about music and music involvement. Teachers at this stage of the student's musical development must be able to inspire the student as a role model through their own exceptional musicianship. Older students, usually by about age 12, can separate their judgments about teacher and music and are willing to tolerate disliked teachers if they respect the teacher as a performer.

The teacher's most important role in developing independent musicians is teaching them how to practice. Practice is not in itself inherently enjoyable, but it is the key to obtaining the intrinsic and extrinsic motivators that fuel continued involvement and success.

Social pressure and recognition can have positive or negative effects on a student's motivation to continue musical involvement. Recognition as a "band geek" may discourage involvement, but identification as a member in a social group, such as "band," may serve as a positive motivator not only for continuation of studies but also for excelling. The difference between these two scenarios depends on the learning environment fostered by the instructor. Social learning contexts that promote excellence can be highly motivational to all members of the group; contexts based on competition may encourage some to excel, but others will become less motivated. Some of the strongest musical motivators appear to be informal activities such as jam sessions or chamber music groups.

It is essential, however, for students to eventually move from extrinsic to intrinsic motivations for musical involvement. It appears that a sense of musical efficacy and musical identity are critical factors in intrinsic motivation.

Personal Attributes

Successful musicians with productive practice habits demonstrate three characteristics associated with self-regulation that extend far beyond simple self-control (Zimmerman 1990):

1. Students continue in music based not only on their prior success and likelihood of future success, but also on their sense of why they have been and will likely continue to be successful. *Attribution theory* suggests that students have many options for explaining their successes or failures, including talent, effort, luck, or task difficulty. Of these, talent and effort are the most common explanations. Those who attribute their success to talent may cease involvement in music if they think they have reached the limit of their gift. Those who attribute their success to effort, derive motivation from both successes and failures; having a belief in effort rather than talent.

2. Those with a *mastery orientation* proactively seek learning opportunities and are persistent in their effort to achieve, knowing that hard work is the key. They are purposeful in their identification of appropriate goals and in the selection of strategies to meet those goals.

3. They proactively engage in self-monitoring and feedback efforts. They assess the effectiveness of their learning strategies by setting goals and assessing their results compared to the goal. They monitor and control their emotional reactions to their efforts, successes, and failures.

This self-awareness and self-regulation promote a cycle in which effort leads to success, which leads to motivation, which leads to increased effort. (See figure 7.4.) Self-regulated learners are aware that the first part of the cycle is effort rather than motivation.

Figure 7.4: The self-regulation-motivation Loop

SUMMARY

While the full implications of the music developmental process will be explored in greater detail in the subsequent chapters, some generalities present themselves.

1. The primary mode for understanding music learning and development must be that of the mental representation. Representations provide the link between the neurological basis of learning and the psychological experience of learning. The way in which these connections develop explains a lot about how music is understood and learned.
2. Parents and caregivers are a child's first music teachers. Early childhood experiences appear to set the stage for future musical involvement and success. At an early age, students can absorb much of their surrounding musical culture.
3. Early formal music instruction should build on childhood musical play. Only gradually are students able to benefit from formalized instruction.
4. Musical development mimics other kinds of learning, especially skill and language development. It is the pairing of knowledge and skill—knowledge in action—that is critical; musicians are unable to perform beyond their level of understanding.
5. Teaching students how to learn on their own—how to practice and the associated self-regulatory attributes—may be a music teacher's most important task.

In the next part of the book, we will explore how teachers create environments in which their students can learn music.

PROJECTS

1. Explain the following concepts:
   - Acculturation
   - Formal and informal learning
   - Musical grouping (especially in relation to general memory abilities)
   - Oral-aural feedback loop
   - Attribution theory
   - Mastery orientation
2. Describe a time when you were at first unmotivated to pursue an activity but became highly motivated after investing some effort. What were the factors that required you to exert some effort despite being unmotivated?

3. At the beginning of this chapter, musical learning was defined as the development of musical representations (sounds along with related factual and procedural knowledge) and corresponding neural connections formed as a response to musical stimuli. Also, toward the end of the chapter, the teacher's primary role was described as creating an environment in which students could learn. In your future music room or rehearsal hall, or in individual or small-group instruction, how will your instruction be different from the kind of K–12 music instruction you received?

4. In development of language, skill, and knowledge, it is often best to know how before knowing about. (This is not always the case. Pilots undergo extensive ground training prior to their first training flight.) First, explain the various reasons why this rule is generally true. Then, list the circumstances that allow exceptions to the rule. Finally, tell a story about a time when you learned how to do something and the learning was subsequently reinforced and explained by learning about it.

5. Do a bit of Internet research and see if you can determine why musical development ceases at about age nine without formal instruction.

6. Use your understanding of the use of music notation to explain how you and your colleagues are able to "sight read" printed text that you've never seen before.

7. You read that the common denominator of musicality is a person's ability to "encode and manipulate musically relevant information, in essence, to construct and manipulate mental representations." In your own words, explain the statement and then either support or rebuff the statement using a nonmusical example.

8. Make a list of specific activities other than formal practice that you could use to improve your performance ability.

9. Make a list of information that would help you prepare to perform a particular work. Explain why each would be helpful.

Long project

Take a new etude, no more than one minute in length, and try to learn it as quickly as possible. Your goal is to move from the motor stage to the autonomous stage of learning in the shortest possible time period. In order to do this, you will have to be as efficient and effective as possible in your practice. After all, you will still have other etudes and selections that need some practice time.

You should complete a Deliberate Practice Pre-planning Form (from Chapter 3) and log your practice time for each session spent on the new etude. In the end, you want to have a detailed mental image of what it sounds and feels like to perform the etude. In order to do this, you will need to develop as many representations of the etude as possible. For instance, if you are an instrumentalist, you will want to be able to sing the piece. If you are a singer, you should learn to play it on an instrument such as the piano. You should analyze and write down the form. You should chart the subtle dynamic changes of the phrases. You should listen to several recordings and try to imitate them. If necessary, you could write a poem or story that matches the emotion of the etude, or even choreograph appropriate movements. Do whatever it takes to internalize the etude. Remember, practice can be considered to be any deliberate effort on your part to get better.

To complete your assignment, submit appropriate documentation of your work, which may include your plans, your practice log, or even a recording. You will also submit a short essay that answers these questions.

1. Describe your learning goal for this week in your own words.
2. Describe the procedures you used in an effort to meet that goal.
3. Show the evidence for why you did or did not reach your goal.
4. Explain what you would do differently the next time you set a similar goal.
5. State whether this project had any impact on your motivation.

You would be wise to consult with your colleagues and your other instructors for insight and assistance with this project.

CHAPTER 8

Meaningful Curriculum

The word *curriculum*, even among educational professionals, often merely means the series of courses students have to complete in order to move onto the next level of instruction or simply the information that gets "covered" during a course. Rarely, the term might refer to a set of educational outcomes prescribed by the state or local school hierarchy. In this chapter, we'll explore the various meanings of *curriculum*, both generically and as it applies to music education.

REDEFINING *CURRICULUM*

All decisions about the goals, content, and methods and materials of instruction must be directly related to the intentional outcomes of instruction. You will recall from Chapter 1 that the four purposes of public education in the United States are academic, vocational, social and civic, and personal (Goodlad, 1984). Teachers are ethically required to assure that their instructional efforts can be reasonably justified against those purposes. Any instruction not related directly to the defined, intended purposes of enabling students to successfully engage in our democratic society detracts from the quality of the students' learning experiences.

A more expansive view of curriculum includes these four facets:

1. The *formal* or *intended* curriculum: the design of the actual subject matter content that is to be taught;
2. The *enacted* or *implemented* curriculum: the materials and activities that are actually delivered to the students, which may not necessarily be the same as the formal curriculum;

3. The *experienced* curriculum: the students' perspective on the enacted curriculum; and

4. The *hidden* curriculum: the often unspoken and sometimes unintended outcomes of participating in the educational system, often consequences of noncurricular decisions such as schedules, discipline plans, and the priority of extracurricular activities.

Teachers soon discover that the academic disciplines are far too wide and deep and courses far too brief to cover all of the known information in any one discipline. Thus, they must decide how to invest their limited interaction time with the students to best prepare them for the challenges they will face after instruction is concluded. But this question remains: Who decides? Because the teacher actually implements the instruction, the teacher is professionally responsible for designing the *formal* and *enacted* curriculum that accounts for the concerns of the external stakeholders and the best interests of the students; it also is aligned with the best knowledge and practices of the discipline. Curriculum, then, is fundamentally about values; all classroom decisions reflect *somebody's* philosophy and values. Whose values? Those of the local community, school authorities, parents, students, and the teacher. For now, we'll focus on the teacher's values.

INFLUENCES ON THE TEACHER'S PHILOSOPHY AND VALUES

What factors influence the teacher's philosophy and values?

1. The teacher's understanding of the value and role of music in society; thus, how understanding music and participating in authentic musical activities leads toward the accomplishment of the purposes of public education.
2. The teacher's knowledge and understanding of music itself.

All classroom and rehearsal activities are value-laden, and it is the teacher whose values are conveyed during instruction. Teachers need to be aware, however, that there is a subtle line between educational and musical leadership and indoctrination. What are the student's interests in the curriculum, and how are they attended to? In the end, students want to be successful *by their own definition of success*. What they really want from the teacher is help in attaining their own educational goals. But students do not always know what they want or what they need to learn in order to attain success, nor do they get to decide the exact course content. For example, students do not decide what they are assigned to read in literature courses, but it's the teacher's job to make Shakespeare meaningful to the students so that they define success to include understanding Shakespeare's writings. With this in mind, one view of the teacher's job would be to create and communicate a *vision* of curriculum and success to students.

In this chapter you'll learn about some instructional techniques that help make the curriculum meaningful for students, and you'll examine several preexisting visions of musical curriculum.

EARLY CHILDHOOD INSTRUCTIONAL METHODOLOGIES

While it is beyond the scope of this book to detail the implementations of these visions, two important points must be considered. The first point is that they have unique strengths and numerous commonalities, they represent a spectrum of views of the purposes of music in society and in individuals' lives. The second is that each curriculum is the product of a particular vision that may or may not translate well to specific instructional contexts. Ultimately, it is each teacher's responsibility to develop a coherent, comprehensive curriculum for his or her unique instructional context based on a knowledge of the context and the students who inhabit it.

Dalcroze

Émile-Jaques Dalcroze (1865–1950) was a Swiss composer and professor at the Geneva Conservatory. As a composer, he had a particular interest in the folk songs of the Suisse-Romande, an area of western Switzerland. As a result of his teaching, he became concerned about his students' apparent lack of "inner hearing." After reading extensive reports for educational and musical theorists, he became convinced about the integral link between human movement and musical rhythm. He felt that walking was the natural analog to the musical measure and that breathing correlated with musical phrasing. When integrated, he believed, these connections would help his students develop a natural sense of musicianship.

Curricular Vision

Dalcroze believed that musical learning should occur as naturally as a child learns language. Therefore, his method is based on children's play.

The system that he developed, *eurhythmics*, which literally means "good rhythm," is based on the premise that the movement of the human body can provide substantial insight into the nature of music prior to learning the formal rules and symbols of music. The system is designed to educate the whole body and mind, not simply to develop performance skills.

The Method

The Dalcroze Method is based on three co-equal components: eurhythmics, solfège, and improvisation. The eurythmic exercises, which include moving through space and stationary gestures, are meant to develop body sense and musical awareness and to inform vocal and instrumental performance. Movement is also used to measure musical duration and pitch distance, especially distance from the tonic, while singing solfège. Musical improvisation incorporates musical movement, such as dance and rhythmic movement, to inform musical expression. Complete musicianship is expressed through the complete integration of movement, singing, and improvisation.

Kodály

Zoltán Kodály (1882–1967) was an important early twentieth-century Hungarian composer, educator, and philosopher. Like many composers of the time, Kodály and his fellow composer Béla Bartók were concerned that their native Hungarian folk music was not being passed along to future generations. Together, starting in about 1905, they led an effort to document this music and to incorporate many of its elements into important compositions for orchestra, opera, and a variety of other musical forms. Appalled by the quality of musical instruction in Hungarian schools and concerned that Hungarian culture was gradually being pushed aside by Viennese and German perspectives, Kodály developed a system for teaching musicianship based on traditional Hungarian folk songs.

Curricular Vision

To Kodály, all children are innately musical; therefore, people are incomplete without music. Music promotes emotional, spiritual, and intellectual growth. Children should learn music in their mother tongue, in the same way they learn spoken language. Instruction should begin with singing, which enables all other musical learning because it develops inner hearing.

The Method

Although Kodály believed that children's musical skills should develop naturally, as their spoken language skills do, he nonetheless developed a highly regimented, sequential system for developing these skills in students. Thus, each skill should be learned first through singing, and the notation is introduced afterward. The materials for these musical skills are Hungarian folk songs, dances, and singing games. The songs are learned by using a movable-do sol-fa system to teach pitch and recognition of intervals and harmonies, reinforced by Curwen hand signals for each pitch. A separate syllable system is used for analyzing and counting rhythms. The end goal is a musical literacy that is equivalent to language literacy; students should be able to read sheet music and hear or produce sounds as effortlessly as if they were reading in their native language.

Orff

Carl Orff (1895–1982) was a German composer perhaps best known for the monumental *Carmina Burana*. The piece is now usually performed in a concert hall as a cantata, but the original conceptualization of the composition was as a staged work including choreography and visual design elements. The important links between music and dance are reflected in Orff's ideas about musicianship and musical education. These ideas were the result of his collaboration with Dorothee Günther when they formed the Günther School of Gymnastics and Dance in 1924. The curriculum at the school included influences from early twentieth-century ideas about dance. Orff eventually began to collate materials involving music, dance, and improvisation into publications known as Orff-Schulwerk. Multiple volumes were eventually produced, the most common being *Elementary Music* and *Music for Children*.

Curricular Vision

According to Orff, all learning is the result of doing. Much of the music is intended for Orff instruments, smaller-than-normal marimbas, xylophones and glockenspiels, simplified by the use of removable bars. Students use simple rounds or ABA form songs to sing, dance, and improvise. As the students advance, they move cyclically through musical exploration, imitation, improvisation, and composition.

The Method

Unlike Kodàly and Suzuki (see below), Orff developed more of an *approach* to instruction than a detailed sequential method. In fact, many believe that the Orff approach is not commonly followed correctly, in that the music is often inappropriately decontextualized from the dance and improvisational aspects. Music, language, and dance were intended to serve as seeds for individual musical activity and growth; the publications were simply designed to serve as models for the kinds of activities Orff envisioned.

Suzuki

Shin'ichi Suzuki (1898--1998) spent much of his childhood in his parents' violin assembly plant. He confessed later in life that, at that time, he viewed the violin as nothing more than a toy that could be tossed at any one of his eleven siblings. Although he had played the violin throughout his childhood, he did not take the instrument seriously until age seventeen, when he heard a Mischa Elman recording of Schubert's "Ave Maria." During the rest of his long life, Suzuki became a highly respected music philosopher and educator. He believed that studying music in a nurturing environment could enable "noble character."

Curricular Vision

Suzuki based his approach, which he called "Talent Education," on the "mother tongue" concept---that all children learn best through observing their environment. Thus, modeling, imitation, and repetition are the core learning activities in the method. Students are encouraged to start their musical learning at a very early age. Because of the need for encouragement and support for young learners, parents are often required to attend and participate in the child's earliest lessons on the instrument. The parents function as musical and learning role models for the child. Students also listen to multiple performances of each piece they are studying in order to learn phrasing and musicality.

The Method

In order to enable musical study by very young students, violins are made in a series of sizes to fit their hands. (Full-size violins are about 23 inches long; 1/64 size violins are just under 12 inches.) Student begin their studies by learning simple songs by imitation rather than by reading notation. These tunes include Dr. Suzuki's *Variations on Twinkle, Twinkle, Little Star* and various easy works by noted composers such as Bach, Handel, Mozart, Schubert, and Brahms. Once a piece is mastered, the students move on to new music but the old music is not forgotten. Part of the Suzuki Method requires that previously learned music be revisited in order to gain new musical insights. This required repetition results in a highly-structured learning sequence.

Gordon

Edwin Gordon (1927–2015) was a more contemporary music education visionary. Like the others discussed in this section, he, too, developed and implemented his own concepts about music learning and teaching; they are known as Music Learning Theory (MLT). Gordon started his music career as a string bass player, performing briefly as the bassist for Gene Krupa. Subsequently, Gordon turned his interest to music education. He was a member of the faculty at Temple University in Philadelphia for eighteen years.

Curricular Vision

Gordon's vision for musical curriculum is founded on his ideas about *audiation*, a type of inner hearing not unlike hearing a voice in one's head when reading text or thinking to oneself. Audiation is more than merely perceiving music; it is hearing and understanding music in the absence of sound in the environment. All subsequent facets of MLT are based on the concepts of audiation and the equivalence between musical thinking and language.

Accordingly, Gordon stated that children gain musical understanding by the same processes they use to learn spoken and written language. That is, they learn the patterns to the sounds of language prior to the written patterns of language. The rules of grammar and syntax are the final stage of the process.

Although individuals audiate many facets of the musical experience—timbre, meter, dynamics, form, and so on—Music Learning Theory is focused primarily on perceiving (differentiating) and audiating ever more complex tonal (melodic) and rhythmic patterns.

The Method

In order to develop an understanding of the instructional methodology employed in MLT, it is first necessary to understand the curricular content. According to MLT, tonal patterns and rhythmic patterns should first be learned separately. The tonal content patterns are, therefore, taught as only a series of strong beats. Similarly, rhythmic patterns are initially taught using a single indeterminate pitch. The Skill Learning Sequence defines a whole-part-whole process for teaching tonal or rhythmic patterns. Only later in the process are the tonal and rhythmic patterns synthesized.

SECONDARY INSTRUCTION

Several important concepts discussed so far in this book will come into play as you consider curriculum in the context of secondary instruction. The first is that, barring some sort of intervention, novice teachers will teach as they were taught. In essence, their curricular vision will be tacitly determined by their previous secondary-level teachers. Second, research concerning music teacher behavior has determined that, with some exceptions, in-service large-ensemble conductors spend extremely little rehearsal time interacting with their students regarding fundamental musical knowledge—perhaps as little as 3 percent of rehearsal is devoted to conceptual knowledge and learning.

Ensemble conductors spend the vast majority of rehearsal time on activities that result in immediate improvement in student performance. On the surface, focusing on immediate results might seem like an efficient way to teach. But if you consider for a moment what you already know about how people learn music and how expertise develops, you might begin to think that the focus on immediate results, rather than on long-term growth, might not be the most *effective* long-term curricular choice.

Several viable curricular visions for teaching young musicians have been developed in the past century. Similar such visions for large ensemble instruction have been developed over the past few decades. The instructional practices of the three main large ensembles—band, chorus and orchestra—have, by and large, been etermined by the performance histories of those ensembles. The band tradition is based on the military band, the choir's on religious vocal ensemble practice, and the orchestra's on concert hall performances.

Two of the most prominent contemporary curricular visions for large ensemble instruction result directly from the development of the national standards. These are the *Teaching Musicianship through Performance* series, from GIA Publications, and *Comprehensive Musicianship through Performance*, an approach developed by a group of music teachers in Wisconsin and outlined in *Shaping Sound Musicians* (O'Toole, 2003). These two visions have many commonalities, but they also have one critical difference. The first is designed to help instructors teach the musical content of literature they have already selected for performance. The second outlines a process through which instructors determine *a priori* the music knowledge, skills, and attitudes they wish their students to develop, and then select musical literature and design instruction to meet those goals.

How should we envision those long-term outcomes and the processes that promote these outcomes? Perhaps the best curriculum would prepare students for lifelong musical participation and independence free from the constraints of large ensemble instruction. Independent musicians should be able to select, arrange, compose, or improvise appropriate music in a variety of venues (religious institutions, community ensembles, and so on) and be able to seek out and absorb new musical learning. Those who choose no longer to actively make music should be prepared to make informed decisions about what music to listen to and to evaluate its quality.

What must music teachers do to promote these ends? They must provide students with opportunities to develop authentic representations of the underlying principles of musicianship and provide amble opportunities to practice implementing these representations. The process outlined in *Comprehensive Musicianship through Performance* (CMP) documents is a good place to start.

The CMP process is an expansion of previous efforts such as *Teaching musicianship in the high school band* (Labuta, 2000), *Blueprint for Band* (Garofalo & Garofalo, 1983), and the *Teaching Musicianship through Performance* series (GIA Publications). The process is symbolized by the five points on a star: (1) analysis, (2) outcomes, (3) strategies, (4) assessment, and (5) music selection. What follows is a brief overview of the curriculum design components found in CMP—music selection, analysis and outcomes—along with a commentary about the strengths and weaknesses of this approach.

Music Selection

Secondary ensemble directors usually consider a number of factors when selecting performance literature. These factors may include the performance context (for example, holiday concert, contest performance, or formal concert), the technical challenges for the students, group motivation (the students' interest in performing the piece), and the amount of allotted rehearsal time. Previous curriculum design models assisted directors in finding meaningful content after the literature had been selected. The CMP model encourages directors to think strategically about their literature selections over the length of a student generation, that is, the typical four-year high school experience. The concept is that, during each student's tenure in the program, he or she should have an opportunity to perform music of a variety of time periods (Renaissance, Baroque, Classical, and the nineteenth, twentieth, and twenty-first centuries), genres (marches, overtures, symphonies, concertos, program music, and so on), forms (sonata, suite, canon, fugue, ABA form, and so on) and instrumentation (such as full ensemble, chamber group, jazz ensemble, and a cappella).

Given the limited rehearsal time allotted to most ensembles, it becomes important to select the compositions of the best quality that fit into these various categories. So, directors are encouraged to examine potential works n the basis of several criteria: uniqueness, form, design, unpredictability, depth, consistency, orchestration or voicing, text, and transcendence. A director's selection of music provides significant insight into his or her musical values and understanding of the purposes of the music program. Imagine for one moment the outcry if a literature teacher were to select comic books instead of Shakespeare for his or her curriculum. Why shouldn't music teachers be held to the same standard?

Analysis

The kind of analysis needed for developing instructional curriculum goes beyond the typical analysis requirements found in a collegiate music theory class. Analysis of the musical elements of the work—listed as form, rhythm, melody, harmony, timbre, texture, and expression in CMP—is essential, but the director also should search for factors that will make the musical work meaningful to the students and look for opportunities for in-depth study of underlying musical principles. This step might include the cultural context of the work and the composer, the implications of any original text, the composer's musical intention and the devices used to create those musical moments, and other reasons to perform the work.

Outcomes

In the CMP model, outcomes are based on the three domains of Bloom's Taxonomy: (1) cognitive, (2) psychomotor, and (3) affective/aesthetic. As described here, the term *outcomes* refers to the products of instruction during a given unit of time (a period of weeks, perhaps) rather than the vision of musicianship outlined in Chapter 4 of this text. Thus, directors are defining outcomes as the result of studying and learning to perform given musical works. These unit outcomes are more sophisticated, however, than merely the knowledge, skills, and motivation required to deliver a musically satisfying performance; these unit outcomes are specific instances of the kinds of knowledge, skills, and attitudes that are emblematic of the vision of musicianship described above.

All of these unit outcomes are entirely driven by the musical literature. The appropriate skill outcomes are those necessary to enable performance of the work; even in *Shaping Sound Musicians* (O'Toole, 2003), directors are left to their own devices to determine those skills and select appropriate materials and methods for teaching them. It is in the knowledge and affective outcomes that the CMP model far exceeds what usually passes for instruction.

Knowledge Outcomes of CMP

Students cannot perform meaningfully beyond their level of understanding. For example, students can be trained to crescendo and decrescendo to approximate a musical performance of a given phrase, but without an understanding of the phrase, the musical potential of the phrase, and the underlying principles of musical expression, their performance will not be personally musical or meaningful. Imagine, for example, if students were trained to perform a play in a foreign language but they were never told the meaning of the lines they were saying. Again, the result might approximate a satisfying performance, but the meaning of the play would be minimized. So one of the first knowledge outcomes would be for students to understand the overall form of the work and the underlying phrase structure. Only then can they begin to contribute to the musical conversation.

But the conversation should go even further. The study of the particular work should be as an instance of a particular form and genre of works. For example, if an ensemble of high school choral students were studying a Bach cantata, they might compare the structure and compositional devices of several cantatas, including the one they will eventually perform.

Ultimately, however, the goal is always to increase the students' individual and collective musicianship as defined by the national standards, and to prepare them for eventual musical independence. This requires that the students operate at the highest levels of Bloom's taxonomy and *create* new musical products. One of the models supplied in *Shaping Sound Musicians* provides an excellent example. In this scenario, the ensemble students are studying and preparing to perform Gustav Holst's *First Suite for Military Band*, of which the first movement is a chaconne. The author listed several levels of possible outcomes for a portion of this study (2003, p. 35):

1. Students will define chaconne. (Knowledge)
2. Students will analyze an unfamiliar score and discover a chaconne. (Analysis, Application)
3. Students will take a theme from one of their scores and construct a chaconne that uses this pre-existing theme. (Synthesis)

As you can see from this simple example, the last outcome is far more sophisticated than either of the other two, and it requires that the students function as creative musicians (listeners, dancers, composers, improvisers, or conductors) rather than merely trained performers.

Affective Outcomes of CMP

Imagining affective outcomes is often more difficult than stating knowledge or skill outcomes. This is the consequence of commonly held misunderstandings about the affective domain. Often, an affective response is considered to be synonymous with an emotional response. But, in reality, it is more about valuing the cultural and personal role of music than the value of a specific musical performance. The authors of the CMP process suggest three lenses through which students can study the affective value of a work as an instance of a larger body of works. The first area to consider is the composer's craft. In this type of assessment, the students analyze, compare, and evaluate the writer's compositional decisions. For example, they might evaluate the composer's use of musical elements such as text or form and how the composer created the potential for musical meaning. Through the second lens, the students consider how they might enhance (or detract from) a performance of the work as a result of any performance decisions they might make such as phrasing, style, or tempo selection. Finally, the students create a view of their individual and collective relationship with the musical work, how it reflects their own musical knowledge or might artistically represent their understanding of life and their community.

ENSEMBLE EXPERTISE

One potential criticism of the CMP model is that, owing to its literature-driven view of curriculum development, it appears to emphasize verbal and written knowledge while neglecting authentic musical thinking—thinking in sounds—and fundamentals of ensemble performance; those are left for the director to develop. Reprising the look at expertise in chapter 6, the following section consider what 'expertise' means in the context of ensemble performance.

As you have read, expert musicians have two musical representations that facilitate learning new literature quickly. First, they have the fundamental performing skills to manipulate their instrument or voice to match their musical imagination. Second, they have basic musical knowledge that allows them to decipher new music quickly. In the context of ensemble performance, they are able to obtain musical information from their sheet music as easily as one might read a book; they easily develop a sound representation of what their music sounds like *without* playing or singing it out loud. And they are able to quickly determine how their part fits with the rest of the ensemble through study of the a score and recordings, along with deliberate listening during rehearsal—an internal representation of their part and its role in the work.

Development of Individual and Ensemble Skills

As you will recall, effective teachers have detailed knowledge of their students' current individual abilities and challenges. Yet large group instruction rarely allows teachers to assess individual students' abilities and provide individual feedback. Some large group instructors are able to effectively deploy technological solutions such as SoundCloud, SmartMusic, or other media to listen to and assess individual student performances. We know, however, that the asynchronous communication provided by these technologies is not a reasonable substitute for the kind of interactive communication that is mediated by individual and small group instruction.

Developing effective individual instruction can be as challenging as large group instruction. The specific feedback that is available in individual and small group instruction provides the student with the self-knowledge that enables productive individual practice. Moreover, the interaction in these instructional settings allow the teacher to probe and mold the students' thinking about performance.

Emerging research on the development of ensemble expertise points to the significant learning opportunities of small-group instruction, especially in preparation for chamber music repertoire, provided the instructor's goal is to coach musical understanding rather than simply prepare the group for performance. In these settings, the coach should guide the performers' musical listening and thinking. These small-group settings promote individual musical competence and confidence, along with understandings of how one's part including style and expression, matches and interacts with the other parts to create a cohesive musical expression. These musical understandings, as outlined in the next section, enable long-term musical independence.

Representations That Mediate Rnsemble Performance

In addition to the outcomes outlined in the CMP model, ensemble participation should also result in various generic sound representations that facilitate learning new repertoire—complex understandings of the entire piece, not an individual part—and generic skills that allow the students to present these representations during performance. These are separate from the specific representations and skills associated with a particular piece of literature.

Students perform at the level of their own understanding—their internal sound and skill representations of the performance. Therefore, for all ensemble performance tasks, performers (players and singers) constantly compare their internal sound representation with their actual contribution to the ensemble and automatically make adjustments to better match their imagined musical product. This is the oral-aural feedback loop. The ensemble leader's task is to help the performers develop accurate representations of the final product. If a performer's representations match those of the leader and the rest of the ensemble, then the task becomes simply matching the sound product to the representation.

What kinds of representations and associated skills mediate participation in an ensemble? As mentioned above, the first step is for the individual performers to create an internal sound representation of their part and then execute it during rehearsal. While playing in the ensemble, the performers then constantly compare their sound with the sounds of the others in an effort to match. They must balance their parts with those who may be performing the same line while balancing that musical line against others. They must also match timbre (tone color), pitch (intonation), and style (note length and shape). This sophisticated listening is often stymied by the technical requirements of the part.

From the perspective of skill, individual performers must be able to purposefully manipulate the sound envelopes they produce. In order to

balance with the ensemble (both the same and different lines), performers must be able to control their volume. To match pitch, they must be
able to purposefully manipulate their own pitch, even performing out of
tune to match wayward performers. To match style, they must be able to
manipulate note length and shape. All of this must be done while maintaining a characteristic tone, and the sounds must be executed simultaneously
(exhibiting precision).

It is beyond the scope of this book to discuss these individual and
ensemble representations and skills in detail, but the main points are these:

1. Performing in an ensemble requires a sophisticated musical imagination
   because players and singers perform no better than they can imagine;
2. Players and singers can learn to realize their musical imagination only if
   they have polished skills that are based on the oral-aural feedback loop,
   and the ability to decipher musical notation as sounds rather than performance instructions; and
3. The ensemble leader's main task is to help performers develop a sophisticated musical imagination.

PREPARING STUDENTS FOR MUSICAL INDEPENDENCE

Just as parents have to teach their children to function in society on their
own, and considering the purposes of public education, music teachers
should aim to give students musical independence. Yet current teaching
practices often result in a kind of musical dependence; even after years of
instruction, students still often depend on sheet music to tell them what
notes to perform, depend on someone else to tell them how to perform
them, and cannot determine for themselves how to make musical progress.
As a result, many cease any meaningful musical involvement at the end of
formal instruction because they are unable to locate an appropriate music
ensemble to join; they are dependent on the ensemble setting—with sheet
music and a conductor—to continue enjoying active music-making.

Students should develop two important competencies while under
the care of a professional music educator that will allow them to function
independently as a mature musician at the end of formal instruction. First,
they need to know how to practice and develop fundamental skills; after
selecting a new piece, they should be able to turn the notation into musical sound representations, develop the skill representations, if necessary, to
adequately translate their representations into sounds, and make appropriate artistic decisions to produce a satisfactory musical performance, alone

or with others. Second, in order to be free from the idea that they cannot play or sing without someone else producing notation for them and to be truly musically independent, students should be able to make adjustments to existing sheet music as needed, arrange simple selections for assorted voices or instruments, compose new tunes (even a countermelody for an existing work), and improvise basic melodies and accompaniments.

Music teachers often avoid teaching improvisation and composition because they are uncertain of their own abilities. Recent developments in pedagogical techniques and materials have made the process significantly less imposing. Keep in mind, however, that these outcomes should be included in any comprehensive musical curriculum. Teaching students to practice independently, however, seems so fundamental that the basic ideas are addressed here.

Teaching Students to Practice

If student musicians have a sound idea of a final musical product, then they are often able to perform the selection with limited direct instruction. Considering this fact, one of the most important tasks for teachers in training students to practice is to help them develop a musical representation as the end result of practice. Therefore, especially for young students, teachers should function as musical models and perform themselves or provide recorded examples for their students. This is especially true for beginners, who will be less proficient at converting notation into sound representations. Teachers may sing or play or use audio and video recordings. The use of models has benefited students' ability to identify and match pitch, perceive rhythms, be self-motivated to practice. Video modeling is especially effective in teaching the physical aspects of performing.

It is just as important to model and assist with practicing. At first, teachers should provide supervised practice opportunities, during which they can discuss various strategies for solving particular performance issues. Second, teachers can follow up with structured music practice plans for students to implement on their own. Subsequently, students should prepare and submit their own deliberate practice plans for feedback on their practice process.

Cognitive Strategies, Analysis and Structure

Musicians can significantly improve the efficiency of their practice time by planning their practice session in advance and by selecting effective practice strategies and tactics. Prior to practicing, musicians should specify attainable goals that can be accomplished during the allotted time, select strategies for each goal, and determine how to assess whether the goal has been reached.

Determining appropriate practice goals requires musicians to analyze their music for technical details (for example, key, meter, and rhythmic patterns) and to divide the music into manageable practice units. The best strategy for technical passages is slow practice. Often young musicians are unable to perceive their technical errors; slow practice makes mistakes more obvious and prevents the use of tricks to play the technical passage that may, in the long run, result in bad performance habits.

It may be surprising to young performers that, under certain conditions, mental practice—imagining playing or singing a specific musical selection—can be nearly as effective as actual practice. First, mental practice is more effective for polishing previously learned music than for learning new music because the aural feedback is missing; students must have a strong sound representation of the selection or errors might inadvertently be reinforced. Second, the effect of mental practice is maximized if students thoroughly understand the task and can express the task verbally. Finally, mental practice should be used in conjunction with physical practice; it can be useful in reducing the physical strain of performance, thus enabling longer practice sessions.

Teachers play an important role in developing effective practice strategies in their students. Young musicians may not be able to design their own practice goals, strategies, and assessments and may therefore need their teacher to do so for them at first. These teacher-designed practice sessions later function as models for students to develop their own practice sessions.

Autonomy

There is no denying that there is an integral link between practice and achievement. It is also true that achieving self-determined goals leads to motivation to practice. Teachers would be wise, therefore, to allow their students to select their own goals within predetermined parameters. Doing so provides students with a sense of musical autonomy and control, which is, after all, the ultimate goal of musical instruction. Teachers should take care to include some facets of student self-determination in their curricula.

CONCLUSION

Musical curricula should not only go beyond preparing students to perform at the next student assembly, music contest, or Friday night football game, but should primarily prepare students for a life of independent musicianship. Music curricula should provide opportunities for students to engage in authentic music making—listening, performing, composing, and improvising. After all, the one who does the (musical) work does the (musical) learning.

Finally, it is essential to realize that music teachers don't teach music, they teach students. All curriculum development should be focused on the needs of the students, not on program development or teacher recognition. The teacher's task is to align the music curriculum with the intended outcomes of public education.

PROJECT

1. Explain the following concepts:
   – Meaningful curriculum
   – Explain why the two listed factors influence a teacher's philosophy. What factors influence a music teacher's philosophy and values? In two sentences, explain your current understanding of those two factors.
2. What are the similarities and the differences between each of the early childhood instructional methodologies listed in the chapter? Find out more about one of the methodologies and explain it further.
3. In a previous chapter, competent instruction was defined as helping students understand the big ideas so that they learn how to solve problems on their own. Imagine a music program in which the curriculum promotes musical independence as outlined in this chapter. What new student learning opportunities can you imagine? How does this hypothetical program compare to the program you participated in?
4. Research the five early childhood methodologies described in this chapter. See what additional information you can find on the musical and instructional philosophies of each. What instructional materials or plans can you find? How are each of the approaches similar and how do they differ? Search for professional organizations and professional development opportunities that might exist in your area.

CHAPTER 9

Designing Meaningful Instruction

The goal of Chapter 8, "Meaningful Curriculum," was to have you begin to think about the desired outcomes of a musical education beyond well-done programs and performances. In that sense, of the four unique types of teacher knowledge, curriculum is a form of subject matter knowledge in that it attempts to answer the philosophical question, "What is it about music that makes it important to study?" So far we have examined three types of teacher knowledge. Chapters 4 and 5 examined knowledge of subject matter. Chapters 6 and 7 discussed knowledge of how students learn and some of the implications for pedagogy. Chapter 8 contained a philosophical argument for what should be taught, based on knowledge of subject matter. In this chapter, we begin to examine teaching skills—pedagogy—in more detail and, more specifically, how teachers prepare for successful instruction. The process of instructional design, which is very similar to the process of preparing for deliberate practice, requires a special kind of teacher knowledge that is *not* one of the four key types but is, in fact, the *synthesis* of three types.

PEDAGOGICAL CONTENT KNOWLEDGE

Much of the important, but often hidden, work of teaching involves preparing for student learning experiences, which requires anticipating how students will respond to instruction. Having "profound knowledge" about the fundamentals of music is a prerequisite, but that alone does not adequately prepare one to teach. Effective teachers also have profound knowledge of how students develop musical understanding, or knowledge of students, and the specific instructional skills to help students attain those understandings, or knowledge of pedagogy (Grossman, Schoenfeld, & Lee, 2005, p. 206). The synthesis of these three types of knowledge—subject matter knowledge, knowledge of students, and knowledge of pedagogy—that enables teachers to design meaningful experiences for students is referred to as *pedagogical content knowledge* (PCK). In many ways, PCK involves knowing how students are likely to *mis*-understand the subject, what those misunderstandings indicate about student thinking, and how to overcome them. In summary, music PCK could be represented as a synthesis of the knowledge of the important ideas in music, the ways those ideas can be represented in explanations and demonstrations, and how those ideas can be presented to make them comprehensible to students, depending on their age and prior knowledge (Shulman, 1986).

Instructional empathy is the ability for teachers to put themselves in the place of their students and imagine the new instructional content from their perspective. You will recall that one of the characteristics of experts is that the knowledge associated with their expertise is so obvious to them that they often fail to imagine that others do not comprehend the information exactly as they do. It is important, therefore, that you consciously adopt your students' perspective as you prepare new instruction.

This is especially true if you are working with students whose cultural or socioeconomic background may be different from your own. I discuss this confounding variable further in Chapter 11.

SIX ESSENTIAL QUESTIONS OF PCK

One of the important aspects of PCK and instructional design is anticipating students' responses to instructional experiences. Teachers learn this pedagogical skill by observing how students have responded to previous instructional experiences. How can preservice teachers learn to anticipate student responses to instruction without actual teaching experience? One effective method is to observe the interaction between instructors and students in an authentic instructional context. The goal is to examine the teacher's thinking by observing the students' responses to teachers' instructions, comparing how different teachers work toward similar instructional goals, analyzing a variety of curricular materials and designs, observing students for evidence of understanding, and engaging in-service teachers and students in dialogue about their experiences (Feiman-Nemser, 2001). Through these experiences, preservice teachers are able to answer questions in these six areas that define music pedagogical content knowledge (paraphrased from Grossman, Schoenfeld, & Lee, 2005, p. 208):

1. What is music? According to various recognized experts, what are the core concepts and skills that enable musical understanding? Are there different definitions of music and, if so, does it matter? How do the National Standards define understanding music and the core competencies that are required?
2. What are the purposes and intended outcomes of public education in the United States? Does the study of music align with these purposes? What are the most important aspects that students should study, and do those priorities change with the student's age?
3. What does musical understanding look and sound like? What are the different aspects of musical understanding and performance? How does musical understanding develop? Does music have an age-dependent developmental sequence? What kinds of experiences mediate musical understanding?
4. What are the generally accepted music curricula? Are these curricula (methods) based on differing concepts of music and musical learning? Do these curricula and methods align with the various national, state, and local standards for music? Do these curricula and methods work across various grade levels? Can teachers easily use these materials to design and deliver musical learning experiences for students?
5. How is musical learning—knowledge, skills, and understanding—assessed? What tools and techniques are useful in assessing student musical learning? How can music teachers use the results of assessment to promote effective musical instruction and musical learning?
6. What kinds of instructional techniques are correlated with effective teaching and student learning of particular kinds of musical concepts? Do those techniques vary depending on the students' developmental level or age? Are there certain kinds of examples or analogies (ways of viewing the materials) that are particularly effective in promoting student understanding?

Although teachers often use their PCK to make moment-to-moment instructional decisions during the act of teaching, the supreme value of a teacher's PCK is engaged during instructional design. The processes of delivering effective instruction and observing instruction in an authentic context are each covered in a subsequent chapter. The purpose of the remaining sections of this chapter is to provide you with an overview of the instructional design process—the thinking teachers engage in prior to instruction—and assessment—the kind of thinking teachers engage in subsequent to instruction.

INSTRUCTIONAL DESIGN

You have read that there is no such thing as talent and, therefore, all of your musical skills were learned. Just as there are no naturally born musicians, no person is born with a gift for teaching. In both cases, some may appear to have a gift that makes music performance or teaching seem easy, but their abilities are the result of their prior experiences. The core skills in teaching are instructional design and delivery. As with any expert ability, these competencies can be quite challenging to learn and may require years of practice. For young teachers, the core instructional design skill is to "be able to design or select assessment tasks that probe for students' conceptual understanding and reflect important learning goals" (Shepard, Hammerness, Darling-Hammond, & Rust, 2005, p. 281). In the subsequent sections of this chapter, you will read an overview of the instructional design process and then examine each stage in the design process.

AN OVERVIEW OF UNDERSTANDING BY DESIGN

The Understanding by Design (UbD) process (Wiggins & McTighe, 2005) has been generally accepted as the gold standard for instructional design. Typically, novice teachers tend to begin their instructional planning process by imagining teacher and student *activities*—by deciding *how* they are going to teach rather than first determining *why* they are going to teach, *who* they are going to teach, and *what* they are going to teach. In music classes, for example, instruction tends to be designed around preparation of repertoire for an upcoming program or performance, or for in-class activities. In *Understanding by Design*, Wiggins and McTigue promote a "backward design" process in which the teacher begins by identifying the core understandings—the fundamental knowledge and skills—that will prepare students for subsequent learning and enable them to perform with understanding on their own when instruction concludes. The process has three stages:

1) **Determining desired outcomes.** This is the "backward" part of the design process as compare to the typical planning process. Here, the teacher begins with the end in mind and works backward logically and chronologically to the beginning of the instructional process. The first step in this stage is to determine the goal of the instruction: What national, state, or local standard, program objective, or learning goal will be addressed during instruction? This applies whether the teacher is planning for a lesson, a unit, or a full academic year. Second, what

big ideas or concepts are embedded within those standards, objectives, or goals? What understandings should the students acquire during instruction? What kinds of prior knowledge or misunderstandings are they likely to have prior to instruction that can be leveraged or must be addressed? What are the typical ways in which students misunderstand these new big ideas or concepts? Third, what "essential questions" can be used to drive the students' inquiry process? Finally, what transferable knowledge and skills—understandings—will the students acquire during this learning unit?

2) **Determining evidence of learning.** After determining the intended outcomes, teachers must next determine what evidence they will use to prove "beyond a reasonable doubt" that their students have achieved them. This evidence should arise from authentic performances. In music, this would include performing, creating, and responding in authentic ways. These performances should be the result of their own efforts rather than the teacher's. Second, the teacher must determine the criteria by which the quality of these student performances will be judged: What are the characteristics of emerging, proficient, and exemplary performance? Third, the teacher must decide what other kinds of corroborating evidence must be gathered to determine that the students are performing with understanding rather than as the result of drill and practice. Finally, teachers must design opportunities for their students to reflect on and assess their own performances and their learning process.

3) **Designing the learning plan.** The key task for the teacher now is to create learning experiences *from the students'* perspective rather than simply planning what the teacher will do. First, it is important for the students to have an overview of the entire learning experience (unit or lesson) and what they will be expected to do. The experiences must motivate the students by engaging their prior knowledge and piquing their curiosity and imagination. During the learning process, students must have opportunities to evaluate their work and revise their understanding of the concepts and their approach to the learning task. Finally, as much as possible, the learning experience should address the individual interests, needs and abilities of each student.

STAGE 1: DETERMINING DESIRED OUTCOMES

Perhaps the most important outcome of any music teacher education program is for the future teacher to have a *vision* of what musical classroom instruction *could* be, as opposed to the kind of classroom experience he or she had. The basis of this argument is the original product-based NAfME National Standards for Music Education:

1. Singing, alone and with others, a varied repertoire of music.
2. Performing on instruments, alone and with others, a varied repertoire of music.
3. Improvising melodies, variations, and accompaniments.
4. Composing and arranging music within specified guidelines.
5. Reading and notating music.
6. Listening to, analyzing, and describing music.
7. Evaluating music and music performances.
8. Understanding relationships between music, the other arts, and disciplines outside the arts.
9. Understanding music in relation to history and culture.

One could argue that, in general, current music education practice in the United States is fairly effective at accomplishing standards 1, 2, 5 and, perhaps, 7. (Although one could reasonably argue that the *quality* of literature selection is often questionable.) The other standards, however, are often either neglected or only addressed in certain settings; only students in jazz ensembles, for example, often have opportunities to improvise, and only students in Advanced Placement or International Baccalaureate courses are required to address the other standards.) Reflect for a moment on how many of these standards were addressed in your elementary or secondary musical education or even in your university courses.

Many teachers consider improvisation to be one of the most difficult standards to address. This may be due, in part, to their vision of what improvisation means: the solo improviser with a jazz group. To the untrained player, this type of complex performance is quite intimidating because the performance options are nearly boundless. Improvisation, often considered spontaneous composition, is really no more than playing or singing by ear. In Orff ensembles, elementary-age students are able to improvise simple melodies and accompaniments precisely because they are given limited options from which to choose. In later years, effective teachers are able to leverage this prior learning and help students improvise simple melodies and accompaniments during early instrumental instruction. The key, as it turns out, is for the students to be able to link the sounds they imagine and their skills to produce those sounds to develop a new kind of musical understanding. Similarly, in the other seldom-addressed standards, students are required to link their musical knowledge with their musical skills—what they can hear or perform—to create a meaningful musical understanding.

Your primary goal while defining outcomes is to specify what the students should be able to do after instruction that they cannot already do. In some performance scenarios, the outcomes may include the teacher's functioning as a co-artist.

Understanding Understanding

You have now read about two taxonomies that explain knowledge. First, Bloom's Taxonomy (Bloom, 1956) and its expansion by other scholars indicated that there are three types of knowledge: cognitive, psychomotor, and affective. This framework, however useful it may be in understanding the various types of knowledge, has limited power to assist in designing effective instructional outcomes. Second, Wiggins and McTigue (2005) proposed a six-faceted explanation of how students can demonstrate their understanding beyond a reasonable doubt:

1. **Explanation:** Far beyond simply stating facts, students are able to connect a set of facts or events using sophisticated explanations, theories, or hypotheses by answering complex *how, what,* and *why* questions.
2. **Interpretation:** Students are required to interpret stories, images, or musical compositions to create personal meaning by answering questions about implications for subjective experience, consequences, and making sense.
3. **Application:** Students are required to solve novel problems by considering what prior knowledge or procedural skills would be most effective in this particular setting.
4. **Perspective:** Students are required to grapple with the strengths, weaknesses, and ambiguities of different possible explanations and interpretations, along with their implications for and the potential consequences of pursuing different options.
5. **Empathy:** Students are required to explain another person's or group's point of view, including the feelings that may give rise to that view.
6. **Self-knowledge:** Students learn more efficiently when they have knowledge of their own strengths and weaknesses, what they already know and need to learn, their own most effective strategies for learning particular kinds of knowledge and skills, and their own biases and patterns of thought. To obtain self-knowledge, students must be challenged to reflect on their own learning behaviors, set personal goals, devise strategies for reaching those goals, and then reflect on their successes and failures.

The next step in the process is to develop questions or prompts to which students respond by explaining, interpreting, applying, imagining perspectives, empathizing with others, and reflecting to develop self-knowledge.

Developing Essential Questions

As music teachers plan for instruction, it is quite easy to become distracted and design activities to prepare for an upcoming performance, maintain classroom control, or simply entertain the students. The challenge for teachers, and for students, is to remain focused on the essential elements of instruction: to acquire the knowledge and skills that foster musical understanding and to prepare students for future learning. Developing essential questions during this phase can help focus the plan, motivate students by connecting them with prior experiences, provide personal connections for the students that will make the learning meaningful, and prepare the students to explore similar concepts and skills in more depth at a later date.

So, what are the characteristics of these essential questions? First, they are ambiguous and require complex, reasoned, and nuanced answers. Consider, for example, the question, "How do composers use tension and release in a composition to foster both a sense of forward motion and finality?" Or "How do composers use form to create unity and variety in one composition?" Or "What performance techniques can musicians use to enhance the original intent of a composer?" In order to answer this type of question, students will be required to dig deep into the structure of the piece, speculate about the composer's intent, justify their answers, and expand their understanding of how music is experienced.

Second, teachers should be able to rephrase questions to address students at a variety of instruction levels, from students in an elementary-level Orff ensemble to graduate students in a music theory forum. Essential questions foster not only a sense of centrality of discrete bits of information or isolated skills but also require students to dig into the core of the topic or discipline. One of the core questions in music is, "How can musical form be used in an artistic manner to represent meaning and subjective life experience?" Such a question can be examined by young students as they examine the structure of simple folk songs and rhymes, or by graduate students struggling through serialism or Schenkerian analysis.

Third, these questions are abstracted from the literature or repertoire in question, and this is key. If properly prompted, students can engage their prior learning and use repertoire from previous units to solidify their new understandings. Subsequently, students will be able to transfer what they learned in the current unit to repertoire in future units for deeper understanding. The point is not only for the students to grasp the structure and form of this one selection but also to engage in the larger question about the functions and purposes of musical form and how they relate to listening to, performing, or composing music. Consider, for example, how studying a theme and variation form may inform the task of improvising.

Writing Objectives

The final step in stage 1 of this instructional design process is to reframe the essential questions and instructional outcomes, or descriptions of what the students will understand at the end of instruction, *and* descriptions of the skills the students will have to master and through which they will demonstrate their new understandings. Including both outcomes—knowledge and skills—is especially important in the creative arts. There would be limited value, for instance, in students' knowing and then stating the characteristics of march style or Renaissance madrigal style without having the skills to perform a march with the correct style *and* intuitively performing in the correct style when warranted by the musical repertoire. Musical understanding is a result of the synthesis of some musical knowledge with some musical skill—performing, composing, or listening. Students cannot demonstrate their understanding, in this case of march style or madrigal style, until they *transfer* their knowledge and skills to a new musical selection. The concept of transfer is covered more thoroughly during the discussion of stage 2 of the design process.

One common mistake teachers make when designing objectives is to write "The students will know *how* . . ." Yes, at some point the students will have to demonstrate their understanding some *how*, but it is better to separate the knowledge and skills goals by writing multiple statements that include "Students will understand *that* . . ." and "Students will demonstrate *how* . . ." Another option is to write goal statements in the following format: "Students will understand *that* . . . and demonstrate their understanding *by* . . ."

At this point, it's appropriate to consider the fact that individual students in any class will arrive with different levels of readiness to learn the material, for a variety of reasons. First, each student has a unique collection of educational experiences that impacts his or her readiness to learn. Second, each student has different learning characteristics (such as preferred learning style) and personal interests. Finally, as the general population becomes more diverse, students arrive with differing cultural backgrounds and linguistic abilities.

In order to be optimally effective, teachers must plan for *differentiated instruction* to accommodate students' abilities, backgrounds, preferences, and interests. Although it is beyond the scope of this text to adequately address designing instructional plans to accommodate all of the needs of a diverse student population, several important concepts will help you in understanding the process.

First, differentiating instruction does not imply that students are engaging with different content. The idea is that students should engage with the content at a level and in a manner best suited to them *within* the normal student grouping.

Second, a differentiated learning plan should include information on a specific student's unique abilities, challenges, and interests. Knowledge of the student's interests provides an entry pathway to the content. The plan should detail the best manner for the student to grasp the *content*, which instructional *process* should be used to engage the student, and what student *product* would best demonstrate understanding of the content (Darrow, 2014).

Finally, you should be aware which students in your class have been identified as having special learning needs and any individual educational plans that may have been developed for them. In this case, you should be sure to collaborate with the special education instructors to ensure the best possible outcomes for your students or students.

STAGE 2: DETERMINING EVIDENCE OF LEARNING

After developing the instructional goals, many teachers proceed directly to planning instruction activities. Following this sequence, without having determined what evidence will be sufficient to prove learning, will more likely result in the final assessment task aligning with the instructional activities rather than the instructional goals. In the end, the students might successfully complete their assessment task but not attain the understandings dictated by the instructional goals. To assure *alignment* between the instructional goals and the final assessment, the assessments must be designed prior to the instructional activities.

Before moving on to the process of writing the objectives, we need to agree on some common concepts and terminology regarding assessment.

A Primer on Assessment and Feedback

It is unfortunate but true that most in-service teachers do not follow best practices for assessment as outlined by educational researchers. When queried about their definition of assessment, most teachers jump immediately to the idea of testing students and providing grades at the end of instruction. When following that pattern of instructional design, teachers have no idea if their students are attaining the outcomes outlined in their plan. In fact, these teachers are engaging in *evaluation* rather than *assessment*. Fortunately, there are clear models for designing and delivering various types of assessments—measurements of student progress—that are useful for revising instruction *during the instructional phase of the unit*.

There are subtle differences between evaluation, as practiced by most teachers, and *summative assessment*. The purpose of evaluation is to determine the final outcomes of instruction and to assign a grade. The purpose of any kind of assessment is to provide specific information about student progress to the teacher *and to the student*. Summative assessment happens to occur also at the end of the instructional period, the purpose being to improve subsequent instruction by the teacher and learning efforts by the student. The purpose of *formative assessment*, which occurs during instruction, is to guide current teaching practice and student learning efforts. Any type of assessment is designed to improve teaching and learning. Research suggests that the use of formative assessment may be the single most effective instructional technique for improving learning.

To be most effective, formative assessment procedures should be planned for as a part of the instructional design, be integrated with instruction, and provide students with an awareness of the various levels of learning success. Formative assessment feedback should not merely inform a student whether he or she has have answered a question correctly on a quiz. Formative feedback should 1) compare the student's work to an agreed-on standard or criterion, 2) identify both the strong and weak areas of the student's work, and 3) suggest ways in which the student can improve both the learning product and their learning process (Wiggins & McTighe, 2005).

Formative feedback may involve *formal assessment* methods such as performances, written tests or quizzes, and other results that students may produce, or *informal assessment* methods, such as observation and discussion. Whatever method is selected, the goal of formative feedback is for both teacher and student to be able to answer three simple questions: (1) What are you trying to accomplish? (2) How much progress have you made, and what barriers are holding you back? and (3) What do you need to do to reach the goal? During this formative period, teachers should always be aware of potential misunderstandings that may be impeding student progress.

If the instructional outcomes from stage 1 of the design process are clearly written, it is easier for the teacher to design the summative assessment and feedback mechanisms and to imagine the students completing them. All too often, teachers simply rely on students' written answers to document learning. It is important to use a variety of types of assessment in order to amass a "preponderance of evidence" of student learning and *understanding*. In order to demonstrate musical understanding, music students should primarily be engaged in authentic musical activities— performing, conducting, improvising, or composing—and the necessary activities to prepare the final product. For example, in preparing for a performance of a given work, it may be appropriate for a student to analyze the work, investigate the history of a work and its composer, and then create a written document, but the point is to use the information gathered during the preparation to inform the authentic performance of the work. The student might also develop a long-term deliberate practice plan. In any case, the summative assessment should be performance-based, should mirror a real-world context as closely as possible, should be appropriately challenging, and should require the student to transfer and synthesize existing knowledge and skills to create a new product.

If teachers are going to gather a wide range of evidence to document student learning, then they must use a wide repertoire of assessment tools. One challenge is to select the appropriate assessment tool for the type of student task.

Assessment Instruments

One of the intended outcomes of the entire educational and learning process is for students to become able to function independently. That requires students to set appropriate goals and then be able to design a process for achieving these goals. (This is, fundamentally, the concept behind deliberate practice.) As a step to that end, student must internalize an understanding of what qualifies as good work. Teachers start this process by designing assessment tools that define levels of excellence or accomplishment. Various assessment tools have differing levels of specificity, and there are variables that often make one tool more appropriate than another. For now, we're going to examine three types: checklists, rating scales, and rubrics.

Some types of performance tasks only require simple binary yes-or-no types of evaluation. For example, assembling a clarinet is an easy procedure that can be mastered in a short period of time and assessed without difficulty. For this task, a simple *checklist* of steps in the procedure would be acceptable because there are no degrees of success; either the step was executed correctly and in sequence or it was not.

Once a student has demonstrated the ability to perform a particular skill, it may be appropriate to measure how consistently or how well he or she does it using a *rating scale*. A rating scale provides the evaluator, usually the teacher, with a range of options, perhaps from 1 to 5. The ends of the range must be specified with, for example, "never to always" or "poor to excellent." In a summative assessment, students can then be awarded points for each level of achievement, and from these a final score can be determined. Research indicates that a single assessor is likely to be consistent in the use of a given rating scale. But when that same rating scale is used by more than one assessor, each may be personally consistent but the evaluations may be markedly different.

Three other elements must be considered to determine whether our newly designed assessment tools will be useful for instruction. The first concern is whether the tool is *valid*: Does the assessment tool actually measure the understanding specified in the learning outcome? The second is whether the tool is *reliable*: If we apply the same type of assessment tool to the same student or group of students, will we consistently get the same result? In either case, if the answer is no, the assessment tool needs to be redesigned or replaced. The third and final concern is whether the assessment instrument is *sufficient*: Does it collect enough data to confirm the student's level of understanding—both knowledge and skill—beyond a reasonable doubt? If the assessment instrument itself meets these three criteria, then it is sufficient.

If the assessment instrument is considered to be valid, reliable, and sufficient, then the teacher must decide the criteria that determine how successful the students were at achieving the goals and objectives of the unit.

It is important to understand that sophisticated tasks require sophisticated measurement tools. A *rubric* is essentially a rating scale with detailed descriptions of the various levels of understanding. A rubric may be used to assess a student performance on a single, holistic criterion or on a series of categories for the various facets of the performance. Each level of achievement should have a detailed description of what it entails. For example, what are the *exact* characteristics of a proficient performance? The more detailed the descriptors, the more accurate the assessment by the teacher will be. And, research on the use of rubrics has shown that detailed descriptors of the levels of achievement result in more consistency in assessments by multiple assessors.

The backward design process outlined here suggests a process through which the various assessment instruments can be designed. During the work of stage 1, teachers develop specific learning outcomes. Each learning outcome from stage 1 implies a specific assessment tool to be designed or selected in stage 2, often before the specific performance task has been designated. The words and phrases in the original standards from which the learning outcome is derived can be used as source material for the rubric categories and descriptors.

You will recall that continuous feedback is one of the essential components of deliberate practice and also that feedback may be the single most important variable in student success. However, not all feedback must come from the teacher. In order to develop musical (and personal) independence, it is essential that students learn to perform self-assessment and self-evaluation. of the products of learning and the learning efforts themselves. Because it is so essential, the student self-assessment process must be included in the instructional design. The easiest way to do this is to allow students to self-assess using the same formal and informal assessment tools that the teacher will use. When you designed your deliberate practice plans, you determined which informal feedback mechanisms would be most appropriate depending on the specific practice goal. The same is true for student self-assessment. Students should always be given the opportunity to view or listen to video or audio recordings of mock performances. Older students should always be required to submit formal self-evaluations of final projects or performances.

Finally, you will recall that the purpose of assessment is not only to assign grades but also to improve the entire teaching-learning process. Effective teachers use the data gathered from formal and informal assessments to adjust instruction in the moment and to adjust the overall learning plan. In order to understand their students' thinking, teachers must explain the students' response to instruction, interpret the results, apply the results to future instructional designs, develop a variety of perspectives and explanations for the results, empathize with their students, and reflect on their own strengths and weaknesses as teachers.

A Primer on Feedback

The quality of instructional feedback of any type—formal or informal, formative or summative, teacher-generated or self-evaluation—can be determined by examining three factors:

1. *Timeliness*: feedback should occur shortly after the student effort. Feedback of any type that occurs significantly later than the initial effort has less impact than immediate feedback. That being said, it is also beneficial to reflect on one's effort, process, and product some time after the process is concluded and the product is complete. Doing so allows the emotion and the self-defense mechanisms associated with the performance to subside, often resulting in a more accurate self-assessment.

2. *Specificity*: Even more than positive or approval feedback, students desire specific feedback. Specific feedback helps students hone their mental image of the task or product, which enables them to make independent improvement. In fact, students will often go a long time without approval or emotional encouragement as long as they perceive progress toward a goal based on specific feedback.

3. *Relevance*: In an efficient learning effort, the student is focused on solving a specific knowledge or skill challenge. Feedback that is related to that task, whether teacher- or student-directed, is far more effective than feedback on an unrelated task. Unfortunately, unrelated feedback is often evident during instructional episodes by novice teachers. Generally, these teachers are so delighted that they noticed an issue that would benefit from feedback that they offer the feedback even when it is unrelated to the task at hand. In such situations, novice teachers would be advised to provide timely and specific feedback on the current task and then initiate a new instructional effort to address the newly discovered issue.

Planning for Assessment and Feedback

Translating generic learning outcomes into concrete learning goals is, perhaps, at the very crux of the challenge of teaching. Outcomes, like learning standards, are intended to be global in nature and applicable in a wide range of instructional contexts. Outcomes paint the broadest possible picture of the understandings students will demonstrate at the end of instruction. Objectives, in contrast, should help eachers and students envision how various kinds of knowledge and skills will be applied within a particular instructional setting and what kinds of products will be produced to demonstrate how the outcomes are being accomplished. For example, a learning objective might specify that students will demonstrate an understanding of theme and variation form. A goal might specify that a student demonstrate that understanding by analyzing a specific work in theme and variation form.

Prerequisites and ZPD

One of the most common errors teachers make when designing goal statements is the failure to consider the students' current abilities, along with the prerequisite knowledge and skills needed to succeed at the learning goals. This is usually brought about by failing to use a backward design process and merely designing activities rather than learning opportunities. It is highly frustrating for both teachers and students to get halfway into a lesson and realize that the students are unprepared for the challenges. Considering the prerequisite skills and required knowledge during the design of the learning opportunities will help teachers maintain instructional momentum.

Several related techniques may be useful in avoiding the surprise finding students unprepared for a particular learning activity. First, a detailed task analysis, which includes the sequence of learning tasks required to accomplish the ultimate goal, will help teachers design the proper learning sequence. Second, teachers need to be certain which of these learning tasks students have already accomplished. Third, teachers should have a clear understanding of what the students can currently achieve independently, what they could achieve with proper support, and what they could not achieve even with proper support. This range s called the zone of proximal development (ZPD), a phrase originally coined by Lev Vygotsky. The point of instruction, of course, is for students to be able to achieve independently what earlier they could only accomplish with support from a teacher or a more-capable other. When designing learning activities, teachers can group students such that some are within their ZPD and others are beyond it. Those who are beyond it can function as the more-capable other.

Teachers also need to consider the ZPD in terms of student motivation. Remember that student tasks can be divided into three categories: the comfort zone (what they can already do), the learning zone (what they could do with some assistance or work), and the panic zone (tasks they are not ready for). Students are more motivated and engaged when they are working within their own ZPD—their learning zone. Students are who consistently working on tasks they can already achieve will become bored; those who are working on tasks they cannot accomplish regardless of the support they receive will become frustrated.

Finally, keep in mind that, because of their differing levels of ability and understanding, different students require scaffolding of various types and intensities.

Outcome Statements

After all the careful considerations about outcomes, goals, and assessment tools, it is time to specify *exactly* what the students will do to demonstrate whether they have mastered the intended outcomes. You will recall that your objective statements often are in the forms "Students will understand *that* . . .," "Students will demonstrate *how* . . .," or "Students will understand *that* . . . and demonstrate their understanding *by* . . ." These statements were free of materials and, by design, generic. The instructional plan, discussed in the next section, covers the instructional process. These outcome statements will specify the *condition, content, context,* and *criteria* for the final student product. For example, given a novel line of text (condition), the student will individually (context) analyze each part, write the phonetic notation for each, and then speak the line (content) without error (criteria).

You should pay special attention to the verbs in your outcome statements. These specify what the student will do to demonstrate understanding, in terms of both knowledge and skill.

Performance Tasks

The task of developing final goals and summative assessment activities can be daunting for any teacher, but the task may be especially difficult for novice teachers who have primarily experienced teacher-directed instruction and summative assessments that only require them to recall information. Given that music students demonstrate their understanding through *authentic* musical tasks, it is helpful to consider the real-world context of an active musician. In *Understanding by Design* (2005), Wiggins and McTighe suggest the mnemonic device GRASPS (Goal-Role-Audience-Situation-Performance-Standard) as a way to develop performance tasks.

Let's consider a specific advanced example that might be appropriate for an AP music theory course. Frank Ticheli's *An American Elegy* was written to memorialize the students who were killed in the Columbine High School massacre in 1999. Embedded within the piece is the melody from the Columbine High School alma mater. The vision (lesson goal) is that a high school chorus would perform a new four-part chorale setting of that melody using new text to memorialize those who died and to rail against the senseless loss of life.

> **Goal**: Compose a four-part chorale setting using a pre-existing melody.

Role: You are a composer.

Audience: The audience for the work will be the community and the ensemble members themselves.

Situation: As the composer, you have been asked to create a hymn to be sung by a high school chorus to memorialize students who have died.

Performance: The new work will be performed at the final concert of the year.

Standard: The work will be judged not only on technical and musical merits, but also on the effect on the audience.

Obviously, this project will require a considerable amount of time to accomplish. As compared to a standard recall task, the students working on this project will be challenged to synthesize and transfer their existing knowledge and seek out new knowledge and skills. The teacher's task is to design a school year's worth of learning experiences to prepare students for this culminating project. During and after the project, students will be required to explain the work and their work, interpret the composition to develop personal meaning, apply what they have learned previously to this new project, develop a variety of perspectives and explanations, empathize with others' views, and develop self-knowledge by reflecting on their own strengths and weaknesses.

Acquiring Evidence of Understanding

When designing the final assessment tasks, it may be useful for you to reconsider the six facets of understanding: explanation, interpretation, application, perspective, empathy, and self-knowledge. Within the final project, you should ask the students to explain the general concepts, interpret the value or implication of the new knowledge, apply the new knowledge or skill to a novel problem, demonstrate different perspectives that others may have, demonstrate genuine empathy for other's views, and provide an opportunity for the students to reflect on their own self-knowledge and abilities.

These kinds of tasks can be assessed using a variety of tools. Along with various checklists, rating scales, and rubrics, students could be expected to develop a portfolio of their work that demonstrates the various facets of their new understandings. Or students could be required to keep a personal journal that documents their problem-solving processes as they grapple with each facet of their new understandings. If the students have been working on several projects throughout the course, it may be appropriate for them to create a portfolio of their best work that also documents their growth through the process.

Planning for Feedback Opportunities

The best feedback is always interaction between the teacher and student. Assessment tools can be used to guide the conversation. But since providing quality feedback is one of the most important instructional functions, the task should not be left to coincidence and serendipity. Opportunities to provide formal and informal feedback should be included in the instructional design. Formal feedback should be provided at the conclusion of each major step of a project as identified by the task analysis. For example, if the students are writing an essay, they should receive formal feedback *after* each step of the process is completed, such as selecting the topic, writing the outline, or completing the draft. Informal feedback should be provided *during* each step of the process.

In addition to keeping students on track, feedback provides students with motivation to successfully complete the project. Especially when interacting during informal feedback sessions, the primary goal may be to engage the student in self-assessment. During such sessions, students should be asked to explain their work and the process they are using to complete the task. Gentle questioning, along with checklists and rubrics, might help the students develop more insight into their work, motivate them more, and help them develop a vision of the finished product more than direct critique of their draft.

STAGE 3: DESIGNING THE LEARNING PLAN

Having defined the learning outcomes and designed the goals and assessments, the final task is to design the actual learning plan. This is the point when the backward design sequence provides significant advantages over approaches that begin with designing instructional activities. With the end of the process clearly envisioned, the design of the student learning activities will be both more effective and more efficient in achieving the desired outcomes because of the *alignment* between the outcomes and the activities. Three major concerns must be addressed when designing the activities: prerequisites, sequence, and multiple opportunities to learn. The goal when designing the learning plan is to make sure the plan content and the chosen instructional methods align with the outcomes that were designed in stage 1 and the assessments that were designed in stage 2.

Task Analysis, Skill Development

Musical understanding and musical performance are the products of musical skills synthesized with musical knowledge. All too often, music teachers consider the performance skills to be the end goal of instruction rather than only one indicator of musical understanding. The focus on skill development is inappropriate, but neglecting skill development will inhibit the development of musical understanding.

The instructional design process for skill development is *task analysis*. Task analysis is accomplished by determining the sequence of the discrete tasks required to perform the given skill, along with the bits of knowledge that enable performance of the task. For example, assembling a clarinet requires a certain sequence of tasks. Along with performing specific actions, the students must be able to identify the various parts of the clarinet prior to beginning the assembly, and they must know how particular parts of the clarinet work such as the bridge keys work, but only at the exact moment when they need to connect the upper and lower joints.

In general, tasks should be divided into no more than eight steps. Each step, however, may have sub-steps or bits of information. The information is meaningful to the students if they receive it just when it is useful to them. If necessary, students can practice each of the sub-steps until they can execute a given step fluidly. Only then are they ready to attempt the entire process in sequence. Student learning experiences that are based on this kind of task analysis are highly efficient and avoid the trap of unconsidered prerequisite knowledge and skills.

Keep in mind that students develop skills in three distinct stages:

1. **Cognitive**: During this stage of development, students have to focus entirely on executing each step of the task correctly. Their activities during this stage are directed by the list and description of the steps, even if the steps and actions are memorized. The goal of this stage is for the students to perform each of the sub-steps and then each of the steps the steps correctly and in the correct sequence.
2. **Associative**: During this stage, the students can execute all of the steps included in the entire process, but they still have to attend entirely to the skill task. It is easy to tell when a student is in the associative stage because he or she is still entirely focused on executing the steps of the task. The goal of this stage is for the student to know what it *feels* like to execute the discrete steps as one unified action.
3. **Autonomous**: When the student has reached this stage, one can say that he or she truly understands the task. The student can execute each step fluidly even when distracted or focusing on another activity, like

carrying on a conversation about a different topic. In music, the goal is for a student to be able to perform the skill *and* be able to focus on other musical tasks.

Note that these are not necessarily discrete steps; each step exists along a developmental continuum. The differences in performance between the end of the cognitive stage and the beginning of the associative stage may be subtle. The differences between the beginning of the associative stage and the end, as the performance is becoming autonomous, may be dramatic. Students may even oscillate between stages as performance parameters change. Alterations to tempo, style, or phrasing, for example, may require students to focus on that one performance parameter until it becomes automatic. Keep in mind that these skill achievement levels should be included in the assessment process.

Knowledge Development

There are three aspects of knowledge development that you need to consider when designing knowledge development plans: *acquisition, meaning making,* and *transfer.* Planning for the acquisition aspect requires that you determine the best sources of simple information that the students will need. Many teachers resort to lecturing to share basic information. But it's been said that "Telling is not teaching." Since real teaching is about more than the simple transfer of information, and one of the overarching outcomes of an education is student independence, students will gain more from researching a topic prior to classroom discussion. When students seek out information, they begin to take ownership of their learning, and the information becomes more personally meaningful. Students will be motivated to seek out the information if the teacher poses an interesting and, perhaps, controversial question that "hits close to home."

One method for motivating students during the acquisition phase of knowledge development is to make a connection between the new knowledge and the students' prior experiences before introducing the materials containing the new information. Darling-Hammond and Bransford (2005) relate an interesting example from a high school literature class of preparing students prior to sharing new information. In this example, instead of simply providing an overview of the plot of *Hamlet,* the teacher asks his students to first imagine that their parents had divorced and that their mother had started a relationship with another man, who may also have had a role in removing their father from his job. He did this without mentioning *Hamlet* or that they were about to study a new play. Asking the students to imagine themselves in that scenario would ultimately help them understand Hamlet's perspective when they studied the play.

The second aspect of knowledge development is meaning making. Recall that knowledge becomes meaningful when the students find it to be useful. In many ways, students operate best on a "need to know" basis. Information becomes meaningful when a student has a useful insight into the domain or into themselves, which allows them to see the topic or themselves in a whole new light—a complete change of perspective.

Information becomes useful when they can use it to solve novel problems. The final aspect of knowledge development that you will need to plan for is *transfer*. Transfer occurs when a student applies existing knowledge to a new context or to a novel problem. This is very different from the "plug and chug" kind of math problem that simply requires a student to repeatedly apply a single formula to multiple nearly identical problems.

Since not all transfer opportunities are the same, it may be valuable for you to think of a spectrum of different types of transfer, ranging from near to far. Some tasks, if students simply have to follow directions, do not require any kind of transfer. The next level is similar in that students only have to recall basic information and *apply* a rule or procedure to complete the task, so very little transfer is required. The next level, which is often referred to as *near transfer*, would be equivalent to the analysis and evaluation levels of Bloom's taxonomy, in that students will not immediately recognize the parameters of the problem but, once they see provided cues and make sense of the requirements, are then able to apply known procedures to complete the task. Finally, in a *far transfer* situation, students face a novel task *without* any cues about how to complete it. In this circumstance, the task may initially appear to be unsolvable or impossible but, as they continue to wrestle with the problem, students are eventually able to create a solution. In fact, the first step in a far transfer problem will likely be for the students to determine how to approach the problem. In general, the challenge is to get the students to focus on the fundamentals of the problem and not the immediately apparent details. Also, keep in mind that what may seem to be near transfer or even obvious to you may require quite a leap for your students.

Transfer does not happen magically; students can be taught in a manner that predisposes them to transfer. Students who consistently strive to develop multiple explanations for problems and to view issues from multiple perspectives are more likely to think flexibly when addressing novel problems and to make appropriate far transfers to preexisting knowledge.

During instruction, these three aspects of knowledge development—acquisition, meaning making, and transfer—are not delivered in their entirety in sequence. Rather, they are iterative, in that students should rapidly shift orbit from one to the next. Students should acquire new information from multiple sources, the information should be made available exactly when it is needed in order for it to be useful, meaningful, and insightful, and the students should be enticed to transfer and connect their new knowledge to foster understanding. Ultimately, the best instructional designs foster knowledge development by providing students with multiple opportunities to engage with new information from a variety of perspectives, in a manner that they find useful for solving novel problems, and allow them to assess their own competence against agreed-on standards.

Learning Plans

Curriculum plans, unit plans, and lesson plans come in a variety of formats. They often vary in terms of specific content, the types of headings and sections they include, and the periods of time they cover. Research on the planning habits of in-service teachers indicates that, as teacher gain instructional experience, the level of detail and specificity they require in their plans to teach effectively declines, especially if they are re-teaching particular units or lessons. For many, however, the best instructional design plans, regardless of the time frame they cover, can be thoroughly understood and expertly delivered by a reasonably competent teacher of the same discipline.

It's beyond the scope of this text to specify formats for the various types of plans. The research indicates that effective teachers include several specific instructional routines in their lesson plans (Rosenshine & Stevens, 1986).

- The lesson begins with a short review of previous learning. Students learn new information more quickly if their prior knowledge is activated.
- The lesson begins with a short statement of goals. Students are more focused and on-task if they understand the lesson's intended outcomes.
- The lesson allows for new information or skills to be introduced in small steps with ample opportunity for students to practice after each new presentation. Students are more successful in the long term if they are allowed to attain competence before moving on to subsequent knowledge or skills.
- The teacher provides clear and detailed instructions and explanations.

- The teacher provides opportunities for active practice by all students. In order for students to be prepared to tackle subsequent knowledge or skills, all students must be given an opportunity to practice.
- The teacher plans for and asks many questions to check for understanding and obtains responses from all students. In order for teachers to ascertain that all students are ready to move on, all students must be given an opportunity to demonstrate competence.
- The teacher provides guidance to students during their initial practice. Students are more likely to be successful if their initial practice is free from significant mistakes or errors.
- The teacher plans for and provides systematic feedback and corrections. Engaged students want to be successful and will be more successful if the teacher provides specific and corrective feedback.
- The teacher provides detailed instructions for and then monitors students during independent and group work.

Many characteristics of effective instructional design, such as principles of assessment, have been discussed in this chapter. Other characteristics of effective instruction will be discussed in detail in Chapter 10, "Delivering Engaging Instruction." The point for now is that, in order to be effective, teachers must plan for classroom activities rather than hope for them to happen through serendipity. Teaching is a subjective human activity and, therefore, subject to the capricious nature of life. But, as Seneca wrote, "Opportunity favors the prepared."

PUTTING IT ALL TOGETHER

Designing learning opportunities for individuals or groups of students is an iterative process, in that you may cycle through stages 1, 2, and 3 several times before you are satisfied that the results from each stage are acceptable and that each stage is aligned with the others.

Likewise, there is an integral (read: integrated) relationship between curriculum selection, instructional design, instructional delivery, and assessment and evaluation, both of students and of oneself. After instruction, as you assess and evaluate students' success at achieving the predetermined outcomes, you will likely find that, however successful the students were at achieving the outcomes, the final results could have been improved. Using student results and student feedback, you may imagine better, more effective activities in which the students engage with the content. You may determine that refining the sequence in which the content is presented could help students avoid various initial misunderstandings. You may, in the end, determine that the entire lesson must be redesigned from scratch, or even that the content itself somehow distracts from the long-term goals of the course or institution.

In terms of your own long-term development as a teacher, such an occurrence should not be considered a failure. The most effective teachers revise their curriculum and lesson designs, and reconsider their instructional delivery for maximum effectiveness. Deciding which aspects of instruction to retain and which to revise is a facet of *adaptive expertise.* Some instructional behaviors and routines that are beneficial early in one's career may, at a later date, constitute a barrier to improving one's art as a teacher. Decisions about what to retain and what to modify are also highly dependent on the instructional context; what does not work in one context with one specific student population may be the ideal instructional solution in another context with a different student population. The height of professionalism is the consistent willingness to evolve for the students' benefit.

PROJECT

1. Explain each of the following terms:
   - Pedagogical Content Knowledge
   - Activities
   - Goals
   - Objectives
   - Alignment
   - Evaluation
   - Assessment
   - Summative assessment
   - Formative assessment
   - Instructional empathy
   - Backward design
2. Answer each of the six PCK knowledge questions.
3. Explain essential questions and how they can be used to motivate students to seek learning opportunities.
4. What is the link between musical knowledge and musical skill?
5. Explain why formative assessment may be the single most important pedagogical technique for improving student learning outcomes.
6. What kinds of student learning outcomes should be assessed by the checklist, the rating scale, and the rubric?
7. To conclude this chapter, you will develop a short instructional design. The first part of this section is the sample design for a lesson on clarinet

assembly. At the end of this section, you will be provided with instructions on how to complete the project.

SAMPLE PROJECT: CLARINET ASSEMBLY LESSON PLAN DEVELOPMENT AND PRODUCT

As you read this section, you'll begin to understand that designing instruction, no matter how trivial the task may seem at the onset, is not a linear process.

The first step in the development of this lesson is to consider the desired outcomes. In this scenario, let's pretend that you are teaching a single middle-school-aged student who has never touched a clarinet before.

Stage 1: Determining Outcomes

Standards: Given the limited scope of this lesson, the only consideration of any standards would be that successfully accomplishing this task would allow the student to pursue more sophisticated understandings later on.
Desired Understandings: At the end of instruction, students should be able to

1. Identify the parts of the clarinet;
2. Explain the assembly steps;
3. Explain the potential consequences of not following the sequence properly; and
4. Demonstrate the proper assembly and disassembly of a clarinet.

Essential Questions:

1. What are the various parts of the clarinet and how do they relate to one another?
2. What are the steps for properly assembling the clarinet?
3. What are the potential consequences of not following the assembly sequence properly?

Stage 2: Determining Evidence of Learning

In order the teacher to assess whether the student has a complete understanding of the process, the student must demonstrate competence in knowledge of the process and the skills required to complete the process. It is also reasonable to assume that these competencies develop in stages.

1. a. When shown one piece of the instrument, the student can name it;
   b. When asked to locate a particular part of the instrument, the student can correctly locate it;
   c. The student can properly identify each instrument part without prompting.
2. The student can perform each step of the assembly process while providing running commentary.
3. a. The student can list each step of the assembly process on paper;
   b. For each step of the assembly process, the student can list the details of that step and the consequences of not attending to the details on paper.

Stage 3: Designing the Assessment

Since the student will be providing running commentary during the second full assembly process, you will be able to assess both knowledge and skill at assembling the clarinet. You should make note of any coaching the student requires so that you can review the knowledge and skills with the student, if necessary.

Because you are assessing lower-level knowledge and a stepwise procedure, a checklist should suffice as an assessment instrument.

1. When shown one piece of the instrument, the student can name it.
   ____ Bell
   ____ Lower joint
   ____ Upper joint
   ____ Barrel
   ____ Mouthpiece
   ____ Ligature
   ____ Reed
2. When asked to locate a particular part of the instrument, the student can correctly locate it.
   ____ Bell
   ____ Lower joint
   ____ Upper joint
   ____ Barrel
   ____ Mouthpiece

_____ Ligature

_____ Reed

3. The student can properly identify each instrument part without prompting.

_____ Bell

_____ Lower joint

_____ Upper joint

_____ Barrel

_____ Mouthpiece

_____ Ligature

_____ Reed

4. The student can perform each step of the assembly process while providing running commentary.

_____ Bell to lower joint

_____ Upper joint to lower joint

_____ Mouthpiece to barrel

_____ Reed to mouthpiece

_____ Ligature to reed and mouthpiece

Stage 4: Designing the Learning Plan

In a lesson involving such a short time frame, it's wise to not only provide the instructional steps but also the expected student responses. Thus, the lesson plan shown in table 9.1 outlines the ideal interaction between teacher and student. After you have taught this lesson a few times, you may discover that students have a common set of misunderstandings or make common mistakes. Subsequently, you could revise this lesson to anticipate and prevent these errors. Note that this lesson sequence assumes that you have access to two clarinets so that the student can imitate the teacher's model at each step of the process.

INSTRUCTIONAL DESIGN ASSIGNMENT

For this assignment, you will develop a short lesson plan. Follow the basic instructional design steps as listed in "An Overview of Understanding by Design" above. Your final product should be similar to the Sample Project, but it need not be identical as long as you can justify your instructional design decisions.

Table 9.1: MODEL LESSON PLAN

Teacher action	Anticipated student response
Starting at the bell, indicate the name of each part to the student. Ask him or her to repeat the name.	The student observes and repeats each part name. The Student names each part.
Point to each part and ask the student to identify it.	
Ask the student to identify the bell. Ask the student to watch, imitate, and follow your actions. Grasp the lower part of the lower joint with the right hand, keeping the lower keys closed to avoid bending them.	The student identifies the lower joint. The student imitates your actions.
Ask the student to identify the bell.	The student identifies the bell. The student imitates your actions.
Ask the student to watch, imitate, and follow your actions. Grasp the clarinet bell with the left hand and gently place it on the lower joint with a slight twisting motion. Do not force it.	
Ask the student to identify the upper joint.	The student identifies the upper joint.
Show the student the bridge key relationship between the upper and lower joints. Demonstrate how to raise the bridge key on the upper joint by depressing the ring keys. Demonstrate how the upper joint must be slightly counterclockwise compared to the lower joint for the joints to join without bending the bridge keys. Return the upper joint to the case.	The student observes your actions.
Ask the student to watch, imitate, and follow your actions: Grasp the upper joint with the left hand, holding the bridge keys down with your fingers. Align the upper joint slightly counterclockwise in relation to the lower joint. Gently place the upper joint onto the lower joint, aligning the bridge keys after the upper joint is fully inserted. Gently set the two joints and the bell on the case.	The student imitates your actions.
Ask the student to identify the barrel. Ask the student to watch, imitate, and follow your actions. Grasp the barrel in the right hand and the mouthpiece with the left hand. Then, insert the mouthpiece into the barrel with a gentle twist.	The student identifies barrel. The student imitates your actions.

(Continued)

Teacher action	Anticipated student response
Ask the student to identify the reed and ligature.	The student identifies the reed and ligature. The student observes your actions.
Demonstrate to the student how to put on the reed and the ligature. Hold the mouthpiece-barrel assembly with the right hand with your thumb poised over the table of the mouthpiece. Center the stock of the reed on the table and hold it with your right thumb. Align the top of the reed just slightly above the tip of the mouthpiece.	
Grab the ligature with your left hand. While keeping the top of the ligature in contact with the top of the mouthpiece (away from the reed), gently place the ligature in the correct location on the mouthpiece. (Note that the location of the ligature screws of screws will depend on the design.) Tighten the screws or screws. If there are two screws, the lower screw should be finger tight to hold the reed in place and the upper screw should be tight enough to stay in place and not vibrate. If there is one screw, it should be just tight enough to hold the reed in place.	
Ask the student to watch, imitate, and follow your actions. Repeat all of the actions in the previous step.	The student imitates your actions.
Ask the student to watch, imitate, and follow your actions. Reverse all of the above steps to return the clarinet to the case.	The student imitates your actions.
Optional: If the student will be attempting to make a sound after reassembling the clarinet, begin soaking the reed.	
Reverse roles and ask the student to guide you through the clarinet assembly process. Provide only as much scaffolding (coaching) as is necessary for the student to successfully complete the process. You may need to prompt or question the student in order for him or her to share all of the information, especially the potential mistakes and consequences.	The student, with only necessary guidance, teaches you how to assemble a clarinet.
Finally, provide the student with a diagram of a clarinet. Ask him or her to identify the parts.	The student identifies the parts on the diagram.
To check for recall, ask the student to list the assembly steps without assistance.	The student writes down the procedure without assistance.

CHAPTER 10

Delivering Engaging Instruction

Pre-service teachers consistently indicate that *classroom management* is their primary concern as they enter the classroom setting. Although their concerns may be well founded, they often harbor simplistic ideas about the nature of classroom management. Owing to their own experience as students and their perhaps limited discussion about classroom management in their methods course, pre-service teachers are inclined to believe that the primary issue is establishing and then enforcing various classroom rules, which is really the far more limited topic of classroom *discipline*. According to Darling-Hammond and Bransford (2005), effective classroom management begins with a meaningful curriculum and engaging pedagogy, which enable the development of a community of learners. The design of meaningful curriculum has been addressed in previous chapters, and the development of community is addressed in Chapter 12. After a quick overview of discipline and management concepts, the primary focus of this chapter is delivering engaging instruction.

CLASSROOM MANAGEMENT

The students of teachers who approach classroom management as a "process of developing and maintaining [an] effective learning environment" (LePage, Darling-Hammond, & Akar, 2005, p. 344) are more engaged than those of teachers who emphasize their own authority. And, in general, experienced teachers are more effective at preventing classroom disruptions than are novice teachers. Based on their experience, teachers learn to anticipate situations when students are most likely to disrupt instruction, and they make subtle changes to their approach to head off disruptions. No matter how experienced the teacher, however, disruptions will occur. How they are dealt with determines whether they are likely to continue or be extinguished. Disruptions, in increasing order of seriousness, may include the following:

1. goofing off or being indifferent to tasks;
2. defiance of authority, or opposing the teacher's expectations;
3. class disruptions, acts that are against set rules or routines;
4. immorality, such as cheating, and
5. physical or verbal aggression.

Interventions to reduce inappropriate behaviors, such as using body language, physical proximity, eye contact calling the student by name, should be as unobtrusive as possible. Classroom-wide off-task or inefficient learning behaviors can be reduced with ambiguous "I-statements" such as, "I am concerned about the noise level in the room." Ideally, students should be redirected toward more appropriate behaviors, perhaps even by simply changing to a slightly different teaching strategy. High-level disruptions may require instruction to cease so that they can be dealt with immediately.

Finally, most schools have a set discipline management strategy, in which various infractions result in standardized responses. Young teachers, especially, would be wise to follow those disciplinary routines until they have established their own repertoire of responses to classroom disruptions.

CLASSROOM ORGANIZATION

All teachers, regardless of their level of experience, are well advised to establish effective classroom routines and procedures at the beginning of the academic year in order to reduce disruptions and maximize instructional effectiveness. Several organizational factors have been identified in the research literature that tend to promote effective learning environments:

- The physical setup of the room;
- Efficient procedures for particular classroom routines, such as taking attendance and passing out or collecting materials;
- Effective procedures for dealing with transitions in or out of the room and between various instructional activities; and
- Established routines for teacher-led, student-led, or learning group activities.

It's beyond the scope of this book to explore detailed room setup guide-lines for each of the various types of instructional settings, but teachers should consider the functional, pedagogical, and sociological implications of various setups, including seating arrangements, opportunities for small group work, and options for showcasing student work. In general, music rooms should be set up so that the students can enter, work, and use any instrument, and then leave the room without encountering any safety hazards, including dangerous acoustical conditions. Instructional spaces should be arranged to encourage students to remain on-task by minimiz-ing potential distractions. In addition, teaching materials and equipment should be available in such a manner that accessing the equipment does not result in a break in instructional momentum.

The way students enter and leave a music classroom is often indicative of the music learning environment. So, teachers should either provide a rou-tine for transitioning in and out of the room or provide guidelines for these transitions. For example, elementary-level students might enter the room using a group singing activity that results in the students' being positioned in the classroom for their first management or instructional activity. Older students should be given explicit guidelines and expectations for transi-tioning in and out of the music room. In secondary settings, teachers may find it advantageous to greet the students as they enter the room.

The research concerning the relation between classroom organization and instructional effectiveness indicates that teachers should establish their classroom procedures, including discipline rules, at the outset of each new term. Although teachers are under extraordinary pressure to produce measurable results, the investment of the time necessary to focus on these classroom procedures will pay dividends during the remainder of the term as the teacher and students are able to focus on the academic and musical goals and avoid unnecessary distractions. Once various classroom rules and procedures have been set, teachers can set hand signals to remind students of the agreed-on rules, procedures, and routines.

INSTRUCTIONAL CYCLES

If curriculum planning represents teachers' thinking and decision making prior to instruction, and assessment practices represent teacher thinking that occurs in response to or after instruction, delivering engaging instruc-tion often requires teachers to make decisions during instruction, as when jazz musicians make improvisational decisions during a performance. Both the instructor and the jazz musician have prepared extensively for the moment, but nonetheless the decision must be made in response to others whose actions cannot be entirely anticipated. As expert jazz performers know how to respond to various chord changes, effective teachers employ general guidelines for making temporal decisions to reach proximal instructional goals. At the smallest time frame, these decisions mediate interactions between instructors and students—how teachers present information or instructions to students, how students respond, and how instructors provide feedback to their students' responses.

The study of instructional cycles in music education was undertaken in response to theories of direct instruction that gained prominence during the late 1960s. While some of these theories have become somewhat dated, the concepts are still useful for analyzing the basic effectiveness of interactions between teachers and students. At its most basic level, an instructional cycle consists of a three-part series: teacher *presentations* are followed by student *responses*, which culminates in the instructor's providing specific *feedback* to the students. In each of the next subsections, each portion of the instructional cycle is examined in detail.

Complete Instructional Cycles

Instructional cycles are generally considered complete if they include each of the three components (presentation, response, and feedback) and correct if the feedback is specific and related to the presentation. Incomplete cycles usually are due to teacher failure to provide feedback on the original presentation as a result of getting distracted by an unrelated error during the student response. Subsequently, the teacher will either provide unrelated feedback or will skip the feedback altogether by moving on to a new presentation on a different topic. Self-observant teachers will simply make a mental note about the newly observed error and address the new issue after closing off the current cycle.

In practice, however, instructional cycles do not provide a 1-2-3 recipe for designing and controlling teacher-student interaction. Effective teachers will often use complex patterns of interaction with their students as they, perhaps, alternate between various types of presentations and student responses until they ultimately provide specific, related feedback. For example, if a teacher asks a question and the student responds in a manner other than exactly what was hoped for, then the teacher might provide additional preparation, reformulate the question, or probe the student's response for clarity before providing specific feedback. Regardless of the approach, the concept of instructional cycles provides a conceptual framework in which teachers and their mentors can discuss and assess teacher-student interaction.

Presentation

Instructors who clearly present information and instructions to their students are perceived to be more effective than instructors who use vague terms, sequence their thoughts poorly, include irrelevant information, or interject verbal tics such as "um" and "uh" into their speech. Teacher presentations can be categorized as instructions, directions, questions, demonstrations, social directives, or off-task.

Instructions and *directions* are similar in that they both inform students about something they are now expected to do in response. They differ in one critical way, however. Instructions provide student with musical or academic information that describes how they should perform, what they should listen to, or how they should be thinking musically. Directions, in contrast, only provide students with minimal information about what they are supposed to do next, such as what to perform or do next without any musical information. If we consider that the instructor's primary role is to guide students' thinking, as opposed to merely their actions, instructions are vastly superior to directions. Excellent conducting is analogous to excellent instructions in that the performers are receiving information on how to perform musically rather than simply when to perform.

Many teachers, including music teachers, use specific instructional *signals* to prompt specific student responses and *routines*. For example, many elementary-level students are trained to respond to a clapped rhythm signal by echoing the rhythm and subsequently focusing their attention on the teacher and remaining quiet. Secondary ensemble conductors often indicate that it is time to commence rehearsal by simply stepping on to the podium or time to end rehearsal with a catch phrase, which prompts the students to begin their end-of-rehearsal routine. Like all classroom management standards, these signal-routine responses must be taught.

Depending on the anticipated student response, *demonstrations* or *models* can be used in conjunction with instructions or questions and may be aural or visual. Since a primary goal of musical instruction is for students to develop the ability to think in sound, aural demonstrations, when used correctly, can be especially powerful teacher presentations for developing students' musical understanding. Teachers should strive to relate models and demonstrations to musical concepts. In other words, the use of demonstrations should be like show and tell.

When using either aural or visual demonstrations or both, it is vitally important for the students to notice the details of the demonstration and to differentiate between the details of intentionally different models. To this end, the teacher may ask the students to attempt to assess and evaluate the demonstration by describing different characteristics of the various models before explicitly calling attention to the details of the demonstration. Demonstration can be employed in a variety of pedagogically sound manners. Rather than only demonstrating by themselves, effective teachers may use student models as the basis of comparison. In addition, students may be asked to echo aural demonstrations, compare performances with supplied notation, or produce their own notation through melodic or rhythmic dictation. In the end, students should be able not only to imitate the teacher's demonstration but also exhibit musical understanding by explaining the concepts behind the demonstration. It is important for teachers to understand that the ability to discriminate between subtly different performances develops slowly. And, a musician's ability to discriminate those subtle differences, understand their significance, and then create similar musical subtleties is a factor in the development of musical artistry.

Some teachers are disinclined to use modeling as a teaching technique owing to a misguided desire to avoid rote instruction. Their well-intentioned goal is to require students to learn to decipher musical notation, but their efforts run counter to the idea of "sound before symbol," which is closely linked to language acquisition. Rote instruction, in fact, is more closely evidenced by teachers who primarily use direction presentations to achieve immediate performance gains. You will recall that using modeling and call-and-response echoing methods can be an especially effective method to teach melodic and rhythmic patterns in order to build students' musical vocabulary.

Other types of teacher presentations are, one hopes, observed less frequently during effective instruction. *Social directives* are used to address discipline issues such as those addressed above. While all teachers use *off-task* presentations or tangential comments at one point or another, they should be avoided in order to maintain instructional momentum. Humorous comments, appropriately applied and not used to embarrass students, can be effective social directives.

One off-task verbal behavior that is common among young teachers is a *verbal tic*, is the unnecessary inclusion of filler syllables or words such as "um," "OK," and "All right." Sometimes these verbal tics are merely habits, but at other times they indicate that the teacher is filling the silence as he or she considers what to say next or how instruction should proceed. In extreme cases, these verbal tics can become a distraction from instruction. The research on eliminating verbal tics is quite interesting and provides a classic example of the value of data and self-assessment in driving behavior modification. The research indicates that when others inform teachers of any level, pre-service or in-service, that they are using verbal tics, the teacher will normally agree that the tics are a problem but will fail to change their verbal behaviors. The best way to eliminate verbal tics is to have the teacher observe a recording of his or instruction and count the verbal tics. Often, a single self-assessment is enough to significantly reduce or completely eliminate them.

A well-formulated *question* or series of questions, like excellent instructions, can be used to guide students' musical and academic thinking toward more sophisticated understandings. Sometimes, teachers use questions simply to force students to remain engaged in the classroom activities. But using questions as a form of instruction can be surprisingly complex (see below).

Along with other types of formative assessment, the primary goal of questioning is to assess student understanding with an eye toward when remediation or other adjustments to instruction should follow, and when the students are adequately prepared to proceed to the next instructional goal. To this end, effective teachers design more questions in advance for various instructional scenarios and assure that all students in the class are involved in answering.

With all types of teacher presentations, the primary concern for both teacher and student is clarity. An unexpected student response may be indicative of an unclear presentation. Often, students and teachers in specific instructional contexts develop their own vocabulary of presentations and responses. Indeed, certain context-specific phrases can be used to help students recall and apply prior learning in a particular instance.

Response

The second step in an instructional cycle is a student response. When students respond to an instructional presentation, the teacher must closely observe the response to decipher the student's level of understanding of both the presentation and of the academic or musical content. It is quite possible for students to not clearly understand what was expected of them. In such a case, the teacher needs to back up and say it differently so that the student understands how to respond. Typically, an inappropriate response means that the instruction, question, or demonstration was not properly prepared and placed in context by the teacher.

When a student does not respond appropriately to the presentation (in the manner anticipated by the teacher), the teacher must then consider whether the response demonstrated a lack of skill or understanding on the part of the students and then determine what to do next to elicit a correct response. Consider a scenario in which the teacher is modeling a melodic pattern for the students to echo back on an instrument. If the students consistently respond correctly to that pattern, the teacher can reasonably assume that they understand the melodic pattern sufficiently. At this point, the teacher can either model a more complex variation of that pattern or use that melodic pattern in another way, such as having the students notate the pattern as performed.

If the students or a subset of the students are not able to consistently respond correctly to the model of that melodic pattern, then the teacher must attempt to find out why and design a remedy. In this case, the mistake could be caused by a discrimination error, in that they cannot understand what they are hearing, or by a performance error, in that they cannot determine exactly which pitches to play to reproduce the pattern. The challenge is that the error looks the same, but the cause is different. To determine the cause of the error in this particular scenario, the teacher might next ask the students to sing back the melodic pattern on nonsense syllables. If they cannot, the mistake is a discrimination issue. If they can, the next step might be to have them sing back the melodic pattern in solfeège syllables, as this might help them reproduce the melodic pattern correctly on their instruments. Finally, if they can sing the solfège syllables but cannot yet correctly perform the pattern on their instruments, the error is likely of a technical nature, such as an incorrect fingering. (This scenario reflects an efficient use of informal assessment to guide instruction.)

Feedback

The third and final step in an instructional cycle is teacher feedback. Early studies on teacher feedback, which were based on theories of behavior modification, suggested that teachers should provide approximately 80 percent approval feedback and 20 percent disapproval. According to these studies, higher percentages of disapproval were thought to reduce student motivation. Studies of the effects of teacher feedback on students' perceptions of teacher effectiveness and motivation indicated, however, that students are willing to tolerate high ratios of corrective feedback provided that it was *specific* to the musical or academic task and, perhaps more important, not personal. In fact, what students desire most from feedback is the perception that it enables them to become more competent at the academic or musical task. Teachers can also use the feedback they give to students to monitor the effectiveness of their instructional presentations; if the students are unsuccessful on their first attempt more than 20 percent of the time, the teacher needs to make adjustments. It could be that the presentations are too challenging, that the students are unprepared to respond (owing to a lack of prerequisite knowledge or skills), or that the presentation is unclear, leading to a misunderstanding or miscommunication.

Along with being specific, instructor feedback should be *related* to the academic or musical task as opposed to an unrelated skill or concept. This characteristic of well-formed instructional cycles is important for several reasons. First, when students are not provided with feedback on the task from the presentation, they tend to assume that their performance was acceptable and that they successfully incorporated the changes suggested by the instructor. Second, and perhaps more important, when a teacher provides a specific musical or academic task during the presentation and then provides specific, related feedback, students are then able to assess their own response, which fosters critical musical thinking, self-regulation, and a sense of self-sufficiency. When done properly, the sequence of specific presentation, student response with self-assessment, and specific, related feedback teaches students to self-monitor, which should increase their ability to monitor and improve their own performance, thus reducing the need to interrupt the music-making for instruction and feedback.

Compared to a higher-level task such as designing the lesson, the instructional cycle should be considered a lower-level technique, in that it enables the teacher to more capably manage the instructional interactions and the setting. But effective instruction should be student-focused rather than teacher-focused. The research on higher-level learning suggests that teachers should strive to create instructional contexts in which students function as musical and cognitive apprentices. This type of setting promotes musical independence rather than musical dependence. One appropriate use of questions may be to allow students to assess their own performances and those of others.

All too often, both teachers and students believe that student learning is a direct result of teacher feedback when, in fact, students are often quite capable of providing their own feedback with the appropriate help. The challenge is to include students in the musical assessment process by giving them opportunities to self-observe and self-assess. As you may recall, the trick to continuous feedback is to select the appropriate feedback mechanism for the musical or academic task. This process can be as simple as allowing a student or a small group of students to observe and assess other students by not performing for short periods of time. Given the ubiquity of smartphones and the music applications that are available for them, teachers and students alike should not hesitate to use these devices as metronomes, tuners, and audio or video recorders—as group and individual feedback and assessment mechanisms. Students must be taught to use them correctly, however. For example, while tuners should be used to correct individual intonation issues, students should also learn that intonation is relevant to other performers and learn how to tune appropriately in an ensemble setting. (In this case, audio recordings can be used as an effective feedback mechanism rather than the tuner.)

Finally, there is also significant evidence that students provide more accurate and more effective self-assessments when they use such simple assessment tools as checklists, rating scales, or rubrics. These tools help students focus on specific performance issues and help define levels of success. Consider, for example, the complex process of teaching a student proper stringed instrument bow hold and arm movement. Since this is a psychomotor skill, the proximal goal is for the student to learn how it feels to hold and move the bow. The learning process, however, requires that the student focus on each discrete characteristic of the hold and movement. Therefore, students could work in pairs to take pictures or video of each other's bow hold and then they could self-assess using s checklist, and even provide reliability by checking each other's work. Later, they could repeat the process to assess bow movement using video or a mirror. If the ultimate goal of music instruction is musical independence, students must be taught to design their own feedback mechanisms and to provide their own feedback so that they can set their own subsequent goals and objectives. Using these techniques helps students develop self-regulation and efficient practice techniques.

Questioning Techniques

Research on teacher development indicates that novice teachers can learn to use effective questioning techniques by observing more expert teachers demonstrate these skills and through targeted self-observation. There are two lower-level questioning techniques that, once mastered, enable instructors to develop more sophisticated techniques. The first involves the timing of the students' response to a question. Teachers should, after asking a question, allow a few seconds of wait time—classroom silence—so that students can more thoughtfully consider their response to the question. And teachers should use a signal to indicate that the wait time is over and choose the student who should respond to the question.

The second and slightly more sophisticated technique is to properly prepare the students to respond to a question by placing it in some academic or musical context. Pre-service teachers often, when reminded by a professor or cooperating in-service teacher to use more questions, will simply launch unprepared questions at their students such as, "Who can tell me the counting syllables for this rhythm?" or "Who can tell me the key signature?" Preparing students for these questions by stating, "You may remember that we learned how to count complex meter rhythms last week" or "Recall that there is a pattern to the names of sharp keys" will activate the students' prior learning and reinforce new concepts. This is especially important for students who may not have mastered the new material. Those who have mastered the materials, and can already respond to unprepared questions, are the ones who are most likely to skip the wait time and yell out their response.

While these lower-level pedagogical techniques help teachers manage the questioning process, the academic content of the teachers' questions has significant impact on the quality of the classroom discourse. You will recall from Bloom's Taxonomy that there are lower-order and higher-order types of knowledge. Just as in the process used to write goal statements, the selection of the verb in the question, which describes exactly what you wish the students to do, determines whether the question is considered lower-order or higher-order and whether it requires a lower-order or higher-order response. Lower-order questions will require students to recall, demonstrate or describe, or apply facts or knowledge. The way in which teachers respond to students' answers is also vitally important. Since questioning can function as a form of informal formative assessment, teachers can gather significant insight into students' thinking, especially their misunderstanding of academic or musical concepts, with effective questioning. Therefore, the way a teacher provides feedback to a student's *incorrect* response can be instrumental in diagnosing a misunderstanding and designing a corrective intervention. Instead of simply informing a student that his or her response is incorrect, effective teachers will ask the student to explain the response until the teacher comprehends why the student got it wrong. Then, the teacher might reformulate the question to frame the content in a way that allows the student to develop a new and, it is hoped, correct perspective on the concept. Other options would be to explore the consequences of the student's misunderstanding until the student realizes an incongruence, or to reset the assumptions or premise on the part of the student that led to the misunderstanding.

The sequencing of questions is important in guiding students' thinking about the academic or musical content. For example, an effective teacher might prepare a lower-order question with a statement about prior knowledge, ask the question, wait three seconds, and then signal for a response. Then the teacher would follow up with a more complex question. In effect, the teacher was using the lower-order question as the preparation for the higher-order question. Effective teachers could use this type of questioning technique to design a series of content-appropriate questions to engage all of the students at their own level of competence. In addition, asking students to summarize the materials in their own words requires them to blend various ideas into a holistic view and provides yet another check for student understanding.

OTHER VIEWS OF EFFECTIVE INSTRUCTION

One significant marker of effective instruction, as mentioned above, is active student engagement in the academic and musical endeavors of the class or ensemble. In this respect, effective instruction is student-centered rather than teacher-centered. For some teachers, creating a student-centered musical environment may require a significant change of mindset. There are numerous lenses, views, frameworks, or constructs that may be useful in assessing whether a learning environment is student-centered. A few such useful lenses are listed below.

Student Engagement

Perhaps the most important factor in student engagement is a meaningful curriculum. Students are not likely to commit their time or energy to curricular goals or activities that do not appear worthwhile to them. Even the most meaningful curriculum, however, will not engage students if poorly delivered. The research on students' perceptions of effective instruction indicates that they are more motivated by intense instruction, even if it is rife with musical errors, than by accurate instruction delivered without enthusiasm. Intense teachers demonstrate consistent control of their interaction with their students. Intensity is, by itself, difficult to measure. But there are other specific markers for intense or engaging instruction.

One factor that is generally associated with engaging presentations of any sort, including public speaking and teaching in large group settings, is eye contact. Teachers or presenters who use a high level of eye contact are generally perceived to be more effective and engaging. In an instructional setting, teachers must observe their students to assess their progress, so eye contact with students has two uses: engagement and assessment. Research suggests that teachers should strive to engage their student visually between 80 percent and 90 percent of the time during active instruction. But most teachers do not do so. As with elimination of verbal tics, teachers can easily increase their use of eye contact through targeted self-observation.

Other factors that may be useful in assessing student engagement involve measuring time use and the interactions between teacher and students. As mentioned above, students learn best when they, rather than the teacher, are actively engaged in the academic and musical processes. So one simple measurement of student engagement would be the percentage of time students spend responding rather than listening to teachers' presentations or feedback. Of course, there are topics that might require an extensive presentation of new material. Effective teachers will, however, avoid direct lecture and will seek to engage their students in conversation instead by asking questions that probe to assure that students understand the new material by relating it to prior learning. To analyze such conversations, teachers should measure the length of their " teacher talk" episodes. Longer talk lengths might indicate a slide toward teacher-centered instruction and student disengagement.

The measurement of the average time between the change of focus between teacher and student is indicative of the pace of instruction. A rapid exchange of focus is reflective of a higher instructional pace and is generally thought to be indicative of engaging instruction. Thoughtful teachers can also use instructional pace to manage the activation level of the group. For example, some groups of students can become unfocused if they are over-stimulated by a high instructional pace. It is possible under those circumstances to calm a group of students by lowering the instructional pace by, perhaps, allowing them to perform without interruption for a longer period of time than usual. Similarly, a group that has grown somewhat lethargic can be activated by increasing the instructional pace.

Principles of Guided Practice

In the section on developing lesson plans in Chapter 9, I noted that effective lesson plans incorporate several important teaching routines, including the following:

- The teacher provides opportunities for active practice by all students; and
- The teacher provides guidance to students during their initial practice.

In an academic context, where students tend to work independently more often, this might involve the teacher's presenting new information, such as a mathematical formula, and then giving students time for individual practice. During this practice time, the teacher would likely circulate among the students and provide guidance during their initial practice. Because of the noise and distractions, this model of guided practice does not translate well to music performance contexts, especially for extended periods of time.

Guided practice, however, is still a valuable technique for music instruction, especially in larger ensembles. The question is how to translate the principles of guided practice into such a setting most effectively. After extensive analysis of expert ensemble music teachers, Robert Duke (1994) developed the concept of the rehearsal frame as a lens through which ensemble instruction could be analyzed. Conceptually, the rehearsal frame consists of three sequential phases:

1. **Target Selection**: In this phase, the instructor identifies a performance issue to be addressed. In practice, target selection may occur during instruction or during prior score study or recording analysis of a prior rehearsal. Based on all that we know about how students acquire musical understanding and on the principles of deliberate practice, the instructor should, rather than simply identify the mistake, strive to determine whether the performance error is caused by the students' misunderstanding of a music fundamental or failure to apply their correct understanding to this particular instance. This is a critical choice because it guides the instructor toward the most effective instructional strategy. In fact, if the error is caused by a lack of knowledge or a fundamental misunderstanding, the best strategy may be to design a new lesson for a later day that addresses the fundamental issue. Failure to apply prior knowledge to this particular instance can be effectively addressed by guided practice.

2. **Decontextualization and Guided Practice**: During the second phase of the rehearsal frame, the instructor designs a practice sequence in which the magnitude of the task is reduced. To do so, the instructor might identify a sub-group of the larger ensemble to perform, select a short music excerpt for scrutiny, or simplify the performance task by slowing the tempo, performing only the rhythm, and so on. This phase may include multiple instructional cycles in which the instructor presents a musical task, allows for student response, and then provides feedback. This phase concludes when the instructor deems further guided practice unwarranted because either the immediate performance goal has been met or further practice is unlikely to be productive. In the second case, the instructor should consider incorporating fundamental instruction in a subsequent lesson.

3. **Recontextualization**: The third and final phase of the rehearsal frame is a process in which the students incorporate the previously simplified musical excerpt back into the original context. This process may include successive approximation of the full-ensemble performance of the excerpt by gradually including more members of the ensemble, gradually increasing the performance tempo, or using ever longer musical excerpts.

The research on the use of rehearsal frames by expert ensemble conductors indicates that they typically last between 1 and 1.5 minutes. It is important to consider that the use of rehearsal frames does not by itself indicate instructional effectiveness. The analysis of rehearsal frame use is merely one lens through which rehearsals can be assessed. Teachers would still be well advised to analyze their musical and verbal interactions with their students to determine the extent to which students are engaged in musical thinking during instruction.

Differentiated Instruction

As you gain experience as a teacher, you will develop a repertoire of instructional routines that save you significant time and are effective for the majority of your students. Your understanding of the instructional process and of your students—your pedagogical content knowledge—and your ability to design new student learning opportunities will become vastly more sophisticated. As your ability to assess and understand your students expands, you will likely notice that some of them are more successful than others. It will bother you that some of them are less successful and you will seek ways to reach all of your students. You will begin by focusing on the needs of your students rather than the subject matter itself. You will need to provide *differentiated instruction.*

It may be difficult to imagine, but there was a time when teachers generally taught one-size-fits-all lessons and they simply hoped that the students would acquire the information. In the latter part of the twentieth century, school systems began experimenting with incorporating students with special learning challenges into the general classroom rather than isolating them all day in self-contained classrooms, which was the original impetus to provide differentiated instruction. It is the process of modifying instructional opportunities, subject content, student projects, and assessment processes to meet the needs of the students—to provide them with a variety of ways of learning and demonstrating competence. This is now the norm for all classrooms.

First, students enter classrooms with a variety of home and educational experiences that may be wildly different from your own. Because of their varied backgrounds, students need different entry points, different pathways into the subject matter. You will need to design entry points that spark the students' imaginations and make the subject matter accessible and meaningful to them by relating it to their existing knowledge and experiences.

Second, not only are their backgrounds different, but so are their current abilities. As you remember from your study of the zone of proximal development, learning challenges that are too difficult are frustrating to students, whereas a lack of challenge results in boredom and perhaps misbehavior. How can you differentiate your instruction to match your students' levels? As always, your challenge as a teacher is to provide meaningful instruction in an engaging manner. But, now, you have to think about providing this instruction for students with a variety of abilities and interests.

Lesson Content: Since your students are at a variety of levels, you have to present the information at a variety of levels. One way to consider these levels, and to allow every student an opportunity to be successful, is to start at the lowest levels of Bloom's Taxonomy and gradually move to the highest level attained so far in the class. Each student needs the optimum entry point into the content. And, of course, you can provide instructional scaffolding to encourage each student to achieve at a higher level than the one reached during the previous lesson. Likewise, you may also have secondary goals for individual students, such as completing work in a timely manner or working well with others in group settings.

Lesson Delivery: Even if your students all achieve at a similar level, they likely have a variety of backgrounds and interests, resulting in a variety of motivation levels and interests for any given topic or task. These motivational concerns are likely expanded with a group of students who have significantly different ability levels.

Lesson Activities: The lesson activities will be driven primarily by the content. But you can divide the class into smaller groups. This presents options: you can group the students of similar ability together, or you can design groups of students with different abilities so that they can work together on tasks that are appropriate for each student. You may want to consider multiple groupings, in which each student will have an opportunity to shine.

Assessment: As you implement assessments, you have to remember that you need to know what their new current abilities are and prepare for and enhance future instruction. Likewise, you have to remember that you have different goals for each student and you need to assess them for those outcomes. So you will want to access both *process* and *product*. During the learning process, the students should engage in formative self-assessments. At the end, you want to give all an opportunity to show off what they've learned and be convinced beyond a reasonable doubt that they have met the instructional goals.

From the perspective of pedagogical content knowledge, this means that you, as the teacher, need to know exactly where each student is on multiple developmental strands, what each student's next challenge should be, how he or she can best attain that knowledge or skill. Additionally, you will need to be aware of each student's motivational and work characteristics so that you can design effective student learning groups. In some ways, successfully migrating from simple group instruction to differentiated instruction is like moving on from checkers to three-dimensional chess.

SUMMARY

As noted at the beginning of this chapter, student teachers and novice teachers state that they perceive classroom management as the greatest challenge to their success. Yet their naive ideas about classroom management—falsely equating it with discipline—can prevent them from developing a more comprehensive understanding of the relations between curriculum, pedagogy, management, and discipline. The research on teacher education and the processes through which pre-service teachers can acquire sophisticated understandings and classroom management skills is clear: Just like every other kind of expertise, the ability to successfully manage a learning context requires an understanding of the underlying principles and opportunities to practice.

Several factors and experiences in particular have been shown to have a positive effect on novice teachers' preparation to manage a classroom. The first, not surprisingly, is to have excellent models, both from their days as K–12 students and from their mentors.

Second, future teachers need basic knowledge of the frameworks for classroom management and opportunities to engage with the frameworks before working with students. In order to avoid inefficient periods of trial and error in the classroom, pre-service teachers should examine case studies of classroom management. Doing so allows them to apply their theoretical knowledge to various scenarios and to reflect on their hypothetical management decisions. It allows them to examine their own understandings and misunderstandings of the critical processes of classroom management.

Finally, pre-service teachers must be given extensive opportunities to work with actual students (not peer students) under the direct supervision of a master teacher. Even five-minute micro-teaching experiences during the first or second year of a pre-service teacher's educational experience can have a positive impact on subsequent development. These preclinical teacher experiences allow emerging teachers to try out various strategies under a variety of circumstances. Afterward, pre-service teachers should engage in extensive self-evaluation along with debriefing with their mentors.

PROJECT

1. Explain the following terms:
   - Classroom management
   - Discipline
   - Presentation
   - Instruction and direction
   - Social directive
   - Off-task presentation
   - Student response
   - Feedback
   - Verbal tic
   - Student engagement
   - Differentiated instruction
2. Explain the logic behind a well-formulated question. Explain the logic behind a well-sequenced series of questions.
3. Differentiate between management and discipline. Without using any names or other identifying details, write two stories, one about observing a teacher using excellent classroom management and a time when you saw a teacher using effective discipline.
4. Develop a mind map of discipline versus management.

CHAPTER 11

Instructional Context

In this chapter we'll take a look at the variables that have an impact, sometimes significant, on the interactions between instructors and students. During the course of the chapter we will start in the music room and, during each subsequent section, examine the ever-larger contexts that surround each classroom and rehearsal hall. In the first section, you will learn basic concepts about observing teacher-student interactions in an instructional setting. In the next section, you will think about how the music program interfaces with the school and the community, along with some of the concerns about how the context may impact teachers and students. In the third section, you will read about the contemporary issues that face music education as we march further into the twenty-first century. Finally, you will receive a short introduction to the contemporary issues in education that influence how music is taught and valued in the United States.

OBSERVING EXPERT INSTRUCTION IN CONTEXT

What is the goal or purpose of observing in-service teachers? You may recall that, via apprenticeship of observation, pre-service teachers often believe they understand what it means to be a teacher because they have informally observed teachers for their entire educational career and can, perhaps, even imitate their teacher's actions. But, as you also learned earlier, simply watching a teacher from the viewpoint of a student does not give one access to the teacher's planning process, decision-making process during the act of teaching, or habits of reflection on his or her work. The purpose of observing and interacting with experienced in-service teachers is to attempt to gain a perspective on the teacher's pedagogical thinking that heretofore had been inaccessible to you as a student. You may find it advantageous to review the six essential questions of pedagogical content knowledge in found in Chapter 9.

Effective ways to examine teacher thinking include observing the students' responses to teachers' instructions in authentic instructional settings, comparing how different teachers work toward the same instructional goals, analyzing a variety of curricular materials and designs, observing students for evidence of understanding, and engaging in-service teachers and students in dialogue about their teaching and learning experiences (Feiman-Nemserb 2001).

The only way to learn to observe instruction is to prepare for an observation, watch a teacher in action, reflect on what you saw, and then receive feedback on your insights.

Caveats and Guidelines

Several caveats must be shared with those who are unaccustomed to doing live classroom observations. First, it is possible to become distracted and drop back into the role of being a student. Second, it is also possible for an instructor to mask ineffective teaching by a particularly engaging presentation. Finally, any time we observe instruction, our perceptions are colored by our own biases, values, feelings, and experiences. In order to avoid these pitfalls, we generally use various predesigned observation instruments that help us focus on discerning the interactions between instructor and students. Observation instruments also limit the number of variables being observed at any given time to help us avoid becoming overwhelmed. The goal is for emerging teachers to become competent at completing observations that are accurate and rich but not tainted by personal bias. Instructors must learn how to observe other instructors in this manner before they can turn a critical eye to their own instruction and interaction with students.

There are several important guidelines that can help keep you focused on observing the instruction and not getting distracted or jumping to conclusions: Clements and Klinger (2010, p. 19) suggest that you (1) go into an observation knowing *exactly* what teacher-student behavior or interaction process you intend to observe, (2) record only *data* during the observation, and (3) only record relevant data rather than trying to record everything. Finally, after the observation, you should (4) draw inferences about the teaching-learning process and context based on the entirety of the data.

You will likely have to complete many of hours of observation and other field experiences before student teaching. You may complete field observations in a group or individually. In either case, it is important for you to follow professional protocol for obtaining any needed security clearances, arranging for, and then completing the observations and any follow-up activities. Your professors may make the necessary arrangements for you, or you may have to make them yourself from an approved list of in-service music educators. Appointments to complete the observations should be made well in advance of the observation date and well before the due date for the assignment, because real-world circumstances, such as inclement weather or teacher illness, may require the observation to be rescheduled. You should arrive at the school well before the scheduled time and complete the school's security protocol, for example, registering in the main office and acquiring a conspicuous visitor's badge. You should always present yourself as an aspiring professional educator and dress accordingly.

Complete guidelines and protocols for completing field observations may vary across institutions and far exceed the scope of this text. Your instructors will certainly provide more detailed information for each of your field experiences.

Types of Observations

There are almost unlimited ways to observe teachers in different instructional settings. These various methods can, perhaps, be reduced to two types: quantitative and qualitative. Both types should include basic school and class information, the physical layout of the instructional context, demographic information about the student population observed, and data about the instructor, along with the date and time of the observation.

In a quantitative observation, the observer simply counts or quantifies the instances of specific teacher behaviors. For example, the observer may have a checklist of behaviors and instructional routines that have been associated with effective lesson presentations, such as starting the lesson with a statement of goals and a review of previous student knowledge. Or the observer might count the number of complete and incomplete instructional cycles. Another example is a time-use study. In this type of observation, different classroom activities are timed or counted so that the durations and ratios of time dedicated to specific teacher and student behaviors, along with their average time length, can be compared with norms or discussed in relation to teacher effectiveness.

Qualitative observations, on the other hand, are more focused on the variables that guide teachers' decision making in the classroom and the human factors the enable or constrain the interactions between individuals and sub-groups within a given instructional context. It is often difficult to generalize qualitative findings to other settings because the defining issues are the context and the individuals who inhabit it. During qualitative obser-vations, you should look for the defining characteristics of meaningful curriculum and engaging instruction as outlined in the preceding chapters. Recall that the defining characteristic of expert teachers may be their abil-ity to recognize patterns of interaction between themselves and their stu-dents and, therefore, become better able to predict their students' responses to instruction than novice teachers. Because you are most likely unable to observe the teacher's planning or decision making process during instruction, you may wish to follow up your in-class observation with questions designed to uncover those processes during a post-observation conference.

In reality, many observations include both quantitative and qualitative information. For example, observations that are designed to decipher class-room management and student behavior issues may include a count of the number of instances of student misconduct and a qualitative assessment of the effectiveness of the teacher's responses and interventions. Finally, pre-service educators should take great care not to pass judgment on the instruction they have observed. The instructional behaviors you observe in the classroom may not align exactly with the instructional theories from your courses but may, rather, be pragmatic enactments of the theories based on the realities of the context.

THE SCHOOL CONTEXT

Research on student teachers and first-year teachers of music indicates that most experience a kind of culture shock when they become embed-ded full-time into an instructional context. They often are overwhelmed by the professional requirements of their new role. Some of these issues result from the challenges that all teachers face, such as the diminishing respect for the teaching profession, the severe financial constraints found in some instructional settings, and the significant needs of some student popula-tions. But there are other challenges that may be unique for music educa-tors, such as the public perception that arts instruction is an "extra" that can be jettisoned during financial cutbacks, along with the very public nature of performance-based programs. In addition, music teachers often face sub-standard instructional environments (such as having to teach in non-music rooms or even travel from room to room or school to school), along with additional administrative challenges such as fundraising, inventory, and travel (Miksza & Berg, 2013).

The same body of research shows, however, that first-year music teach-ers who have had extensive pre-service field experiences, including obser-vations and micro-teaching opportunities, find this transition into the profession far less challenging than those who did not. More important, perhaps, these "experienced" first-year teachers have been found to be significantly more effective in the classroom when they start their professional careers.

The characteristics of instructional settings vary widely; the country has schools that are urban, suburban, and rural; private (both religious and non-religious), public, and charter; large and small (in terms of student enrollment); and subject to varying state requirements and regional differences. They also have statistically significant differences in student demographics such as race and affluence. Each school setting is the product of the unique interaction of these national, regional, state, and local variables. As you first visit various schools and then embed yourself in a particular learning community, it is vitally important to remember that each will provide its own unique joys and challenges.

Community of Practice

Regardless of their unique characteristics, the best instructional settings constitute a "Community of Practice," a grouping of "people who share a concern or a passion for something they do and learn how to do it better as they interact regularly" (Wenger-Trayner, n.d., n.p.). Members of a community will work together to improve their instructional practice by sharing resources, planning together, sharing information about students, and providing various kinds of support. Teachers may, therefore, belong to a variety of communities of practice. They may be grouped by the facility in which they teach or by other factors, such as grade level or discipline. These groupings may extend across facilities and even school districts.

Within each instructional community of practice, various administrative structures exist to support and enable teaching. For example, teachers may report to department chairs or any number of school administrators, such as principals and assistant principals, along with superintendents and other district-level administrators. Schools and school districts also include a wide variety of support staff, such as school counselors, media librarians, bookkeepers, security officers, maintenance and custodial staff, bus drivers, and curriculum coordinators. The school system itself exists within the larger community, which provides oversight of the district via an elected school board. Most schools and school systems also include a formal parent organization, which provides both support and input.

The list of roles within a school community is extensive, and it is important for you to understand that your role is largely defined for you by the rest of the community. As you enter into any school community, you should

take great care to seek to understand all that is expected of you, professionally and personally. At various times in your career, you may choose to leave
a particular community or to not join one in the first place.

While you receive the benefits of joining a community of practice, you
also will have certain responsibilities to the other members. Primarily, you
will be responsible for maintaining and even improving the quality of the
interactions within the community. You must at all times comport yourself
within the guidelines of your professional dispositions, as discussed in the
introduction to this book. But, any professional interaction is also a social
interaction and, therefore, has a personal component. You must realize that
others in the community are likely as motivated as you are to be recognized
as influential, effective, and successful. The more you contribute to the community, the more you will benefit from it. Working with other members of
the community of practice can multiply your efforts; working in isolation
or against each other will likely be destructive. Establishing common goals
within the localized culture is, therefore, essential.

Administration and Community

The primary governing authority for any school district is the elected Board
of Education, also known more colloquially as the school board. The board
is charged with representing the interests of the local constituents—those
who pay taxes to support the school district—by supervising the school
district's administration, approving the district budget, setting local policies while assuring compliance with state and federal law and policy, and
defining and promoting excellence in the district. Some school boards even
have to approve the hiring of any instructional or support personnel. All
local districts report to the state board of education. The geographical area
of the school district may range from a small village to a city, a group of cit-
ies, or a county. Some states include primarily city districts, while others are
entirely county districts.

School districts also have a superintendent, who is the executive admin-
istrator for the district. Some superintendents are hired by the school
board, and others are elected by the district's constituents. Regardless, the
superintendent reports to the school board and is responsible for the day-
to-day operations of the district and for assuring compliance with all district, state, and federal regulations. Larger districts are likely to have either
area superintendents or assistant superintendents, who are in charge of
specific aspects of the district administration. Districts may also have officers in charge of various administrative functions such as finances, facilities,
and technology. You can think of the superintendent and the rest of the

administration as the executive branch of the school district and the school board as the legislative or policy branch.

Likewise, schools have their own executive and policy structures. The primary executive at a school is generally known as the principal (not principle) because during the era of very small schools, the lead teacher was known as the principal teacher. Now, principals generally do not have instructional responsibilities. As with districts, schools have certain administrative structures. These may include assistant principals or other junior administrators, bookkeepers, facilities coordinators, event coordinators, curriculum coordinators, and athletic directors. As any experienced teacher will likely tell you, the most important personnel for you to get to know are the principal's secretary and the head janitor. (As an aside, it is important to understand that the school support staff do not work for you. You would be well advised to treat them as colleagues with whom you share an educational mission.) Each school will also likely have a board or organization of parents and community members who guide but do not determine policy and also promote the school and encourage community engagement. Moreover, schools often have parental and community groups such as athletic boosters and music program boosters, to assist with and financially support specific programs.

The main point is that schools have complex bureaucratic structures by design. Working within these structures can be frustrating in that change and progress usually are slow and incremental. But when implemented correctly, these small bureaucratic processes mediate systematic change and can protect one from individual whims and personal interests. The keys to any productive bureaucratic system are leaders who ensure that all voices are heard equally and for all constituents of the system to understand how the system works.

Finally, it is important to realize that you also become a member of any community when you accept an instructional position, even if you choose to live outside of the school district or attendance zone. Every community has various groups who are not directly affiliated with the schools yet may provide significant support for the schools and the community in general. One effective way of becoming embedded in the community is to join one or more of these groups.

CONTEMPORARY ISSUES IN EDUCATION
Standardized Testing and Standardizing Curriculum

Over the course of the past century, various educational reform movements have emerged in the United States as a consequence of a particular contemporary crisis or of a report, any of which seemed to indicate that the educational institutions in the country were failing in some manner. Either they were not successfully educating the population for the modern needs of society or they were lagging behind the educational systems of other countries. The first crisis was the result of the Soviet Union's successfully sending a man-made satellite into orbit in October 1957. The thought was that *Sputnik* indicated that the educational systems in the USSR were superior to those in the United States, especially in the area of technology. The federal response was the National Defense Education Act, which provided additional funding to improve science and mathematics instruction at educational institutions at all levels.

Until the 1970s, individual school districts were empowered to determine the educational outcomes for the students in their charge and to design their curricula to assist students in achieving those outcomes. Even then, school districts used standardized tests of basic skills such as the Stanford Achievement Test or any number of other *norm-referenced standardized tests* to determine relative student achievement. (*Norm-referenced* means that the test determined an individual student's rank within a defined population. Students were often given a score that might indicate, for example, that they scored better than 75 percent of the other students at their level at a given task, such as spelling.) Subsequently, however, many states began to move toward a system of minimum competency tests. Passing such a test supposedly showed that a student had met a set of predefined minimum standards for completion of graduation requirements or to move from one grade level to the next.

As a part of President Lyndon Johnson's "war on poverty," Congress passed the Elementary and Secondary Education Act (ESEA) in 1965. The primary goal of the act was to reduce the achievement gap between students in more affluent and less advantaged school systems. In addition to providing funding, the act set standards for student resources such as school libraries and provided funding for educational research, training, and support. The ESEA is renewed by Congress every five years. The Head Start program, designed to more adequately prepare disadvantaged students for primary instruction, was also initiated during this same time period.

Once standardized testing became the norm, it became possible to review and compare testing results over time. In 1983, President Ronald Reagan's National Commission on Excellence in Education, an eighteen-member panel appointed by the Secretary of Education, issued a report titled "A Nation at Risk: The Imperative for Educational Reform," which indicated that scores on standardized tests had dropped significantly over the course of several decades. The report stated that the quality of teaching and learning at the primary, secondary, and post-secondary levels, in both private and public institutions, represented a "rising tide of mediocrity that threatens our very future as a Nation and a people." The report went further to state, "If an unfriendly foreign power had attempted to impose on America the mediocre educational performance that exists today, we might well have viewed it as an act of war." The report initiated a wave of education reform and included recommendations in five categories: content (curriculum), standards and expectations (more standardized testing), time (lengthened academic years), teaching (increasing the stature and pay for teachers but requiring documented instructional competence), and leadership and fiscal support (federal standards for educational institutions, which would be rewarded with increased financial support).

Since 1990 the U.S. Department of Education has administered the National Assessment of Educational Progress (NAEP), which tests sample student populations from across the United States and from select urban school districts in an effort to analyze long-term educational achievement trends. Students in the fourth, eighth, and twelfth grades are examined via standardized pencil-and-paper tests in mathematics, reading, science, writing, the arts, civics, economics, geography, U.S. history, and in technology and engineering literacy. Data from the NAEP can be disaggregated, which means specific student populations, such fourth-grade females or twelfth-grade Hispanic males, can be analyzed. The overall data from the NAEP are reported annually as a part of "The Nation's Report Card."

The 2001 renewal of the Elementary and Secondary Education Act is referred to as the No Child Left Behind Act of 2001 (NCLB). The logical basis of the NCLB Act was that setting mandatory high standards, to be assessed annually by standardized tests, would result in higher achievement. Schools and teachers that did not meet the designated standards would be subject to budget cuts and other sanctions. Parents of students attending schools that did not meet the achievement standards would be empowered to send their children to other, presumably more effective, schools and might even be awarded vouchers to send their children to private schools. Proponents of the act claim that improved test scores, especially those of minority students, prove the effectiveness of this particular model of reform, but its critics claim that the high-stakes nature of the standardized tests has encouraged teachers to teach only to the test and to neglect other forms of innovative pedagogy. Others point out that instructional time spent on areas outside of reading, math, and science, such as physical education and the arts, has been severely reduced, because these subjects are not assessed and scored by the standardized tests.

The Race to the Top initiative was a part of the American Recovery and Investment Act of 2009 (ARRA). The ARRA provided $4.35 billion to the

Race to the Top Fund to serve as a carrot to promote various educational reforms designed to improve student achievement by

1. Adopting standards and assessments that prepare students to succeed in college and the workplace and to compete in the global economy;
2. Building data systems that measure student growth and success, and inform teachers and principals about how they can improve instruction;
3. Recruiting, developing, rewarding, and retaining effective teachers and principals, especially where they are needed most; and
4. Turning around our lowest-achieving schools. (*Race to the Top Program: Executive Summary*, 2009, p. 2)

To apply for funding, states submitted lengthy, detailed applications that were scored against a complex rubric. Not all states submitted applications and, of those, only a portion received funding. In the first round, only two of the sixteen states that applied received funding: Delaware was awarded $100 billion and Tennessee received $500 billion. In the second round, only ten of thirty-six applicant states were awarded funding, with the awards averaging $33.25 billion. These awards provided significant assistance to these states but, of course, came with stringent requirements. States were required to submit annual performance reports, which documented progress toward the goals outlined in the grant application.

Naturally, there have been some harsh criticisms of the reforms mandated by the Race to the Top. Teachers and teachers' unions have primarily argued that standardized tests are hardly the best measure of student learning and teacher impact. State policy makers have resisted the requirement to relinquish local and state control of the educational process in order to receive supplemental federal funding. Many have also argued that the standardized testing mechanisms contain cultural biases that disadvantage minority and under-resourced students.

Unrelated to the federal Race to the Top initiative, a proposal for the Common Core Standards (CCS) was developed by the National Governor's Association and the Council of Chief State School Officers. They were concerned about the inconsistent standards adopted by the various states, which made it difficult to compare academic achievement rates and for students to transfer between schools in different states. Together, they proposed a process by which the states would first agree on college- and career-readiness standards and subsequently on K–12 standards. The only connection between R2T and CCS was that the grant process for R2T awarded additional credits to the states that adopted standards aimed toward college readiness and career-readiness. Development of the CCS, which only provides standards for English and mathematics, was completed in 2014. Many of the states and US territories that adopted the CCS are working toward implementation.

As with the other educational reform initiatives outlined in this section, there have been concerns and criticisms regarding the CCS, some of which have been the result of misunderstanding their nature. First, the standards do not outline curriculum for teachers but only outcome standards. Each participating educational system—state or local—must still devise its own curriculum, so the CCS do not amount to a national curriculum, as some have protested. Second, because the CCS do not dictate curriculum, they also do not dictate pedagogical approaches. The standards are designed, however, to promote pedagogical approaches that are aligned with best practices and current research. Third, there is not a direct correlation between the adoption of the CCS and the unfortunate proliferation of standardized testing. Some states have even now withdrawn from the CSS initiative after considerable complaints about the time students spent in standardized testing. All this means is that the students may take different tests. Finally, there are those who have protested that the CCS constitute overreach by the federal Department of Education, thus eliminating local control. The nature of the Common Core development process clearly indicates that it was not a federal initiative, but it was promoted by state governors and chief education officers.

In December 2015 Congress passed an update to the Elementary and Secondary Education act, this time named the Every Student Succeeds Act (ESSA). The act is quite different from the NCLB Act, which it replaces, in that it reduces the emphasis on standardized testing in math and reading and, instead, emphasizes that all students should receive a "well-rounded education" in multiple disciplines, including music. In fact, federal dollars are available to meet any identified deficiencies in providing a well-rounded education to all students. Documents available from the NAfME website note several other advantages to ESSA, including the use of federal funds for professional development for all teachers and protection from students' being pulled out out classes in other areas for remediation in math and reading.

Because the stream of school reform ideas is broad and seemingly unending, many such ideas—such as block scheduling, blue ribbon schools, and the small schools initiative—are not discussed in this section; the topic is expansive enough to fill a book by itself. And reform ideas tend to be trendy; what appears to be a good idea one year is implemented and subsequently discarded when the next great new idea surfaces. Pre-service music teachers would be well advised to contact local educators to find out which reform programs are currently being implemented in their districts.

Teacher Evaluation

I have stressed that there are significant, observable differences between highly effective and less effective teachers and that the instructional behaviors and dispositions of the former can be deliberately acquired. This argument is strongly supported in the literature about teacher effectiveness and in the teacher-practitioner community. In many ways, these theories of effective pedagogy have been developed by observing and interviewing teachers who have obviously been effective and then developing theories and frameworks to explain their effectiveness. Now I turn to the formal processes that are employed to evaluate the effectiveness of individual teachers by school systems, the implications of individual teacher evaluations on their continued employment and merit pay, and whether such evaluations can be considered valid and reliable.

We do know that, whereas teachers can contribute positively to the lives of their students, other factors in the students' lives also have significant impact on their academic success. It is generally estimated that teacher effectiveness accounts for only a small percentage of an individual student's success. Other factors include

- School factors such as class sizes, curriculum materials, instructional time, availability of specialists and tutors, and resources for learning (books, computers, science labs, and more);
- Home and community supports or challenges;
- Individual student needs and abilities, health, and attendance;
- Peer culture and achievement;
- Prior teachers and schooling, as well as other current teachers;
- Differential summer learning loss, which especially affects low-income children; and
- The specific tests used, which emphasize some kinds of learning and not others and which rarely measure achievement that is well above or below grade level. (Darling-Hammond, Amrein-Beardsley, Haertel, & Rothstein, 2012, p. 8)

Yet many school districts and so-called experts advocate for and implement teacher evaluation systems based in part or in full on standardized testing. They insist that teacher accountability is the best mechanism for increasing teacher quality by rewarding effective teachers with merit pay and punishing ineffective ones, including removing them from their positions. These experts advocate for improving school-wide test scores via market-based logic, which would allow parents to choose to send their students to higher-achieving schools.

Social Justice and Diversity

You will recall from Chapter 9 that, in order to be most effective, teachers need to develop a sense of instructional empathy, which means that they need to be able to understand their students' perspective on the curricular content. But, as we move from the narrow view of the musical curriculum and consider the entire instructional context *from the students' perspective*, you will also recall that professionals in all domains must evince an ethical and moral commitment to their clients (Shulman, 1998). Allsup expands on this idea and states, "At the heart of teaching others is the moral imperative to care" (Allsup & Shieh, 2012, p. 47). He goes even further to state that, as one cares for another, he or she develops an empathetic sense for the social injustices many students face that affect not only their ability to learn but also their ability to thrive in society. In short, teachers must advocate and take action for social justice for their students in particular and social justice within their community, however they define their community. These ideals are at the heart of the purposes of public education.

We begin to develop a vision of social justice only when we become acutely aware of the parameters of its opposite—the often tacit injustices and barriers that students face in their daily lives. What exactly might those parameters be? Estelle Jorgensen states, "Among these [parameters] are matters of language, age, gender and sexual orientation, social class, ethnicity, race, color, physical characteristics such as size, weight, height, and dexterity, personality characteristics such as introversion, independence, sensitivity, and anxiety, intelligence, wealth, geographic location, culture and country of origin, and family background including religious and political affiliation and orientation to education" (Jorgensen, 2007, p. 169). She further states that these injustices constitute societal oppression, which prevent some people from individually or collectively pursuing the lives they might wish to lead. These differences result in individuals or groups being treated differently as a consequence of "capricious factors out of one's control, namely, accidents of birth and social standing" (2007, p. 171).

Why should and how can professional music educators address these issues within their community? One might be tempted to simply look away and let others deal with the consequences, or to simply hope that these matters remain tacit. This view is not only unprofessional, it's impossible. Consider for a moment what may be the most overt form of oppression: physical violence or physical bullying, which is often accompanied by verbal abuse. Can one simply look away? Of course not. Educators have a moral responsibility to create a safe learning environment. If these injustices cannot be ignored, where does one draw the line? Should we deal with physical bullying but not merely verbal bullying? How about race and gender but not other physical characteristics? There is no line. Where there is a perceived injustice, it must be addressed. But how?

Again, the professional educator's responsibility in this circumstance is to work to develop empathy—a nuanced understanding of the students' perspective. While some insight into their viewpoints can develop from reading any of the numerous texts on social justice and diversity in the educational setting, true empathy and understanding for a particular student or student group can only develop through dispassionate, nonjudgmental dialogue. This dialogue may, at times, extend to additional stakeholders within the community. Likewise, students must develop an understanding of their responsibilities to the community and for their own education through dialogue.

As important as an empathetic disposition is to addressing issues of social justice, we also must be aware of the positive impact it has on outcomes for students—the ultimate goal of education. While empathy can mediate positive outcomes, it must be paired with pedagogical skills. Teachers report that, after receiving professional development relating to empathy in instructional relationships, they were able to create more positive relationships with students, had improved classroom cultures, and were better able to engage in student-centered instruction (McAllister & Irvine, 2002). In sum, empathy is important for purposes of effective instructional design, productive classroom climate, and promoting social justice.

Finally, there are the issues of authority and power. By virtue of their professional license and employment, educators are authorized, empowered, and often legally obligated to protect students from injustice, oppression, and abuse. The full gamut of social justice and diversity is far beyond the scope of this text. Many books and articles have been written about social justice in education and specifically in music education. Curious and resourceful students should have no problem locating additional contemporary reading materials. And it is highly probable that you will have specific coursework on diversity at some time during your licensure process. You should not, however, merely consider these issues of social injustice only when required to by an instructor or by coursework. As all other skills and dispositions, you will become more competent and comfortable addressing the issues of social injustice the more consistently and thoughtfully you engage with them.

Charter School Movement

Over the course of the past twenty-five years, the charter school movement has been a leading force for reform of the traditional public school model in the United States. In function, charter schools fall between the traditional public school and private schools. In general, charter schools are exempt from many of the state mandates that apply to public schools (as are private schools) but are funded primarily with public (that is, state) dollars. Instead of an elected school board, charter schools are administered by private individuals or groups. These groups may be for-profit or nonprofit. The administering organization applies for a charter from the state to receive state funding and offer instruction and credits. These charters are offered for a given time period, during which these schools must demonstrate academic success at least on a par with the public schools in order to retain and renew the charter. Charter organizations with demonstrated success are often authorized to expand by adding seats or opening new locations. If demand for enrollment exceeds the available capacity, charter schools employ a lottery system to select students.

Because of the private-public nature of charter schools, they must attend to some mandates while other mandates are waived. For example, charters are supposed to have fair and open admissions, but are often not required to serve students with special needs, and they can essentially expel students who are not successful. There are those who contend that charter schools are not competing on a level field with traditional public schools, which must accept all students. Many charter schools are organized like magnet schools, in that they have a certain curricular focus such as technology, the arts, or a foreign language.

Those who support the charter school movement contend that the competition it offers public schools will force them to improve. The supporters of the charter school movement have been some conservative state legislatures, parent's groups, school reform–focused nonprofit policy organizations and foundations, and some corporate school leaders. Although the agendas for each organization have not necessarily aligned, together they constitute a formidable advocacy movement.

Parents are primarily supportive of charter schools because of the belief that they provide school choice options that may be more compatible with their ideas for the child's education. State legislatures have bought into the charter school concept for several reasons: (1) to promote student achievement by allowing charter schools to experiment with curricular offerings and methods, (2) a belief that for-profit charter school organizations, because of the profit motive, will find more efficient educational systems, and (3) it is an effort to counterbalance the power of teacher unions, since many charter schools are exempt from the requirement to hire professionally licensed teachers. Corporate supporters by definition are interested in charter schools for the possibility of making money.

Many individual teachers and essentially all professional teacher organizations (unions) are opposed to charter schools because they are exempt from many of the standards imposed on public schools. Note that the states do not generally supply funding for charter school facilities, so the charter organizations must secure that funding. In some cases, nonprofit charter organizations rent facilities from for-profit organizations, and both are owned by the same personnel.

Charter schools have a mixed track record of academic success. Some easily exceed the achievement levels of nearby public schools, whereas others have very low achievement levels. Because of the lottery system for student selection and the fact that motivated parents have self-selected the charter school, it is sometimes difficult to compare the educational outcomes of charter and public schools. In general, however, charter schools in urban areas have generally outperformed comparable urban public schools.

CONTEMPORARY ISSUES IN MUSIC EDUCATION

Just as in education generally, music education has experienced periods of reform as the consequence of various national reports and studies. Many of these reforms occurred because of gatherings of interested and informed professionals, who are guided by the intention of discerning and defining the future of music education and producing a manifesto. One of the first of these gatherings was the Yale Seminar on Music Education of June 1963. The genesis of the seminar was a call by the federal Panel on Educational Research and Development to examine why the music education system in the US had failed to produce a musically literate society. A diverse group of thirty-one music professionals met for twelve days to examine the current state of music education and propose a path forward. In the end, they produced a list of ten recommendations, which were focused primarily on curriculum and musical materials:

The seminar also led to the development of the Juilliard Repertory Project, in which 230 samples of "high-quality" music were curated for use in K–6 music education. A second such gathering was the Tanglewood Symposium of 1967, during which the participants' main focus was on music instruction. They, too, produced a list of generic recommendations.

After a hiatus of nearly thirty years, June Hinckley, then president of MENC, determined that as a consequence of tremendous changes in society, technology, and the educational system since the Tanglewood

Symposium of 1967, along with the ratification of the first National Standards for Music Education, a new vision was needed to usher in the twenty-first century. The results of the Housewright Symposium on the Future of Music Education, held on the campus of Florida State University in September 1999, were the Housewright Declaration and the symposium archive, "Vision 2020: The Housewright Symposium on the Future of Music Education." During the conference, leaders from the education system at all levels (pre-K through university), along with officers of MENC and music industry organizations, plus performing musicians, met to consider the content and context of a musical education. The declaration reads in part:

We agree on the following:

1. All persons, regardless of age, cultural heritage, ability, venue, or financial circumstance, deserve to participate fully in the best music experiences possible.
2. The integrity of music study must be preserved. Music educators must lead the development of meaningful music instruction and experience.
3. Time must be allotted for formal music study at all levels of instruction such that a comprehensive, sequential, and standards-based program of music instruction is made available.
4. All music has a place in the curriculum. Not only does the Western art tradition need to be preserved and disseminated; music educators also need to be aware of other music that people experience and be able to integrate it into classroom music instruction.
5. Music educators need to be proficient and knowledgeable concerning technological changes and advancements and be prepared to use all appropriate tools in advancing music study while recognizing the importance of people coming together to make and share music.
6. Music educators should involve the music industry, other agencies, individuals, and music institutions in improving the quality and quantity of music instruction. This should start within each local community by defining the appropriate role of these resources in teaching and learning.
7. The currently defined role of the music educator will expand as settings for music instruction proliferate. Professional music educators must provide a leadership role in coordinating music activities beyond the school setting to insure formal and informal curricular integration.
8. Recruiting prospective music teachers is a responsibility of many, including music educators. Potential teachers need to be drawn from diverse backgrounds, identified early, led to develop both teaching and musical abilities, and sustained through ongoing professional

development. Also, alternative licensing should be explored in order to expand the number and variety of teachers available to those seeking music instruction.

9. Continuing research addressing all aspects of music activity needs to be supported, including intellectual, emotional, and physical responses to music. Ancillary social results of music study also need exploration, as well as specific studies to increase meaningful music listening.

10. Music making is an essential way in which learners come to know and understand music and music traditions. Music making should be broadly interpreted to be performing, composing, improvising, listening, and interpreting music notation.

11. Music educators must join with others in providing opportunities for meaningful music instruction for all people beginning at the earliest possible age and continuing throughout life.

12. Music educators must identify the barriers that impede the full actualization of any of the above and work to overcome them.

Pre-service music teachers certainly need not memorize these twelve points, but they must grasp the importance of such achievements. The primary take away from this cursory glance at these historical reform movements is that educational systems, including the enterprise of music education, are in a constant state of flux. Sometimes these reforms are the result of internal motivations and movements; at other times they they result from outside influences—changes in both governmental policy and societal forces. As a music educator, you will be expected to respond to them professionally, in that you will always have the best interests of your students in mind. Over the course of your career, you will be expected to evolve from a novice teacher who complies with educational policy into a master teacher who promotes change by advocating for music students and music education. You may at some point be responsible for developing a new vision for music education within your school, your district, your state, or the country.

Advocacy

As reflected in the manifestos produced by the various symposia, the primary issues in music education in the past and in the future are what they have always been: What shall be the content and context of music education? Unfortunately, the policy discussions often devolve into questions about the value of music education for learning *other* content, such as math and science, or for raising general achievement test scores. It is important to keep the focus on the value of an education in music and on active participation in music. You will recall that one accomplishment for MENC and the original National Standards for Music Education was to have music and the arts in general classified as a core subject as opposed to an extracurricular activity.

It is essential, then, that all music educators learn to initiate and guide conversations about the role of music education with their communities, whatever the parameters of those communities may be. For instance, it may be appropriate for novice music teachers, those with five or fewer years of experience, to participate in a highly localized community—one that includes students, their parents, school administrators, and the local stakeholders. As they gain mastery in the classroom and rehearsal hall, their judgment about the direction of the program also gains credibility. Subsequently, it may be wise to partner with more experienced teachers within their school district or nearby districts on particular advocacy projects. It is certainly important to attend your state MEA conferences to obtain information and guidance from state leaders.

The disconnect between music education advocates and policy makers at various levels (local, state, and national) is the result of differing perspectives on the educational process, appropriate educational outcomes, and the value of an education in the arts. It is vitally important for you, as an advocate for music education, to learn how the complex educational enterprise works and how to speak the language—the jargon—of the local and state administrative mechanisms.

The National Association for Music Education has a large collection of advocacy materials and writings in the "Take Action" area on its website. Young teachers are especially encouraged to view their "Advocacy and Music Educator" document on the NAfME website (http://www.nafme.org/about/position-statements/advocacy-and-the-music-educator-position-statement/advocacy-and-the-music-educator/) for a more detailed rationale for music education advocacy and descriptions of specific actions that music educators can take.

Music Education Reform

The issues of justice and democracy during the eighteenth and nineteenth centuries led directly to the American Revolution and subsequent significant upheaval in Europe and around the world. Of course, not all of the issues were solved as a result of the political revolutions. Specifically, the issue of slavery led directly to the American Civil War. Other issues such as women's suffrage, civil rights, various anti-war movements, LGBT rights, same-sex marriage, and inequality continue to rock and reform our society. Only willful ignorance would lead one to expect that music education and music performance could somehow avoid facing the forces of societal change.

Within the academic world of university-level music education researchers, philosophers, and music teacher educators, a music education reform movement has coalesced around the ideals of social justice and democracy. Members of this movement ask that we all critically examine our practices in music performance and music education to determine whether they conform to these ideals. In practice, the reformers advocate for expanding participation in music making, valuing all varieties of music making and contexts in which musicking occurs, and reforming music instruction with these goals in mind. It would be difficult to argue with the idea that all music is important, as are those who make that music.

As the music reform movement has matured, some have argued that current music education practice and some music performance arts are elitist and actively attempt to exclude the "less talented" from participating. Their arguments are not without merit. Some have argued that the traditional musical ensembles, because of their inherent power structures, are beyond reform and should be eliminated from public school music education offerings.

The response from those who view themselves as performing artists has been furious. They argue that the reformers simply do not understand the sustained effort and musical understanding required to consistently produce high-level artistic performances. Some reformers argue that traditional ensembles should be eliminated because only 20 percent of school populations participate. Performers argue back that those 20 percent see a value in electing to participate in those ensembles. Moreover, the argument exists that, if one of the goals of the reform movement is to respect all music making and the contexts in which it occurs, traditional large ensemble deserves the same respect.

Because performers and reformers have accepted certain ideals not only as worthy goals but also as a part of their identities, what should be a purifying and enlightening discussion about music, music making, and society has devolved into personal invective and name-calling. As has been the case with many reform movements, the younger generation—younger teachers, in this case—has often found ways to implement reform ideals in ways that are not revolutionary but evolutionary, in ways that feel as obvious to them as other social changes do. Many school music programs now include music study and music performance that more accurately reflect the cultural practices and interests of their communities. They have found and created new pedagogies that allow students to participate in and be guided by the process of musical and artistic decision making.

You are about to embark on a career that is fraught with opportunities. Not only will you be responsible for guiding a generation of students through their musical pursuits, but you will also be responsible for fostering an inclusive, artistic musical environment for subsequent generations. The more you understand music, the contexts in which music is made, and the personalities of those who inhabit those contexts, the better prepared you will be to make the critical decisions you will face.

PROJECT

1. Consider and attempt to unpack the various meanings and interactions between the ideas of power, authority, oppression, diversity, freedom, liberty, fairness, justice (in general), social justice, and mercy. How do these concepts apply to and impact musicking, music education and music instruction? Consider how these ideas affect the individual, interactions between individuals, and groups. In order to view the wide variety of perspectives, you will need to seek out the writings of the authors on all sides of the issues. Your instructor should be able to provide you with citations for the most salient and appropriate resources. Some of the most provocative articles in the reform movement can be found at maydaygroup.org.
2. Contact a local music educator and find out what the current music education issues are in their school, district, and state. Ascertain his or her reactions to these issues. Ask what strategies he or she has used to address these issues. Which strategies have been successful and which have not? It may be useful to inquire how the issues have evolved and changed over the course of the educator's career and how his or her strategies have evolved along with them.
3. At about this time during the semester, you should complete a simple field observation. (A sample form is included as figure 11.1.) During your field observation, make special note of both the classroom management and classroom discipline efforts of the in-service teacher. Were these efforts effective? Did they match the ideals outlined in this chapter? Why or why not? Speculate about the next class sessions; will the students' behavior be better, or could the teacher's decisions have unintended consequences? Explain.

Date: _____

Teacher: _____

School: _____

Class: _____

1. Transition to class or rehearsal:
   Take note of how the teacher and students behave during the transition before the class session.
   Are the students on-task during the transition?
   What is the teacher doing to set the tone of the rehearsal?
   What is the teacher's signal to begin rehearsal?

2. Checklist of effective instructional behaviors:
   Look of each of the following instructional behaviors used by the teacher. Take notes to document your observation. The teacher:

   _____ begins the lesson with a short review of previous learning;

   _____ begins the lesson with a short statement of goals;

   _____ presents new material (information) in small steps, with student practice after each step;

   _____ gives clear and detailed instructions and explanations;

   _____ provides a high level of active practice for *all* students;

   _____ asks a large number of questions, checks for student understanding, and obtains responses from all students;

   _____ provides related feedback;

   _____ guides students during initial practice; and

   _____ provides closure for the rehearsal.

3. Other observations:
   Are the students on-task throughout the rehearsal?
   Are the teacher and students obviously following any set routines?
   Did the teacher have any classroom management issues?

4. Teacher Knowledge Base:
   Your task is to look for evidence in each of these categories of teacher knowledge:
   1. Subject matter knowledge

   2. Pedagogical knowledge

   3. Knowledge of students

   4. Knowledge of context

Figure 11.1: Music Instruction Observation Form

CHAPTER 12

From Student to Teacher Revisited

At the beginning of this book, we explored the idea that almost all of what pre-service music teachers know and believe about being a music teacher is the direct result of multiple years in the music classroom as a student and that, unless these ideas and beliefs are challenged in some way, novice music instructors will mostly teach as they were taught, except they will not have access to the kinds of thinking and instructional decisions that guided their teachers' teaching. The purpose of all of the prior chapters in this book was to begin to challenge these tacit ideas you brought to your studies. I hope your ideas about the intellectual basis for music making and music teaching have become more sophisticated as a result.

And yet, all of the research on music teacher development shows that, despite engaging with these kinds of ideas in the university classroom and expressing an appreciation for their value and potential use, many novice teachers still fail to incorporate these ideas into their teaching! How is it that novice teachers fail to enact what they already know about music teaching and learning in their musical routines and pedagogy? In short, the problem appears to involve how pre-service and novice teachers see themselves in their musical and educational landscape: how various experiences define and refine how they view themselves, how they interact with and change their local subculture, how they harmonize the various public and private identities they choose to embrace—such as musician, educator, mentor, leader, community member, and family member—and whether they proactively seek to develop their musical and pedagogical abilities to consciously make sense of themselves as musicians and pedagogues.

DEVELOPING A VISION OF THE TEACHER-SELF

You have read that, according to Linda Darling-Hammond and John Bransford, perhaps the most important outcome from a teacher education program was for the pre-service teacher to develop a vision of what curriculum should and could be for their students. Equally challenging and perhaps just as important is for future teachers to have a vision of themselves as teachers and, at this point in their career, to create a role for themselves within a future hypothetical instructional context—to create a vision of their future selves. Research on pre-service, student teacher, and novice music teachers indicates that they struggle even with determining whether they are primarily a musician or a teacher. There is also evidence that the ability to successfully negotiate and create a coherent self-image may be a determining factor for either developing and maintaining a successful career as a music educator or ultimately leaving the profession.

Before we explore the processes through which teacher identities develop, let's take a look at a few of the basic ideas and terms that underpin the concepts of self and identity.

Self, Identity, and Role

Within the extensive body of research on the subject, researchers and writers note the challenge of providing consistent definitions of the terms *self,* *identity,* and *role.* So, of necessity, what follows is a simplified overview that remains true to the research and literature concerning teacher identity. These constructs should be useful to you, however, for ongoing discussions and debate about your self, your teacher identity, and the roles you may play as a music teacher.

Your self is the person you recognize as you: yourself. As children develop, they go through several stages as they become self-aware. Initially, infants are completely unable to differentiate between themselves, including their own bodies, and their environment. At about the age of eighteen months, a toddler is able recognize that the person she sees in the mirror is herself and not another person. Finally, at about age five, young children begin to develop a sense of self as a unique person as they are able to recall prior events in which they played a role. A more unified awareness of self continues to develop through adolescence. Some theorists argue whether the self is immutable, whether it changes over time, or whether only our perception of self can evolve. Regardless, very simply, your self is the person whom you are with when you are alone.

On the other end of the spectrum is the concept of role. A *role* is your understanding of the socially constructed expectations and require- ments of a particular part that you may play on the stage of life. As you choose to be or become a teacher, musician, parent, member of a par- ticular self-identified community, or any number of other roles, you have an idea of what taking on that role means to you and to others. You may base your understanding of a given role on another person, a role model, from your past. You may have certain understandings of a role based on discussions with others or materials you have read about others who play a particular role. Regardless, your understanding of the role is mutable and incomplete. In fact, you can only understand a particular role as an outsider until you play the role yourself. By defini- tion, your understanding of a role becomes more complex and nuanced over time as you play the role, interact with others, and reflect on your experiences.

Identity stands between the self and a role. This is how you present your- self to others. At various times in your life, you will decide to play a particular role and, at some point, say, "I am a(n) _____." At other times you may say "I am not a(n) _____" or "I am no longer a(n) _____." These are the moments at which you choose or reject a particular role as part of your personally constructed identity. Of course, your understanding of a particular role may differ significantly from that of others. And, therefore, they may have different expectations of the way you will play that role as you identify yourself. As might be expected, these misunderstandings may even remain tacit and may cause significant conflicts between you and others.

These conflicts inform the idea that the formation of one's professional identity is an ongoing, dynamic process. Beijaard, Meijer, and Verloop (2004) suggest that the self-definition of one's identity is never an answer but rather the constant reengagement with the questions "Who am I at this moment?" and "Who do I want to become?" Thus there are often two understandings of self-identity: the realized identity and the imag- ined identity. Music educators undergo a significant and often challenging shift in identity as they transition from student to teacher. Because teach- ers work within a particular instructional context with its unique culture, a teacher's self-identity is often modified by and negotiated against local role expectations. This, too, can be a cause of conflict both internally and with others, depending on potential values conflicts and on the magnitude of the conflict.

Within a music teacher's understanding of his or her professional iden- tity, there may exist sub-identities. These sub-identities may harmonize nicely, or there may be significant dissonance between them. Student teachers and novice music teachers report real personal conflict because they often feel compelled to abandon their self-identification as a musician-performer and adopt the identity of teacher.

Identity Development

The research shows that a music teacher's self-identity often begins to take form as a by product of his or her K–12 music instruction. Many future music teachers decide during high school or even middle school that they intend to become music teachers. As we have seen, pre-service music teacher's ideas about music curriculum and instruction are first based on the apprenticeship of observation that occurs while they are students. Their identities as music teachers are also formed as a result of having music teacher role models and, therefore, pre-service music teachers' idealized self is often a reflection of their role models.

Pre-service music educators often face their first identity conflict on matriculating as a music education major. This conflict revolves around the potential conflict between self-identifying as a performer and self-identifying as a future music teacher. The gateway into college-level music study is always a performance audition of some sort. Often, financial aid and scholarship dollars are attached to this audition. Some institutions, in fact, do not accept students as music education majors unless they are able to perform at the same level as potential music performance majors. By using such a process, institutions communicate a powerful message to their students that their initial value to the school is based on their performing ability. And because of their prior identity development, which is based on their secondary ensemble conductors, young music majors often attach themselves to their new university-level ensemble conductors or their applied instructors, further reinforcing their self-identity as music performers rather than music teachers. Sociological research on university-level music units indicates that significant peer social recognition is attached to perceived performance ability. Simply put, the organizational and social aspects of most music units practically require all music majors to see themselves primarily as performers.

There is ample evidence that many novice music teachers will also experience significant music-performer versus music-educator role conflict during their first years of teaching. As they experience the conflict between their self-identity as a performer and the role expectations placed on them by the instructional context, they experience a kind a *praxisschock*, or practice shock, that can ultimately result in frustration, burnout, and leaving the profession.

Researchers Francis Fuller and Oliver Brown (1975) describe a model of the stages of concern that novice teachers pass through as they develop, which may have implications for their vision of self and their identity. The stages are self-concern, task concerns, and impact concerns. During the first stage, *self-concern*, novice teachers tend to focus on their appearance, how they might be judged by others, and their ability to control student behavior. During the second stage, *task concerns*, novice teachers will tend to focus on their basic instructional skills and their ability to properly execute particular instructional tasks according to a preexisting model, as if following a recipe. For example, they will judge their own instruction more positively if they follow their written lesson plan rather than deviate for any reason. During this stage, they find it challenging to react and adapt to their students' responses during instruction. Finally, during the third stage, *impact concerns*, teachers focus more on the impact of their instruction on student achievement, which leads to a willingness to examine and modify instructional curriculum and their pedagogical skills. It is during the third stage of concern that the role and identity of teacher are established and reinforced. You should understand, though, that experienced teachers don't jettison self-concerns, nor do they stop attending to their basic instructional skills. As you mature as an educator, you'll spend a higher percentage of time in the second and third stages. It is also important to understand that, since even experienced teachers are often resistant to change, teachers will likely revert to behaviors more characteristic of the earlier stages during their career as they are assigned different topics to teach, change instructional positions, or must work outside of their comfort zone.

It is preferable, however, for music teachers to begin advancing through the stages of concern *during* their pre-service education and thereby avoid the most severe consequences of *praxisschock*. They can do this by engaging in activities that are designed to encourage them to reflect on their role and identity as a teacher. It has been shown that pre-service teachers are disinclined to reflect on their instructional role, identity, or pedagogical skills unless they are placed in situations that challenge them to fulfill the role of teacher. Thus, there is a reciprocal relationship between seeing oneself as a teacher and being willing to examine one's own potential instructional impact as a teacher.

The models for music teacher development, which are based on general theories of teacher development, indicate that a continuous cycle of planning, teaching, and reflecting is the only way pre-service music teachers can develop a self-identity as teacher and focus on the impact of their instruction. Earlier in their development process, they should engage in the relatively safe experience of peer instruction. It is during peer instruction episodes that pre-service teachers can become desensitized to the discomfort of standing in front of others, practice delivering instruction according to their plan, and develop habits of reflection by watching and analyzing video of themselves teaching. According to the research literature, even music education majors understand that developing these lower-level instructional skills—teaching to a plan and analyzing the results—requires the same kind of dedication and practice that is required to develop performance skills. After these skills have been habituated in the safe environment of peer teaching, pre-service teachers should have many chances to plan and teach short lessons with small groups of real students and then to reflect on their teaching. Repeating this cycle of plan-teach-reflect under the supervision of a university professor or school-based master teacher allows pre-service music teachers to enact the instructional theories they have learned in their methods classes and to develop the situated knowledge and situational awareness that enables them to make instructional decisions during the act of teaching.

Relationship between Self, Context, and Instructional Practice

Teacher identity development is a dynamic rather than a linear process. As much as theory may inform our understanding of the process in a general sense, the journey of each emerging teacher is a unique excursion. Each pre-service teacher brings his or her unique experiences and understandings to the teacher education process. Every music institution has its own distinct culture that emphasizes some facets of the role and diminishes others. And, perhaps most important, every instructional context has a one-of-a-kind collection of individuals—faculty, administration, students, and parents—who have their own input into the role expectations for the music teacher. The result is often a messy interaction of miscommunicated role expectations and role conflict—praxisschock. Given the cacophony of internal and external voices, how should a novice teacher go about deciding on a course of action?

The first step is simply to accept that becoming and being a teacher is a messy, dynamic, personal journey. The second step, of course, is to remember that your personal and professional development is not the ultimate outcome. You will recall from the beginning of this text that your task as a professional musician-pedagogue is to create an instructional environment in which students can develop the academic, vocational, social and civic, and personal knowledge and skills that will enable them to become functioning and contributing members of our democratic and musical society. Third, you should identify mentors both in and outside of your school, both musical and nonmusical, and identify a cohort of colleague-friends who are at a similar point in their career. Together, they will help you determine common role expectations and suggest options for meeting those expectations.

BECOMING A PROFESSIONAL MUSICIAN-PEDAGOGUE

From the previous chapters in this book, you know that effective teachers have expert knowledge of four distinct areas: subject matter, pedagogy, students, and the instructional context. But you also know that expertise is a product of deliberate practice over an extended period of time. The research on teacher effectiveness indicates that it takes a minimum of five years for a novice teacher to develop instructional competence (Roulston, Legette, & Trotman Womack, 2005), which means being able to consistently provide effective instruction. The goal of a teacher education program is to prepare novice teachers to be at least minimally effective during their first years as teachers—to execute effective instructional routines—even if they do not yet fully understand the impact of their instruction. This begs the questions, what are the characteristics of experienced teachers as compared to novice teachers, what are the characteristics of a professional, and how do these characteristics develop over time?

Characteristics of Experienced Pedagogues

We know from understanding the Fuller and Brown model for stages of concern that novice teacher progress from concern about self to concerns about the task and ultimately to concerns about the impact of their instruction on their students. If we assume that first-year teachers, as the result of their university education, are primarily concerned about the task, what are the instructional characteristics of these first-year teachers and how might their teaching change over time? Researcher David Berliner has described a series of instructional characteristics that are seen as novice teachers develop competence and, eventually, expertise (Berliner, 2004).

Competent novice teachers have a well-developed set of instructional rules and routines that they can follow and implement consistently. This type of teaching, because it is rule-based, does not allow for any variation or adaptation in response to the instructional context or the idiosyncrasies of the students. Only gradually are novice teachers able to identify important variables in the instructional context and develop the competence to adapt their teaching to the context. *Proficient* teachers can consistently and consciously adapt their instruction for a particular context and yield positive outcomes. *Expert* teachers are able to react to instructional variables and apply their professional judgment with such ease and fluency that to outside observers the instruction appears to be almost magical and intuitive. In this sense, expert teachers demonstrate instructional virtuosity in a manner similar to the way virtuoso musical performers do.

Compared to the expert teacher, the novice teacher's use of rules and routines may seem to have negative implications. Yet it is these very routines that enable the development of expertise. How is that possible? Consider what a learning environment might look like *without* these routines. What you would see is a chaotic place in which neither the teacher nor the students would know what to expect next. Routines are clearly the key factor in effective classroom management. By having control of the instructional process via routines, the novice teacher is enabled to notice the students' response to instruction and empowered to enact instructional innovations. The key is finding the right balance between routine and innovation. Without innovations, instruction becomes stagnant; without routines, the context becomes chaotic.

As a corollary, the use of instructional routines might enable the development of expertise, but it does not guarantee it. First, novice teachers must be willing to experiment in their instruction. (You may find it valuable at this time to review the concept of adaptive expertise.) Second, the innovations they implement must be based on sound educational and musical theories. And, finally, they must use the same process (plan-teach-reflect) that they used during their undergraduate education to implement a process of professional development via deliberate practice.

Leadership

Unlike their novice teacher peers in other disciplines and subject areas, novice music teachers are often saddled with the unique administrative requirements of running a music program. These challenges may include course and student scheduling, budgeting and purchasing, inventory, organizing public performances, supervising student travel and field trips, and negotiating with parent or booster organizations. All of these efforts are, of course, in addition to the time requirements of teaching. As with teaching, it takes time to fully understand how these systems work and to manage them effectively. Sometimes, it become necessary not only to manage systems but to change them—to become a leader.

Becoming a professional musician-educator is, on the surface, a long highly prescribed process involving auditions, course work, field work, recitals and exams, student teaching, professional exams, and induction. But, at its core, it is also a highly personal process. Not only does the process require the development of the knowledge and skills necessary to be effective in the classroom, but it also requires the development of a personal and professional identity as a musician-educator. In addition to the other factors of self-identity discussed previously, such as a personal sense of agency, the ability to imagine and effect change appears to be a key factor in the development process.

The best pre-professional and novice educators are aware that the development of their own knowledge, skills, and identity is a *self-regulated process*, that the development process does not primarily happen to them but, rather, they make it happen as the result of their deliberate effort.. This emerging sense of agency has an interesting by-product: a stronger sense of self-sufficiency. As developing teachers realize their ability to effect change, that sense of agency is incorporated into their self-image. Ultimately, there is an inextricable link between identity and agency:

> What may result from a teacher's realization of his or her identity, in performance within teaching contexts, is a sense of agency, of empowerment to move ideas forward, to reach goals *or even to transform the context*. It is apparent that a heightened awareness of one's identity may lead to a strong sense of agency. (Beauchamp & Thomas, 2009, p. 183, emphasis added)

According to the Fuller and Brown stages of concern, the concerns of young teachers gradually move from the self to the task and ultimately to their impact on student learning. It's not unreasonable to speculate that teachers might eventually develop a concern about the implications of the larger educational systems outside of their immediate orbit for their carefully structured classroom environment. Over time, one's areas of concern expand in ever widening circles as one perceives the interrelationship between instructional systems and instructional contexts. This awareness prompts competent teachers to test their leadership skills and their ability to promote change both within their instructional context and in the overall system.

Researchers who study management and leadership in the business realm make a distinction between management, transactional leadership, and transformational leadership. Transactional leaders view change as essentially a barter or exchange: If you do this, I'll give you this in exchange; If you do your job, you'll get paid and potentially promoted. Those who operate with this mindset are not leaders but managers. They believe there is a defined system and that within that system there are defined roles and identities. Within this model, goals are attained if all parties play their defined roles and fulfill their responsibilities.

Transformational leaders, on the other hand, often have a powerful vision of what could be. In order to effect change, these leaders inspire others, via modeling and empowerment, to make meaningful, systemic change. Those who are led by transformational leaders experience changes in their perceived self-identity as they allow the well-being of the group and the mission to supersede their own interests.

> [T]ransformational leaders motivate their followers to commit to and to realize performance outcomes that exceed their expectations. Achieving such outcomes entails three principal leadership processes: (1) these leaders heighten followers' awareness about the importance and value of designated goals and the means to achieve them; (2) they induce followers to transcend their self-interests for the good of the organization and its goals; and (3) they stimulate and meet their followers' higher order needs through the leadership process and the mission. (Marotto, Victor, & Roos, 2001, p. 6)

You can understand these two models of leadership more clearly if you imagine them as the model of individual adaptive expertise that has been expanded to an organizational or systemic level. As with a classroom guided by an adaptive expert, there is a certain value to established routines that allow an organization to function. A stagnant, nonadaptive organization, however, can be as stifling as a learning environment that is based entirely on established routines. The goal is to find a balance between roles and routines that foster efficiency and innovations that foster expanded effectiveness. One of your challenges as an emerging teacher and future leader is to establish these habits of efficient routines and effective adaptations for yourself.

One way to think of your instructional context is as a complex, dynamic, interactive system of variables. Every student, every grouping of students, each new instructional unit, each change of season, every change of time schedule, or any number of other variables can have an impact on the effectiveness and efficiency of instruction in a given context. Your task during those first five years of instruction is to establish routines that take into account all of these kinds of variables and yet are stable on their own. Learning to manage and modify this system is, in fact, a form of leadership.

From a slightly more elevated viewpoint, you can think of each instructional setting in your school as its own little system of variables that interact with each other and create a larger system of variables called a school. Your classroom system is like a black box inside a larger system. Some variables are controlled within the classroom by your and your students; other variables are determined by the larger system of the school. Only after you have learned to manage the variables in your own classroom can you begin to understand how those outside of your classroom can affect it. From this perspective, it might be wise to resist promoting change to the outside system until you've mastered your own.

One final note about promoting change: as artists, music teachers are often blessed with abundant visions of what should be and how systems should serve their own instructional and musical aspirations. For these leaders, it is often tempting to bring about change through force of will, by the power of their personal charisma. However effective this change may be in the short term, it often leads to significant challenges for the organization when the charismatic leader leaves. Transformational leaders leave a lasting legacy of positive change by improving the system alongside others within it. Their style of leadership is most similar to that of an effective teacher, in that they empower others to do good works within a particular context. You may recall that a teacher's primary task is to create an environment in which students can learn. The primary task of a transformational leader is to create an environment in which the members of the organization can do their work at a high level and effect meaningful change on their own.

Dispositions

Pre-professional teachers become professionals not only by acting as they do but also by engaging in the same kind of professional thinking. So from this list of characteristics of professionals, we are able to distill dispositions for successful music teacher education students:

1. Has regular and punctual attendance
2. Is dependable and responsible (e.g., initiates timely communication with instructors regarding absences, scheduling, or documentation)
3. Demonstrates positive communication style with instructors and colleagues
4. Avoids use of technology in the classroom for non-instructional activities (e.g., not using Facebook, texting, or sending personal emails)
5. Exhibits appropriate professional behavior (e.g., passion for teaching, positive attitude, no inappropriate content on personal pages such as Facebook or Twitter)
6. Maintains an appropriate professional appearance (e.g., proper attire and personal hygiene)

7. Adheres to high ethical standards (e.g., proper citation of resources, not representing others' work as one's own, adhering to the Student Academic Code of Conduct, and so on)
8. Uses appropriate grammar and vocabulary in all documents and emails (avoiding the use of slang, inappropriate humor, and so on)
9. Is responsive to constructive feedback
10. Maintains professionalism during field experiences

Just as with deliberate learning, if you can incorporate these dispositions into your identity—who you are—then you will have mastered the fundamentals of becoming a professional educator.

LICENSURE AND CERTIFICATION PROCESSES

In the closing section of this final chapter, we will circle back to the beginning and discuss the meaning of being a professional music educator along with the various processes through which one develops and obtains both the characteristics and credentials to become so identified.

Characteristics of Professionals

Technically, professionals are those who require some kind of official licensure or certification to practice. Along with educators, this list includes accountants, physicians, and architects. Lee Schulman, an educational psychologist who has written extensively about educational practice and teacher development, indicated that professional educators share six "commonplaces" that characterize all professions (1998, p. 516):

1. An "obligation of service to others": professional educators are bound by certain moral and ethical obligations to place the interests of their clients—their students, in this case—above their own interests;
2. An "understanding of a scholarly or theoretical kind": a recognition that there is a body of scholarly knowledge that guides one's practice in the profession;
3. "A domain of skilled performance or practice": practice in the profession requires the *enactment* of that body of knowledge;
4. "The exercise of judgment under conditions of unavoidable uncertainty": because the needs of students and instructional contexts vary widely, judgment is required as to what and how professional knowledge needs to be applied to solve real-world problems;

5. Recognition of "the need for learning from experience as theory and practice interact": an understanding by all in the educational and teacher education realm that experience and reflection are the keys to developing effective practice; and

6. "A professional community to monitor quality and aggregate knowledge": by development of professional organizations and standards, it is practitioners who define professional practice and regulate membership in the profession.

The processes through which you obtain and retain professional credentials to practice as a music educator vary from state to state and, therefore, are beyond the scope of this book. Certain commonalities are reviewed here, however. are In general, these processes adhere closely to the ideals outlined in Schulman's six commonplaces.

Under the guidance of practicing professionals, each state has developed means by which those who desire to become teachers may obtain and retain the requisite credentials. These processes generally include the following:

1. Acquisition of a required body of knowledge, which is documented by the successful completion of specified coursework. (This coursework must be completed at an accredited institution. Teacher education programs obtain accreditation by meeting certain standards that are set by outside accrediting organizations, such as the National Council for Accreditation of Teacher Education (NCATE) or Teacher Education Accreditation Council (TEAC). Teacher education programs obtain accreditation by submitting significant portfolios of documentation to these agencies, which review the documentation and visit the institutions to determine whether they meet the standards. Only then is the institution authorized to prepare teachers to enter the profession.)

2. Completion, during the coursework, of a prescribed number of field experience hours under the supervision of professionally credentialed educators.

3. The successful completion of a formal mentoring process. Almost without exception, those wishing to obtain professional teacher credentials must spend a length of time working with and then under the direct supervision of a credentialed professional educator. This process is often referred to as "student teaching" or an "internship." This field experience is specified as part of the coursework and must be completed prior to earning a degree from the institution.

4. Passing a professional exam.

On completion of this process, one is generally eligible to obtain a preliminary license or certificate as a professional educator and is, therefore, eligible to be employed by a public school system. In parallel with the medical licensure process, some jurisdictions refer to initially licensed teachers as resident educators. In some states, private schools and charter schools are not bound by the same standards and may hire individuals as teachers even if they have not obtained professional credentials.

Obtaining a Teaching License

All states have statutory requirements that must be met prior to obtaining a teaching position. Meeting these requirements earns one of the various types of teaching licenses. Although the requirements for obtaining a teaching license and the types of licenses vary from state to state, in general the following apply:

1. You must obtain a bachelor's degree from an accredited college or university;
2. You must complete an approved teacher preparation program;
3. You must complete various licensing exams;
4. You must submit to and pass a background check, which will include fingerprinting; and
5. You must complete the extensive license application process.

If you're taking a course that requires this text, there is a very good chance that you either are pursuing a bachelor's degree in music education or you have already completed a bachelor's degree in music and are now in a music teacher preparation program. Either scenario will allow you to complete the first two requirements on the list. Many music teacher preparation programs require credentials candidates to pass some of the licensing exams either prior to student teaching or in order to pass the internship. Some states require national exams such as the PRAXIS exam or EdTPA, whereas other states have created their own exams. By the time you complete your student teaching, you should have met all of the requirements to apply for a teaching license.

The subsequent sections in this chapter include details about and suggestions for successfully completing some of the steps in the licensure process.

Student Teaching

When you have finished your coursework at the university or college, you are not yet authorized to be responsible for students' learning outcomes from the state's perspective because you have not completed the requirements to obtain a license, nor have you proved that are a competent teacher. It's a classic Catch-22: you cannot get teaching experience because you do not have a license and you cannot get a license without teaching experience.

Almost without exception, you will be required to complete a student teaching experience to obtain your initial teaching license or certificate. In the past, this internship was sometimes called "practice teaching." The purpose of this opportunity is for you to practice enacting your pedagogical content knowledge with real students in an authentic instructional context under the mentorship of a cooperating teacher. The school-based cooperating teacher is primarily responsible for assuring that the students in his or her classes are still receiving high-quality instruction and will be fully prepared to complete any standardized tests or other summative assessments at the end of their course. Secondarily, your cooperating teacher will serve as a mentor.

You will have to apply for a student teaching placement, usually through the regular teacher education offices on your campus. You will also have to complete a background check, including fingerprinting. You should pay attention to deadlines, as these applications and the background check often must be completed well before you can be assigned to a school. Some school systems require an interview before they will accept you as a student teacher.

When you first receive your student teaching assignment, you will need to ascertain the particulars such as your daily schedule, the details about the class or classes and students you will be teaching, any non-instructional duties, and the dress code. Before your first day as a student teacher, you will want to learn as much as possible about your cooperating teacher, the school, the school system, and the surrounding community, especially if your student teaching location is distant from where you have been completing your coursework. The more you know about the instructional context and your cooperating teacher, the better prepared you will be to join into the community of practice.

During your student teaching assignment, you will be working closely with your cooperating teacher, so it is essential that you develop a working relationship with him or her. Even if the school system does not require an interview prior to your placement, you will find it advantageous to schedule a meeting with your cooperating teacher prior to your official first day on campus. It is important that you have a clear understanding of the cooperating teacher's expectations of you. Assuming the role of a student teacher can be challenging for some students, especially those who have had leadership roles during the college experience.

It is important for you to understand that, as a student teacher, you are a temporary guest in a preexisting community of practice. Your primary task is to fit into this community as seamlessly as possible. To minimize the impact on the instructional momentum, you will need to learn and use your cooperating teacher's instructional routines, even if you think your way might be more effective. The quickest way to sour your relationship with your cooperating teacher would be to leave even the impression that you believe you know more than he or she does.

During the course of your internship, you will likely start your experience by observing all of your cooperating teacher's classes. During this time, you should attempt to understand the instructional routines and classroom management procedures, so that that you can implement them when your turn arrives. You should also endeavor to learn the students' names. After the period of observation, you may be given the opportunity to mimic these routines, such as the entering and exiting procedures, taking attendance, or the warm-up. Successfully completing these short class segments will inspire confidence from the students and your cooperating teacher and will help you become more comfortable. If you are successful, you will gradually be given more responsibilities and be incorporated into the instructional life of the program. Your cooperating teacher will help you plan for your lessons, observe you while you teach, help you reflect on your teaching, and provide useful feedback. If you wish to continue to have his or her confidence, you will take the advice to heart and implement suggested changes in your teaching.

In addition to the school-based cooperating teacher, you will also have a university-based supervisor. You may or may not have had classes with this person prior to your internship. This person may not even have a music background. If many of the student teachers from your university are placed a considerable distance away from campus, the university may hire someone whose sole task is to supervise student teachers. Whatever particular arrangements are made for you, the university supervisor will also function as a mentor who will critique your lesson plans and give constructive feedback following observations. He or she will also help you complete the extensive documentation that is required to obtain your teaching license. You and the other music student teachers will likely have periodic seminar meetings with your university supervisor. Depending on the logistics, these seminars may take in-person or online. During these seminars, you will have reading and writing assignments, and you will have an opportunity to discuss issues that may have arisen since your last seminar meeting. Sometimes, the best advice you receive might be from your student teacher colleagues. As with your cooperating teacher, it is to your advantage to maintain a positive working relationship with your university supervisor, since he or she may be the final authority to document and sign off on the completion of your licensure process.

EdTPA

As mentioned by Schulman (1998), the sixth of the characteristics of professional practice is a set of standards for practice that are developed by the larger professional community. All states require prospective educators to pass an examination of their professional knowledge in order to obtain a provisional teaching license. Although many states have developed their own exam, the PRAXIS exam has been accepted by many others. This exam allows for reciprocal licensure between participating states. In spite of its name, the PRAXIS exam has been criticized for not requiring teacher candidates to demonstrate effective instructional planning or competence in delivery. In other words, the PRAXIS exam is not an authentic assessment tool since the prospective educators are not required to engage in an authentic instructional task. There has long been a need for a standardized method of assessing whether prospective educators can demonstrate thinking about instructional design, instructional delivery, student assessment, and self-reflection that is similar to the thinking of seasoned professional educators.

To address this need, education professors at Stanford University and members of the American Association of Colleges for Teacher Education collaborated to design and validate the Education Teacher Performance Assessment (EdTPA), which allows authentic assessment of effective instructional tasks. Like the licensing examinations in other professional fields, the EdTPA examination requires prospective educators to demonstrate their ability to enact their pedagogical content knowledge rather than merely document their knowledge of best instructional practices and theory. In each of five categories, licensure candidates are required to submit artifacts to document their instructional effectiveness. These artifacts are assessed by trained evaluators. See table 12.1 for an overview of the EdTPA assessment process (*Using EdTPA*, n.d.).

Preliminary research on the Performance Assessment of California Teacher (PACT), which employs a design similar to that of the EdTPA process, indicates that standardized teacher performance assessments (TPAs) are useful for predicting subsequent instructional effectiveness (Darling-Hammond, Newton, & Wei, 2013). Moreover, TPAs may prove valuable tools for improving the quality of teacher education programs in general (Peck, Singer-Gabella, Sloan, & Lin, 2014). There are those, of course, who contend that the instructional process is far too complex and context-specific to be adequately assessed by a standardized tool, but others contend that the process does not provide comparable, reliable data unless the assessment process is standardized.

Table 12.1: EDUCATION TEACHER PERFORMANCE ASSESSMENT OUTCOMES

	Artifacts	Rubrics
Planning	Lesson plans, instructional materials, student assignments, assessments Planning commentary	Planning for Content Understanding Supporting Student's Learning Needs Planning Assessment to Monitor Student Understanding
Instruction	Unedited video clips Instruction commentary	Demonstrating a Positive and Engaging Learning Environment Engaging Students in Learning Deepening Learning During Instruction Subject-Specific Pedagogy
Assessment	Samples of student work Summary of student learning Assessment commentary	Analyzing Student Learning Providing Feedback to Guide Learning Supporting Students' Use of Feedback
Analysis of Learning	Planning commentary Instruction commentary Assessment commentary	Using Knowledge of Students to Inform Planning Analyzing Teaching Using Assessment to Inform Instruction
Academic Language	Unedited video clips and/or student work samples Planning and assessment commentaries	Identifying and Supporting Language Demands Evidence of Language to Support Content Understandings

Finally, some controversy has developed about the way EdTPA is administered and the way students are assessed. Owing to the great size of the project, Pearson, a corporation that specializes in developing large-scale learning assessment tools, was engaged to participate in the development of EdTPA and to administer the examination. Because each exam requires a substantial fee, which is normally paid by the student, critics contend that Pearson has rigged the examination process to maximize its profits. Although there have been notable exceptions, the evaluators are primarily university education professors who are trained and paid by Pearson to score the results. Some people have suggested that, because the evaluators have no longitudinal data on the licensure candidates, they are unable to predict long-term success on the basis of a single assessment. But it is also argued that the assessors must be independent from those being evaluated.

Any systemic change of this magnitude will always result in controversy. You would be advised to consult updated sources for the latest information on EdTPA policies and procedures in your state.

Alternative Licensure Processes

Many states have authorized alternative procedures for attaining certification or licensure as a professional music educator. They cannot all be covered in this text. However, many such programs allow candidates to attain credits via online courses or night and weekend courses, award credits for "life experience," and sometimes allow candidates to skip normally crucial portions of the educational experience, such as student teaching, by awarding credit for teaching in private schools. This course is often pursued by adult students who may have already been teaching for years in private schools that, until recently, had not required a valid teaching license as a prerequisite for attaining a position. Other programs, such as Teach for America, allow college graduates to attend six-week teaching "boot camps" and then teach in under-resourced districts.

Naturally, there are critics of such programs. These critics suggest that such shortcuts to licensure undermine the professional nature of the educational process and that organizations such as Teach for America are more interested in profits than in high-quality educational experiences for students. Supporters of alternative licensure claim that university colleges of education are out of step with developments in the business models of modern educational systems and that the current models of teacher education produce novice teachers who are not adequately prepared for the rigors of teaching.

Initial Employment and Induction

Most novice teachers describe their first year in the profession as being highly rewarding. They also note that they face a wide variety of challenges, many of them unanticipated. Specifically, they report the trials of classroom management and remaining focused on their instructional goals. But these difficulties are balanced against the satisfaction they receive from their students' general growth. Along with the challenges faced by all first-year teachers, first-year music teachers also must deal with managing a music program, including recruiting, preparing for public performances, travel, working with large numbers of students (compared to most classroom teachers), parent groups, and before- and after-school activities. Some music teachers face the unique challenge having to provide instruction on more than one campus, often without a designated music classroom.

The data concerning teacher attrition indicate that nearly half of all novice teachers leave the profession within five years. In addition to the factors cited above, those who leave often cite the overall school environment, especially in urban districts, and the lack of parental and administrative support as major factors. Specifically, those who leave the profession or seek employment in different schools or districts indicate that a lack of administrative support—such as concert attendance, assistance with scheduling students into the music program, student behavior management, and creating a positive school environment—was a key factor in their decision to seek change. In many cases, these administrative support issues determined job satisfaction among early-career music teachers and affected their propensity to stay in the profession. The best administrators realize that novice music teachers face unique challenges and seek to provide specialized support.

Induction is a formalized process through which beginning teachers in all disciplines receive special mentoring and professional development specifically designed to meet their needs. Almost all states mandate that school districts provide an induction program. The quality of these programs, however, is inconsistent. The majority of them are only designed for generic first-year teachers. It is the exception for a district to provide a unique music teacher induction program. Usually a first-year music teacher participates in a generic induction program along with a music teacher mentor.

Although first-year music teachers have generally positive attitudes toward their training, they generally cite a desire to become more effective teachers, along with a need to become more personally and professionally organized. The survey data indicate that these needs and concerns are primarily driven by the unique challenges of their current instructional context. Novice music teachers should take special care to seek out even informal mentoring from trusted senior music faculty members, friends in the profession, and even family members. These important others can provide significant advice for dealing with novel problems, challenging individuals, and job expectations. Often, attaining permanent licensure is contingent upon satisfactory completion of the induction and mentoring process.

Professional Development

After the long process of completing a music education degree or licensure program, successfully completing student teaching, passing the licensure exams, obtaining an initial license and finding a job, your journey as a music educator will have only just started. As a part of your professional responsibilities, you will have to maintain your eligibility to practice by attending professional development sessions or attending graduate-level courses to renew your license. In-service educators involved in intense professional development programs report "a greater awareness of the students in their classes who are struggling academically and how to help them; a broader and more complex understanding of curriculum planning; [an awareness of] the importance of collegiality and collaboration in professional life; [an appreciation for] the value of feedback and structured reflection; and [a deeper understanding of the] theoretical frameworks of education that [have] enhanced both pedagogy and appreciation for broader educational issues outside the classroom" (Kunzman, 2003, p. 241).

Many school districts offer professional development courses, but these may not be music-specific or, perhaps, even germane to the unique instructional requirements of music. Other opportunities abound, however. In addition to the various state music education associations that are affiliated with the National Association for Music Education, there are national organizations devoted to specific areas such as the American Orff-Schulwerk Association (aosa.org), the Organization of American Kodály Educators (oake.org), and the Gordon Institute for Music Learning (giml.org), all of which have state and local chapters. Each offers opportunities for professional development and networking within their community of practice. Note that additional fees are often required at these workshops in order to obtain professional development or college credits. You should also be aware that many universities offer professional development opportunities, often via summer courses or by awarding credits for attending and then reflecting on attendance at national and state conventions.

In addition to the various formal induction and professional development opportunities, you may wish to seek out informal communities of practice or mentorship arrangements. For example, you might establish professional relationships or friendships with nearby colleagues who are at a similar point in their career, since they are likely to be experiencing challenges similar to yours, along with veteran music educators, even those who are retired, who may have wise advice on how to navigate early-career challenges.

The most important aspect of professional development is to have a growth orientation—a disposition which suggests that you are not enabled or limited by a set of gifts or talents but that you can get better at any aspect of your professional life if you work at it. Likewise, you have to understand that, although your students may face significant challenges with the musical material and other aspects of their lives, if the lesson doesn't work, it's not their fault. You have to determine the best professional reaction to the students' response.

The teachers who make the most progress go through a cycle of planning, teaching, and reflecting followed by study and consultation. You must plan for your instruction, implement the plan as best you can, and then reflect on your students' response and success. The challenge is to determine what did not work, what you need to know in order to do better, study and consult with respected colleagues, and then go through another planning-teaching-reflecting cycle. These cycles occur daily, over the course of an academic year, and over the course of a career.

Finally, you will recall that music education majors often experience role conflict as they decide between identifying themselves as performers or educators. After reading this text, you may have come to the conclusion that the best musician is both performer and educator. You would be well advised, then, to continue your own development and participation in both realms. Conductors often find that it is invaluable to continue as a performer in a community ensemble, which helps them remember the kinds of challenges their students face in their school ensembles. More important, maintaining an active musical life as a performer will help you remember the unique joys and personal insights that come from making music and help you remember why you became a musician and music educator in the first place.

PROJECT

1. Explain the following concepts:
   – Stages of concern
     – Self-concern
     – Task concerns
     – Impact concerns
   – Instructional competence
   – Management and leadership (You might be able to make a connection with proactive classroom management)
2. Explain the difference between instructional systems and instructional contexts.
3. Consider the instructional behaviors you might expect to observe at each of the three stages of concern. How would these behaviors impact instructional effectiveness, classroom management, and other teacher-student interactions?
4. Look back at the reflections you wrote after viewing your observations of in-service teachers and your reflections on your micro-teaching experiences. Look for and cite at least one example of each of the stages from your observations and your reflections. Explain why each represents that stage of development. If you are unable to identify an example of a particular stage, explain why not. What do you need to do as a future music teacher to focus on impact concerns as opposed to the previous two stages?

5. It was stated in this chapter that expert teachers demonstrate instructional virtuosity in a manner similar to the way virtuoso musical performers. State whether you support this statement and then explain your reasoning.

6. Determine the music teacher licensing requirements in your state. Go to the websites for your college or university's education license area, your state department of education, and your state music education association to obtain information on the requirements for initial or permanent music teacher certification. Create a checklist outline of the requirements and add the dates when you anticipate meeting the requirements.

7. Contact a local in-service music teacher whom you can ask about administrative responsibilities. Be sure to ask about purchasing, budgets, fundraising, parent groups, scheduling, performances, inventory, and field trips. Also ask whether he or she has to share in other faculty service, such as lunch supervision or bus duty.

8. Compare the six commonplaces of professionals with the list of dispositions listed in the introduction to the book.

9. Investigate and document alternative licensure procedures in your state.

10. Investigate and report on state- and district-level induction policies and procedures.

CHAPTER 13

Coda

In this brief conclusion, I reconsider some of the key points from other chapters. Previously, you viewed these concepts in your role as a student; now I'm going to ask you to view them from the perspective of your role as future teacher and consider your impact on your future students.

DELIBERATE LEARNING

You will recall the concept of deliberate practice and how successful musicians use deliberate practice to achieve their musical goals. At this point, I want to encourage you to use *deliberate learning* to achieve all of your musical and academic goals.

1. You have to plan how you are going to achieve your goals. Do *not* allow the assignments set by your instructors to be the extent of your goals. Think of your assignments, your lessons, your juries, and your ensemble roles as *minimum* expectations. You will not excel until you set your own long-term goals, but often those goals are so far away that it is impossible to see a clear path. So, we have to set nearer-term goals that move us in the general direction of the long-term aim.

2. You need to focus on fundamental skills and fundamental understandings rather than the details of the literature you are working on or on the details of a given assignment. For example, if you have to write a short paper for a class, rather than allowing the short-term assignment (the paper) to get your focus, you should instead focus on your ability as a researcher, which is necessary for gathering the information for your paper, and your ability to write clearly. As you continue to work on these two abilities, your subsequent papers will be better products without

being nearly as overwhelming to complete. Likewise, as you work on your performance skills, try to avoid focusing on getting through the next performance and instead focus on the fundamental skills and understandings that will allow you to prepare for subsequent performances more quickly while also delivering a better, more musical product.

3. Take every opportunity to get better. Send drafts of your papers to your instructors for feedback so that you make sure you are on track. Send recordings from your practice sessions to your applied instructor for feedback. Perform for your peers. Let the older students read your papers. Send your papers to your parents and let them read them; assuming they are nonmusicians, if they can understand them, then likely your writing is clear and sufficient. As you work in the practice room and on your academic assignments, you are probably not going to notice the incremental improvements or the random bad habits that might creep into your work. But getting feedback from others not only helps you stay focused on the fundamentals, it also helps you notice your improvements and your errors so that you will become less reliant on external feedback and validation. You can, in essence, become your own teacher.

4. Keep in mind that musical performance, no matter how much psychomotor skill is involved, is primarily a mental task, since the mind controls the body. This is also true about writing; despite the fact that you may be pounding the keyboard on your computer, it is still a mental task at its core. Therefore, you have to learn how to remain mentally focused on your task. One useful suggestion is to use a timer: work for twenty-five minutes without taking a physical or mental break and then take a five-minute break. If you think about your work in this way, then you can put off checking your email or responding to a text until your break time. (It may also be useful to turn off notifications on your phone while you work.)

5. Working in this manner is not fun like riding a roller coaster, but it is satisfying. One important goal for yourself is to become a person who gets things done and to incorporate that idea into how you self-identify. Your work ethic or work ideal should be that of the tortoise and not the hare: you may not be the fastest, but you will work until you reach your self-designed goal.

IDENTITY AND MOTIVATION FOR BECOMING A MUSICIAN-EDUCATOR

Throughout the book, you have been challenged to reconsider how you view yourself. In chapter 2, I asked you to reconsider what you know about what it means to be a teacher. When you read about apprenticeship of observation, one reasonable inference would have been that you really didn't know what it meant to be a teacher. Quite frankly, it is absolutely impossible for you to know what it is like to be a teacher and how teachers think until you have been a teacher for a few years. In many ways, the whole point of that reading was to urge you to give up your preexisting ideas about being a teacher and about teaching so that you could build up new understandings to which you could add new knowledge and skills. Because they form the foundation for future learning about teaching, I asked you to read about the four purposes of public education in the United States and about the four kinds of specialized knowledge that effective teachers lean on to make context-specific instructional decisions.

In the third chapter, you read about the myth of talent that many hold dear as the basis of their identity as a musician. If you listen carefully, you will often hear mature musicians talk about how their talent manifested itself while they were still young and how some important person told them that they were special—that they had "the gift.'" If you think about it from that perspective, you can understand how hard it would be for one to give up the idea that they are special and that it is only a matter of time until their abilities are widely recognized. Giving up that part of your self-identity, if you had it, was exactly what you were asked to do, but you were also asked to replace it with the idea that hard work in the form of deliberate practice was the key to achieving what you already imagined that you would achieve.

After a lengthy consideration of the issues of music, music as subject (subject matter knowledge), how students learn and acquire understanding (knowledge of students), curriculum, instructional design, and engaging instruction (pedagogical knowledge), along with the instructional context (knowledge of context), you were finally asked to specifically consider your self, identity, and role as a musician and as a pedagogue. Exactly who are you as a musician and a teacher? How do you want to project your self to your students and the community of practice? Can you find a community of practice where your self and your identity are a match for the role its members expect you to fill? And, as you assume the role of leader in your school and in the profession while considering the contemporary issues in education and music education, can you help improve the quality of life and music making in those communities?

In the end, the assumption is that you want to be both a great musician and a great teacher. The first purpose of all the reading was to have you realize that that you can't simply *be* a great musician-pedagogue. But you can *become* a great musician-pedagogue and you have control of that process. The second purpose of the reading was to give you the understandings that you need to plan that process and to implement it.

PAUSE FOR THOUGHT

Consider your own musical story to this point in your life. What has caused you to dare to be a music teacher? To be a teacher of children and adolescents? How did you arrive where you are today?

What stories have influenced your path? Who has played a role in the various stories of your life? How have your stories and experiences influenced you and your thoughts about music teaching and learning? What do you believe about teaching music and why?

Check yourself. Are you able to explain these concepts and why they are meaningful to you?

How have you used deliberate practice and deliberate learning to transform yourself as a musician and as a pedagogue? Prior to taking this course, had you bought into the myth of talent?

Explain the importance of getting and giving honest feedback.

What have you learned about your self during the semester? Have you changed your identity—how you present yourself to others—as a result of your growth?

Compared to the beginning of the semester, explain how your understanding of what it means to be a musician (artist) and a pedagogue (teacher) has changed. How have you changed as a result of your new understandings? How has your process for approaching learning changed?

REFERENCES

Ables, H. F., Hoffer, C. R., & Klotman, R. H. (1995). *Foundations of music education* (2nd ed.). New York: Schirmer Books.

Allsup, R. E., & Shieh, E. (2012). Social justice and music education: The call for a public pedagogy. *Music Educators Journal, 98*(4), 47–51. doi:10.1177/0027432112442969

Barry, N. H., & Hallum, S. (2002). Practice. In *The science and psychology of music performance: Cognitive strategies for teaching and learning* (pp. 151–166). New York: Oxford University Press.

Beauchamp, C., & Thomas, L. (2009). Understanding teacher identity: An overview of issues in the literature and implications for teacher education. *Cambridge Journal of Education, 39*(2), 175–189. doi:10.1080/03057640902902252

Beijaard, D., Meijer, P. C., & Verloop, N. (2004). Reconsidering research on teachers' professional identity. *Teaching and Teacher Education, 20*(2), 107–128. doi:10.1016/j.tate.2003.07.001

Berliner, D. C. (2004). Expert teachers: Their characteristics, development and accomplishments. *R. Batllori i Obiols, AE Gomez Martinez, M. Oller i Freixa & J. Pages i. Blanch (Eds.), De la teoria. . . . a l'aula: Formacio del professorat enseñyament de las ciències socials*, 13–28.

Bloom, B. S. (1956). *Taxonomy of educational objectives: The classification of educational goals. Handbook 1; cognitive domain.* New York: David McKay.

Bloom's Taxonomy. (n.d.). Bloom's taxonomy. [Web page].

Bransford, J. D., Derry, S., Berliner, D., & Hammerness, K. (2005). Theories of learning and their roles in teaching. In L. Darling-Hammond & J. Bransford (Eds), *Preparing teachers for a changing world: What teachers should learn and be able to do* (pp. 40–87). San Franciso, CA: Jossey-Bass.

Bransford, J. D., & Stein, B. S. (1993). *The IDEAL problem solver* (2nd ed.). New York: Freeman.

Bruner, J. S. (1977). *The process of education.* Cambridge: Harvard University Press. Retrieved from Library of Congress or OCLC Worldcat.

Brunning, R. H., Schraw, G. J., & Ronning, R. R. (1999). *Cognitive psychology and instruction* (3rd ed.). Upper Saddle River, NJ: Prentice-Hall.

Clements, A. C., & Klinger, R. (2010). *A field guide to student teaching in music.* New York: Routledge.

Colvin, G. (2008). *Talent is overrated: What really separates world-class performers from everybody else.* New York: Penguin Group.

Consortium of National Arts Education Associations. (1994). *Dance, music, theatre, visual arts: what every young American should know and be able to do in the arts: National standards for arts education.* Lanham, MD: Rowman & Littlefield Education.

Darling-Hammond, L., Amrein-Beardsley, A., Haertel, E., & Rothstein, J. (2012). Evaluating teacher evaluation. *Phi Delta Kappan*, 8–15. Retrieved from Google Scholar.

Darling-Hammond, L., Banks, J., Zumwalt, K., Gomez, L., Sherin, M. G., Griesdorn, J., & Finn, L. (2005). Educational goals and purposes: Developing a curricular vision for teaching. In L. Darling-Hammond & J. Bransford (Eds.), *Preparing teachers for a changing world: What teachers should know and be able to do* (pp. 169-200). San Francisco, CA: Jossey-Bass

Darling-Hammond, L., & Bransford, J. (Eds.). (2005). *Preparing teachers for a changing world: What teachers should know and be able to do.* San Francisco: Jossey-Bass.

Darling-Hammond, L., Newton, S. P., & Wei, R. C. (2013). Developing and accessing beginning teacher effectiveness: The potential of performance assessments. *Educational Assessment, Evaluation and Accountability, 25*(3), 179–204. Retrieved from Google Scholar.

Darrow, A. (2014). Differentiated instruction for students with disabilities: Using DI in the music classroom. *General Music Today, 28*(2), 29–32. doi:10.1177/1048371314554279

Davidson, J. W., Howe, M. J. A., Moore, D. G., & Sloboda, J. A. (1996). The role of parental influences in the development of musical ability. *British Journal of Developmental Psychology, 14*, 399–411.

de Groot, A. D. (1965). *Thought and choice in chess.* The Hague: Mouton.

Duke, R. A. (1994). Bringing the art of rehearsing into focus: The rehearsal frame as a model for prescriptive analysis of rehearsal conducting. *Journal of Band Research, 30*, 78–95.

Elliott, D. J. (2005). *Praxial music education : Reflections and dialogues.* New York: Oxford University Press.

Ericsson, K. A., & Chase, W. G. (1982). Exceptional memory. *American Scientist, 6*, 607–612.

Ericsson, K. A., Krampe, R. T., & Tesch-Römer, C. (1993). The role of deliberate practice in the acquisition of expert performance. *Psychological Review, 100*(3), 363–406.

Feiman-Nemser, S. (2001). From preparation to practice: Designing a continuum to strengthen and sustain teaching. *The Teachers College Record, 103*(6), 1013–1055.

Fuller, F. F., & Bown, O. H. (1975). Becoming a teacher. In K. Ryan (Ed.), *Teacher education* (pp. 25–52). Chicago: National Society for the Study of Education.

Garofalo, R., & Garofalo, R. J. (1983). *Blueprint for band: A guide to teaching comprehensive musicianship through school band performance.* Hal Leonard Corporation. Retrieved from Google Scholar.

Gembris, H. (2002). The development of musical abilities. In R. Colwell & C. Richardson (Eds.), *The new handbook of research on music learning and teaching* (487–508). Oxford: Oxford University Press.

Goodlad, J. I. (1984). *A place called school.* New York: McGraw-Hill.

Grossman, P., Schoenfeld, A., & Lee, C. (2005). Teaching subject matter. In J. Bransford & L. Darling-Hammond (Eds.), *Preparing teachers for a changing world: What teachers should learn and be able to do* (pp. 202–231). San Francisco: Jossey-Bass.

Grühn, W. (2005). Understanding musical understanding. In D. J. Elliott (Ed.), *Praxial music education: Reflections and dialogues* (pp. 98–111). New York: Oxford University Press.

Hoffer, C., Lindeman, C., Reimer, B., Shuler, S., Straub, D., & Lehman, P. (n.d.). *October 2007 report of the MENC task force on national standards* [Web page]. Retrieved from http://www.nafme.org/my-classroom/standards/national-standards-archives/.

Hovey, N. (1976). *Efficient rehearsal procedures for school bands.* Elkhart, IN: The Selmer Company.

Howe, M. J. A., Davidson, J. W., Moore, D. G., & Sloboda, J. A. (1995). Are there early childhood signs of musical ability? *Psychology of Music, 23*, 162–176.

Jorgensen, E. R. (2007). Concerning justice and music education. *Music Education Research, 9*(2), 169–189. doi:10.1080/14613800701411731

Juslin, P. N., & Persson, R. S. (2002). Emotional communication. In R. Parncutt & G. E. McPherson (Eds.), *The science and psychology of music performance: Creative strategies for teaching and learning* (pp. 219–236). Oxford: Oxford University Press.

Kunzman, R. (2003). From teacher to student the value of teacher education for experienced teachers. *Journal of Teacher Education, 54*(3), 241–253.

Labuta, J. A. (2000). *Teaching musicianship in the high school band.* Galesville, MD: Meredith Music.

Langer, S. (1953). *Feeling and form: A theory of art.* New York: Charles Scribner's Sons.

LePage, P., Darling-Hammond, L., & Akar, H. (2005). Classroom management. In J. Bransford & L. Darling-Hammond (Eds.), *Preparing teachers for a changing world: What teachers should learn and be able to do.* San Francisco: Jossey-Bass

Lehmann, A. C., Sloboda, J. A., & Woody, R. H. (2007). *Psychology for musicians: Understanding and acquiring the skills.* Oxford: Oxford University Press.

Lortie, D. C. (1975). *Schoolteacher: A sociological study.* Chicago: University of Chicago Press.

Marotto, M., Victor, B., & Roos, D. R. J. (2001). Leadership as collective virtuosity. In *Paper delivered to the 2001 EGOS conference.* Retrieved from Google Scholar.

McAllister, G., & Irvine, J. (2002). The role of empathy in teaching culturally diverse students: A qualitative study of teachers' beliefs. *Journal of Teacher Education, 53*(5), 433–443. doi:10.1177/002248702237397

McPherson, G. E., & Gabrielsson, A. (2002). From sound to sign. In R. Parncutt & G. E. McPherson (Eds.), *The science and psychology of music performance: Creative strategies for teaching and learning* (pp. 99–116). New York: Oxford University Press.

MENC. (1996). *Performance standards for music, grades pre-k–12: Strategies and benchmarks for assessing progress toward the national standards.* Reston, VA: MENC: The National Association for Music Education.

Miksza, P., & Berg, M. (2013). Transition from student to teacher: Frameworks for understanding preservice music teacher development. *Journal of Music Teacher Education, 23*(1), 10–26. doi:10.1177/1057083713480888

National Standards for Arts Education. (1994). *Dance, music, theatre, visual arts: What every young american should know and be able to do in the arts: National standards for arts education.* Reston, VA: Music Educators National Conference.

O'Toole, P. A. (2003). *Shaping sound musicians: An innovative approach to teaching comprehensive musicianship through performance.* Chicago: GIA Publications. Retrieved from Library of Congress or OCLC Worldcat.

Oxendine, J. B. (1984). *Psychology of motor learning* (2nd ed.). New York: Appleton-Century-Crofts.

Parncutt, R., & McPherson, G. E. (Eds.) (2002). *The science and psychology of music performance: Creative strategies for teaching and learning.* Oxford: Oxford University Press.

Peck, C. A., Singer-Gabella, M., Sloan, T., & Lin, S. (2014). Driving blind: Why we need standardized performance assessment in teacher education. *Journal of Curriculum and Instruction, 8*(1), 8–30. Retrieved from Google Scholar.

Pink, D. H. (2009). *Drive: The surprising truth about what motivates us.* New York: Riverhead Books.

Race to the Top Program: Executive Summary. (2009). US Department of Education, Washington, DC. Retrieved from http://www2.ed.gov/programs/racetothetop/executive-summary.pdf

Rosenshine, B., & Stevens, R. (1986). Teaching functions. In M. C. Wittrock (Ed.), *Handbook of research on teaching* (3rd ed.) (pp. 376–391). New York: Macmillan.

Roulston, K., Legette, R., & Trotman Womack, S. (2005). Beginning music teachers' perceptions of the transition from university to teaching in schools. *Music Education Research, 7*(1), 59–82.

Shepard, H., Hammerness, K., Darling-Hammond, L., & Rust, F. (2005). Assessment. In J. Bransford & L. Darling-Hammond (Eds.), *Preparing teachers for a changing world: What teachers should learn and be able to do* (pp. 275–326). San Francisco: Jossey-Bass.

Shulman, L. S. (1986). Those who understand: Knowledge growth in teaching. *Educational Researcher, 15*(2), 4–14.

Shulman, L. S. (1998). Theory, practice, and the education of professionals. *The Elementary School Journal*, 511–526. Retrieved from Google Scholar.

Sloboda, J. A., Davidson, J. W., Howe, M. J. A., & Moore, D. G. (1996). *The role of practice in the development of performing musicians*. British Journal of Psychology, 87, 287–309.

Using EdTPA. (n.d.). Retrieved from www.highered.nysed.gov/edtpausing.pdf.

Wenger-Trayner, E. (n.d.). Communities of practice: A brief introduction. [Web page] Retrieved from http://wenger-trayner.com/theory/

Wiggins, G. P., & McTighe, J. (2005). *Understanding by design*. Alexandria, VA: Association for Supervision and Curriculum Development.

Zimmerman, B. J. (1990). Self-regulation learning and academic achievement: An overview. *Educational Psychologist*, 25(1), 3–17.

INDEX

Page numbers in italics refer to figures and tables.

Made in the USA
Las Vegas, NV
27 December 2023

83604206R00141